KT-427-886

The Greek Plays

WITHDRAWN

088860
Aberdeen College Library

The Greek Plays

Ellen McLaughlin

ABERDEEN COLLEGE
GORDON LIBRARY

THEATRE COMMUNICATIONS GROUP
NEW YORK
2005

The Greek Plays is copyright © 2005 by Ellen McLaughlin

Iphigenia and Other Daughters, The Trojan Women, Helen, Lysistrata, The Persians, Oedipus and the Preface are copyright © 2005 by Ellen McLaughlin; the Foreword is copyright © 2005 by Tony Kushner

The Greek Plays is published by Theatre Communications Group, Inc., 520 Eighth Avenue, 24th Floor, New York, NY 10018-4156.

All rights reserved. Except for brief passages quoted in newspaper, magazine, radio or television reviews, no part of this book may be reproduced in any form or by any means, electronic or mechanical, including photocopying or recording, or by an information storage and retrieval system, without permission in writing from the publisher.

Professionals and amateurs are hereby warned that this material, being fully protected under the Copyright Laws of the United States of America and all other countries of the Berne and Universal Copyright Conventions, is subject to a royalty. All rights including, but not limited to, professional, amateur, recording, motion picture, recitation, lecturing, public reading, radio and television broadcasting, and the rights of translation into foreign languages are expressly reserved. Particular emphasis is placed on the question of readings and all uses of these plays by educational institutions, permission for which must be secured from the author's representative: Joyce P. Ketay, The Joyce Ketay Agency, 630 Ninth Avenue, Suite 706, New York, NY 10036; (212) 354-6825.

Cover art is "Fragmentary Head of a Queen," ca. 1352–1336 B.C.E., courtesy of The Metropolitan Museum of Art, purchase Edward S. Harkness Gift, 1926 (26.7.1396). Photograph copyright © 1996 The Metropolitan Museum of Art.

This publication is made possible in part with public funds from the New York State Council on the Arts, a State Agency.

TCG books are exclusively distributed to the book trade by Consortium Book Sales and Distribution, 1045 Westgate Drive, St. Paul, MN 55114.

LIBRARY OF CONGRESS CATALOGING-IN-PUBLICATION DATA

McLaughlin, Ellen.
    The Greek plays / Ellen McLaughlin.—1st ed.
    p. cm.
    ISBN-13: 978-1-55936-240-5
    ISBN-10: 1-55936-240-5
1. Greek drama—Adaptations. 2. Mythology, Greek—Drama.
I. Title.

PS3563.C3837G74   2005
812'.54—dc22
2005028585

Cover design by Kitty Suen
Author photograph by T. Charles Erickson
Text design and composition by Lisa Govan

First Edition, December 2005

Contents

Foreword

By Tony Kushner

Ellen McLaughlin is a dramatist of courage, intelligence, wit and lyricism. Her plays are political and excruciatingly personal. Her drama is the drama of witness, predicated on a deep faith in human sympathy: if she can describe precisely what sorrows our wickedness, confusion or indifference occasions, if she can make it possible for us to empathize with others who are suffering, we will surely change our ways and our world. Because she is a poet, Ellen understands that for these purposes docudrama will not do. The voice of simple fact is not sufficient to pierce our jaded, exhausted sensibilities; the voice of the 6 P.M. newscast is used to soothe us and sell us cars. She is a poet and she knows that it is only through an exploration of language itself, of the very tools of telling, of bearing witness, that we have any hope of finding our way deep inside the pain and longing of other people.

Ellen is one of those uncomfortable writers. She writes because she believes her writing will make an actual difference, for the better, in this terribly troubled world, or, rather, she writes in the hope that it will, out of a faith that writing can have consequence in the world. If she loses her conviction that there is a need to try to write plays that will make a difference, she doesn't write. She falls silent. She prefers silence, I think, to idle chatter, to pointless noise. Ellen is a playwright by trade but one of the essential tools of her trade, as she practices it, is necessity. The weight of necessity pulls at her writing. She makes entertainments for serious people. She wants to provide the particular pleasure that comes from not turning away. She understands that simplicity and brevity are neither the only nor necessarily the surest paths to truth. She has always expected her audiences to be driven, as she is, by a kind of heartbroken curiosity, profoundly respectful of the dark miracle of surviving that which can't be survived, and of the power survivors find within themselves to articulate, or to strive to articulate, against every obstacle, against every mechanism of denial, aphasia, amnesia, testimony regarding survival and its price, varieties of agony offered up by the agon.

To say that Ellen is one of those writers who believes that writing matters is to say that she is one of those whose works issue from a paradox, seldom considered: the writers who want to prompt their audience into action are sometimes those most conversant with the impossibility of doing so, the ones who know despair most intimately. To proceed from an assumption that change is impossible and that art has nothing to do with change is to proceed from a place of resignation indistinguishable, finally, from comfort. To proceed from a certainty that plays can help change the way we see the world and thus change the world, from a certainty that language is as much a key to liberation as it is a prison house, is to proceed with a near-certainty of failure, for a faith in art's transmutational power breeds, in artists who, like Ellen, have actually paid attention to history, who have actually been engaged in political processes of change, a painful awareness of how difficult change almost always is. The hope expressed by such artists that articulation can transform and alter the course of history's flow is infused with anticipatory grief that most articulation, most art, works slowly, indirectly, or not at all. Cassandra fails instrumentally—no one listens to her—and succeeds ethically, leaving behind an altered myth; because of her, people could not say, as they have always wanted to say, "No one warned us, we didn't know what would happen." People are always warned. We *know* what will happen. There are always Cassandras trying to tell us. What drives them to tell is believing that words will affect history. They tell us that this hope is necessary, and slim; we can hear in their voices that they know us, and our resistance to change, our lack of courage, our desire for destruction, all too well. They are uncomfortable, and frequently unwelcome.

Ellen McLaughlin in her role as playwright has always insisted on the primacy of the search for truth, insisted on it over the expectation, so powerful in our times, of politeness and neatness and compactness and the illusion of completeness, those tidy pocketable unities, precious ingredients of the aesthetics of commodity fetishism. Her completely original works—*Days and Nights Within, A Narrow Bed, Infinity's House* and *Tongue of a Bird*—are large, large-hearted, poetic plays, and they've had a tough time on contemporary American stages. They have their fanatical adherents and champions, but they're hard to stage, hard to perform. Audiences expecting quicker and easier gratifications find them frustrating. As for drama critics, well . . . Ellen's plays have a generosity, a patience and a seriousness of spirit that demand a matching spirit from practitioner, audience and critic, and this is not a generous or patient time, nor, for all that our predicaments could not be more serious, is it a particularly good time for serious, as opposed to snobby, people (snobbishness is, finally, silly). It's difficult for a playwright to keep writing without a welcome. Finding a less-than-warm welcome for her writer's voice, Ellen has flirted with silence, with leaving the stage as a writer—she has always had her extraordinary acting ability to turn to. Fortunately, for nearly a decade now, the playwright has resisted the temptation to fall silent; instead, she has enlarged and refreshed her writer's voice by turning to the Greeks.

Part of the allure of the Greek myths, and of the poems and plays that transformed those myths into art, part of the reason we return to them, forbidding as they can be, alien as they can be, difficult as they are to translate, stage, perform—one aspect of their magnetism is that they offer as much as anything can the possibility of returning to origins, of going back to the beginning, where one is both shocked and gratified to see that certain aspects of our wretchedness and our greatness have altered very little in three thousand years. The Holy Scriptures are older than Homer and far older than the great Greek dramas, and the New Testament is almost as old as the plays, and these Jewish and Christian texts too suggest that what we struggle with in the twenty-first century, that which moves us to exhilaration, terror, despair, war, suicide, infidelity, nobility and art, moved tribal people in the mideastern desert in similar ways ages upon ages ago. But the myths of those desert tribes were enlisted to promote a fierce monotheism and a teleological universe. The flexibility and heterogeneity of the Greeks' polytheism, their alarming (to our contemporary sensibilities, anyway) comfort with caprice in their deities, judge less and mirror more. For the progressive person, feeling too close the hot breath of fundamentalist theocracy, threatening to string up all human complexity between bipolar extremities, the Greek plays, aeons before those epistemological earthquakes which gave birth to modernity and the very notion of progress, seem modern, secular, in opposition to very modern political evil. Ellen writes, in her introduction and in many of the notes to the plays, that what has drawn her to these texts is that they were written by war veterans for war veterans. One of her first plays, *A Narrow Bed*, has as a central character a veteran of the Vietnam War, and indeed all her plays have addressed, with horror and deep fascination, the subject of violence, of war, and of gender differences in our relationship to the harshness of human existence.

E. H. Carr describes the march of history as serpentine. Remote periods suddenly loom close to the present as the march of time snakes on. We are in a moment in which classical antiquity feels proximate, and those aspects of human life which have not changed much since the time of the great Athenian dramatists are of particular importance to us now. To some of us the classics are important only because they prove that people don't change. To others, like Ellen, they prove rather that the struggle for change, the desire for change, is ancient and unconquerable.

The voice in these texts, never dogmatic, is recognizably feminist, pluralist, anti-war in the most modern sense. Though it is impossible that it should be so, we discover a similar voice in myths and plays 2,500 years old. Ellen's appropriation of the plays helps us hear that voice.

Hence this book collects chapters in an important act of re-invention and re-invigoration. And it collects under one cover a number of beautiful, remarkable plays, hard to stage, hard to perform, and entirely worth the challenge—as artists and audiences all over America have discovered. As Aeschylus, Sophocles and Euripides knew, as Ellen McLaughlin knows, the social world is grounded in, held together by and nurtured toward future growth through private rage, laughter, sorrow, publicly articulated. As these plays make their ferocious claims on human sympathy, they discover within that ordinary sympathy, that common feeling, paths that expand out toward the infinite and the sublime.

Preface

By Ellen McLaughlin

I should start by admitting that I don't read Greek. This has always presented the nice problem of what I should *call* what I make of the plays. Even if I never call these plays "translations," are they justifiably called "adaptations," which usually involve some knowledge of the language in which they were written? I have generally avoided the issue entirely by calling them "versions" of the plays, but that can indicate that I feel less fidelity to the original texts, as I understand them, than I tend to feel. "Version," to my mind anyway, implies "alternative," which has never been my intention. So, at least for the purposes of this book, I'm forced to leave the distinct appellation to the reader, and am open to suggestion in the future.

I fell into working on Greek plays by a happy accident. I was commissioned by Brian Kulick, then at The Actors' Gang in Los Angeles, to write a new version of *Electra* for them back in 1992, as part of a new *Oresteia* they were staging, each of the three plays to be written by a different playwright. (I was also asked to write a short prologue and epilogue, based on Euripides' *Iphigenia in Aulis* and *Iphigenia in Tauris*, respectively, neither of which was staged as part of that evening, but which I then combined with the *Electra* to make a sort of *Iphigenia*-ia, or rather, *Iphigenia and Other Daughters*.)

The way I went about writing that play became a system I have since employed every time I've approached these texts. I read every English translation I can lay my hands on extremely carefully and then put them all away and start to write. (I have a horror of inadvertently appropriating some scholar's work and passing it off as my own invention.) I have taken liberties with every play, some more than others, but have remained fairly faithful to the fundamental dramatic structure, since the dramaturgy of these plays seems to be unerringly sound.

Each project was written for its own unique reasons and under the influence of its own political moment:

My version of Euripides' *Trojan Women* was originally written for a project I directed as a result of a grant from the Lila Wallace–Reader's Digest Fund during the Bosnian War. The play was performed as a staged reading by refugees and emigrants from the former Yugoslavia, almost none of them actors. Readings were mounted in New York three times with different groups over the course of three years during the mid-1990s.

Helen, based loosely on the Euripides play of the same name, was first written in the spring of 2000 for the Women Playwrights Festival produced by ACT in Seattle and was very much the product of the tenacity and faith of Liz Engelman, who was then that theater's literary manager.

Lysistrata, based on the Aristophanes play of the same name, was written very quickly in response to the startling phenomenon, dreamed up by Kathryn Blume and Sharron Bower, of the Lysistrata Project, which inspired readings of the Aristophanes play to take place all over the world on March 3, 2003, as a form of global protest against the imminent invasion of Iraq. My version of the play was one of dozens performed that day in the New York area alone. I directed it, with the help of Lisa Rothe, at the Harvey Theater at the Brooklyn Academy of Music.

The Persians, based on the Aeschylus play of the same name, was commissioned by Tony Randall's National Actors Theatre in New York City during the weeks after the invasion of Iraq and in response to that event. It was performed in May and June of 2003.

Oedipus, based on the Sophocles play of the same name, was commissioned by the Guthrie Theater in Minneapolis. Lisa Peterson, the director, pitched the project to Joe Dowling, artistic director of the Guthrie, in early 2004, inspired by a desire to grapple with American notions of identity and responsibility in the light of the Iraq War and the ongoing crisis of the Bush presidency. The production opened on January 21, 2005, months after Bush's reelection and mere weeks after the catastrophe of the Indian Ocean tsunami.

My concerns as a writer have changed over the years, but I keep being drawn back to the Greeks. My fascination with them stems from earliest childhood. *D'Aulaires' Book of Greek Myths* was one of the first books I experienced alone, in the sense of reading it by myself to myself and poring over the illustrations so thoroughly that even now I can call most of them up in my mind's eye in stunning detail.

I like to think that in writing these plays I'm doing something not wholly unrelated to what the great tragedians were doing. Each ancient play was a retelling of a myth, a variation on a story that was familiar to the audience. That familiarity with the basic material, which modern audiences experience to a lesser extent, is vital to the way the plays work on us. The stories *already* have a claim on us just as we have a claim on the stories. They belong to no one and to everyone, just as they always have.

What the Greek plays have given me as a writer is a means of taking on eternally relevant issues unapologetically. The Greeks ask the hardest questions, always: What is it to be human? What do we owe to each other? How do we negotiate with the divine? What sense can we make of the inevitability of human suffering? And beyond this, the plays have given me a means to write about war. The great tragedians' intimate, clear-eyed understanding of war and its horrors has been tremendously helpful to me as a writer trying to thrash out my response to the wars of my own time. All of the plays in this volume address war, and that content is probably what, above all, drew me to these particular works.

Whenever Western civilization has contemplated war as a concept, since the beginning of our cultural and literary history we

have thought about the Trojan War. For the Greeks, the Trojan
War was a primary legend, and though it is for us one of the oldest stories going, it was to a lesser extent markedly remote for
them as well, and hence useful. The Trojan War provided them
with the means to consider war in the abstract, as a phenomenon
separate from politics or any sense of patriotism. One has merely
to remember that the only heroes who come off particularly well
in *The Iliad* are the defeated Trojans, such as Hector and Priam,
as opposed to the Greeks—the sulking Achilles, the doltish
Agamemnon, the untrustworthy and conniving Odysseus—to
realize how independent of any predictable nationalistic formulas the myth was for them. And so it is for us. It is a war in which
the most righteous characters are members of an irrevocably lost
civilization.

But if the Trojan War is our template for the notion of war,
what do we learn from it?

1. WARS ARE PROFLIGATE IN WOE, LENGTHY AND VASTLY
   DESTRUCTIVE.

   The Greeks spend ten years besieging a city they
   finally destroy, along with a legendarily noble royal family and a mighty civilization. Though there are sympa-
   thetic figures, like Patroclus, among the Greeks, more
   often than not, the greatest of the heroes, including
   Achilles, conduct themselves hatefully before dying hor-
   rid deaths.

2. THE *CASUS BELLI* CAN HARDLY BE SAID TO JUSTIFY THE
   CONSEQUENT SLAUGHTER AND SUFFERING.

   Even if Helen remains in Troy throughout, can her
   husband's recovery of her really balance out the countless warriors dead? To say nothing of the entire civilization of Troy and the vast majority of its citizens, men and
   women alike? And if she never goes at all, if some cloud
   copy is residing up in the Trojan palace the whole time,
   while the real Helen is sitting it out in Egypt, how is one
   to think of all those deaths and all that mayhem?

3. NOBODY WINS.

Well, of course the Greeks do, on paper. But those who survive have a hell of a time getting home—Odysseus takes ten years to manage it—and find precious little to cheer them when they do arrive home at last. Their kingdoms have gone to ruin and chaos in the interval, and the welcoming committee can be surprisingly brusque—Agamemnon's swift dispatch into the next world comes to mind.

4. THE GLORY OF WAR IS A QUESTIONABLE CONCEPT AT BEST.

Those who exult the most concerning the glory of war—and this is as true now as it ever was—tend not to be the people fighting and dying in the war.

We don't know as much as we'd like about the composition of the audience for the festivals at which these plays were presented, but we are certain about one thing at least: the audiences contained a large number, perhaps even a majority, of veterans. And we know that all of the three major tragic playwrights were veterans. This fact alone—that the plays were written by veterans, and largely for veterans—makes whatever these playwrights have to say about war particularly worthy of our attention, since we haven't had that kind of dynamic between playwrights and their audiences in theatrical literature since. Never again would citizens address other citizens about war in this way. The plays weren't written to please wealthy patrons or producers, nor were they meant to placate or aggrandize political figures. As far as we can tell, there was little or no money involved with the honor of winning the dramatic contest of the festival, and the group of citizens who determined the outcome of the competition was large, amorphous and unpredictable, since they changed completely from year to year.

It is almost impossible for a modern audience to imagine the kind of freedom and privilege such a system conferred on the playwright. One could not only speak the truth as one understood it, but one could be certain of being heard. The festivals were attended by thousands—the Theater of Dionysus near Athens seated fourteen thousand. (Even prisoners were sometimes released to attend the festivals.) Playwrights wrote from an immediate experience of war and spoke to an audience that had no less direct an experience of war. Yet, almost invariably, in the plays that have survived for us, playwrights were speaking through the conduit of a shared mythology and that mythology was the Trojan War. *The Persians* is the great exception, yet even that is a play about the nearly mythical *Other*, the enemy, not the familiar—not the contemporary Athenian experience. (Furthermore, Aeschylus took enormous and obvious liberties with the immediate shared history.) Myth provided the necessary distance, the means by which one could make sense of the baffling reality this burgeoning civilization was up against. Athenians suffered from their own imperialist fiascos, but the way they chose to address that present reality was through this odd reimagining of their shared legend. Similarly, when the Athenians were coping with the plague, which killed a third of the populace, Sophocles gave them *Oedipus*, which is, among other things, a tragedy about one particular political leader's response to the mythical plague of Thebes.

I don't think times have changed that much. I think we are still finding a bearable way of contemplating the unbearable truth of our times by working with a common mythology. We toy with the stories, come up with variations that suit our needs, but that doesn't make much difference to the basic strength of the raw material we're working with. Every age will find its use for these stories. But the stories will never cease to be relevant. They belong to us as human beings and they are as recognizable as the symmetry of our bodies, two eyes, two ears, two arms, two legs, and the familiar tattoo of our beating hearts.

Acknowledgments

I have tried in my introductions to each of the plays to thank specific people who were responsible for each play's inception. There are, however, a few people whose salvific influence spans more than one of the plays and to whom I am indebted deeply.

Of the many friends who have supported me and my work over the years, I must acknowledge one in particular: Jane Lincoln Taylor has not only been an invaluable source of wise and loving counsel but she has edited nearly every one of the plays and indeed almost everything I've written in my professional life. We've known each other since college and meeting her then was one of the greatest strokes of luck in my life. I know that I am a better writer for her influence and I am a better person for her friendship.

I was also lucky in 1995, when I had a chance to direct *Iphigenia and Other Daughters* at the Chautauqua Theater Company in upstate New York and cast Lisa Rothe as Electra. Lisa made not only a brilliant Electra but a lasting impression on me as a savvy, passionate woman of the theater. Consequently, she's been part of virtually everything I've done professionally, either as my assistant on *Tongue of a Bird* and *Helen* at The Public Theater and *Lysistrata* at BAM, or as assistant director to Ethan McSweeny for *The Persians* at National Actors Theatre. Happily, she is currently too busy directing to be assistant to anyone anymore, but I'm fortunate I met her when she could give her time, her intelligence and her inimitable grace in aid of so much of my work.

Finally, I must mention my husband, Rinde Eckert, who has loved me well and wisely throughout all of this, while unfailingly remaining the smartest person I know. I shudder to think where I would be without him.

Iphigenia and
Other Daughters

Introduction

Iphigenia in Aulis

Iphigenia and Clytemnestra should be present on the stage
throughout. The piece should be staged as sparely as possible—the aesthetic leaning toward minimalist dance, rather than
naturalistic theater. Silence is important. The pace of the piece
should be dictated by the text's format, which indicates blank
verse for Iphigenia (with attention paid to end stops) and prose for
Clytemnestra. Stillness is crucial, particularly for Iphigenia herself, who should not move much throughout the bulk of the piece,
until the end, if even then. Her entire climactic action might be
simply to stand. Nothing should interfere with the intensity of
the connection between us and this girl trying to think through
an impossible puzzle. Her tone is quietly curious, wry and utterly
lacking in self-pity. She is, above all, an intellect articulating itself.
Clytemnestra is queenly in her mien and anxiety, never descending into hysteria or vulgarity but not without bitter wit. My
instinct is that there should never be physical contact between
them. Iphigenia's relationship to the audience and her own
thoughts is clear, if interior, whilst Clytemnestra is a public figure, comfortable with direct address.

As the realization of what is actually happening dawns on
Iphigenia, she becomes calmer. All of her intellect and instincts
lead her through the course of the piece to the final awesome

truth, and in that moment of enlightenment, her entire character is confirmed. She has finally figured it out.

Electra

What interests me about Sophocles' version of *Electra* is that he titles it for a character who does not in fact *do* anything, but whose very inability to do anything forms the nexus of the play. He surrounds her with female characters who are difficult to fit into any satisfying feminist ideology. They are prickly and uncomfortable figures, which makes them interesting to me because they force me up against my own demons—the nightmares at the back of my notions of the female. I think that my fears are common to most women, so these characters have been a compelling and difficult bunch of people to take on.

I believe that most women feel, deep down, that they are not part of the real history of mankind, the important stuff, the heroic stuff, the stuff that matters. And we are indeed correct—the his/story of man/kind is precisely that. So we are left to make up our own, gather stories, sift through what we can make out of the unchronicled, the lost lives, quilts, songs, anonymous poems that might have, could have been rendered by people not unlike ourselves. But there is always a certain self-loathing that one keeps at bay—perhaps I am speaking only for myself here—the sense that one would like to be able to identify oneself with something more substantial, more vivid, more, well, powerful. But power in the hands of women has nearly always been perceived as monstrous in terms of his/story (hence characters like Clytemnestra) or as merely sexual (hence, oh, you name it). So one ends up identifying oneself with men. I know I did. Literature, politics, virtually everything that was part of my education involved my identification with the male. This has its advantages. One learns how men think, feel and act. But there are obvious disadvantages—these are not, ultimately, my stories, my triumphs, my terrors.

This play is also an investigation of the notion of history itself. And since this is based on a Greek source, that entails an investigation of tragedy and fate. This is an exceedingly intimate play: familial, female. This is not the kind of sphere within which one is used to examining notions of history. That's what interests me about it. Clytemnestra clearly feels that she is a part of history; Chrysothemis, that she is outside history; Electra, that she *is* history. Orestes has the hatred of history that only one who has been part of its chugging engine can feel.

NOTES ON CHARACTERS

CLYTEMNESTRA

Clytemnestra is a woman of the world in a way that neither of her daughters is. She has seen the great landscapes, been part of politics, known and assessed "great men." Because she feels that she is part of the big drama, she knows that she is ultimately tragic. It is an aspect of the bargain with fate she made knowingly. Such is the price of the grand gesture. Greek myth is quite stringent about such things, which is why everyone knows the name Clytemnestra and few remember Chrysothemis. Clytemnestra is aware that her reign at the top of the wheel of fortune is finite. It has been secured with blood, it will be ended with blood. Her knowledge of this does not diminish her fear of death. Electra is right: she is terrified. And Clytemnestra's life at this point is spent in attempts to forestall the inevitable. She is waiting. She is surrounded by her children, who are her own walking nightmares. Electra reminds her of her most apparent fear—that of an imminent and violent death. But Chrysothemis is equally, if more subtly, terrifying; she is there to whisper into Clytemnestra's ear the awful possibility that her life has been futile and pointless, that because she is merely a woman, nothing she has done has the greatness of scale that *real* history entails. And then there is the constant specter of her absent son, whose inevitable presence her dream prophesies.

Though Clytemnestra is a queen, her identity in my play is principally, oddly enough, as a mother. Those familiar with the myth will notice that I don't include the character of Agisthus, Clytemnestra's lover. That's because he has always muddied the issue for me. Clytemnestra's need for revenge always seemed tremendously clear to me, given Agamemnon's sacrifice of their daughter Iphigenia. Why do we need adultery to explain that murder? Adultery also seems beside the point and vilifying in an unsatisfying way. My Clytemnestra commits murder as an outraged mother and knows that she will die at the hands of her own child. It's an irony of which she's fully aware.

Clytemnestra inspires awe, even in her daughters. She has done things; she has made her presence felt; she has been a part of history. Even her far more famous sister Helen was never so actively involved in events. Helen was merely bundled like a statue from one place to the next, one bed to the next. Clytemnestra, like Antigone, made a stand for her own interpretation of justice. This makes her heroic at the same time that it makes her monstrous. She is formidable and impossible to dismiss.

One note: It is important to me that Clytemnestra live and finally die like the queen she is. She should never tip her hand, not to Orestes, not to Electra, not to us, as to the exact moment of her understanding of Orestes' real identity. I always advise letting the actress make that call and feel no obligation to flag it. Consequently, her death is oddly, but fundamentally, heroic because she goes to it knowingly.

ELECTRA

I see Electra as the eternal child, locked at the moment that she witnessed a crime she will never be able to redress, but that she can never forget either. This is a terrible life to have to live.

She has this effect on clocks—they either stop altogether or are rendered meaningless. Not only can she never seem to enter the world, she can't seem to enter the flow of time itself. She can't seem to grow up and tear her eyes from that bloody hearthside but neither can she forestall the sense that time is whipping past her, turning her older and more useless by the second. The notion of justice is very dear to her, dearer even than the notion of death because justice seems to entail release in a way in which death—her own—cannot. If justice were to be rendered in the form of the appropriate redress of her father's murder, then she could become human perhaps—sleep, eat or simply die. The problem is that the appropriate redress involves Orestes as the murderer, not her, so she must wait and watch and remember. Twenty years is a very long time.

In the meantime, she has devoted her life to being the ultimate scourge and household blight. She cannot kill her mother, but she can make her life miserable and fearful. This is at least as hard on the blight as it is on the blighted. She has driven herself mad and she lives in horrifying squalor and sleeplessness. Technically, I suppose I see her as a manic-depressive, always prowling, never sleeping, seldom eating and always talking, talking, talking.

Electra and Hedda Gabler bear a familial resemblance. They are women who are deeply identified with fathers they never knew and who spend their lives yearning for men who will make *for them, in their name* the great, masculine gesture on the landscape that they don't feel capable of making themselves. They share a terrible contempt for all that is feminine without particularly understanding the masculine, since the men they revered were always remote and are now either absent or dead. They share the tragedy of people whose lives must perforce be lived through reluctant others who never have the same script, and thus don't know their lines or even how to show up on time. Also, no one will ever understand the beauty and power of that script as they do; it is theirs alone.

But Electra is perhaps even more tragic than Hedda because she is smarter, more woefully enmeshed in a punishing myth, and she does not have the luxury of an escape into suicide.

Electra's sense of justice is directly linked to her sense of history. History, and by extension, life itself, is bearable only if it has meaning, ethical meaning. If there are no gods to assign that meaning then she will have to step in, mortal though she is. She never has any doubts as to what her mother's crime demands in terms of punishment, but she may occasionally doubt her own abilities to see such a punishment through. She has no confidence that, should her vigilance fail, justice would still prevail.

Electra's sense of the world is tiny; she has never been allowed outside the confines of her own house and yard. She does not know what is around the bend of the road she looks at through the fence of the property. But her sense of the issues of justice and history is proportionately enormous and rigid in its very abstraction. As I say, this play is overwhelmingly intimate, and yet it is all about history and justice.

CHRYSOTHEMIS

Chrysothemis is the character that no one ever remembers after reading the Sophocles play. So she has become the center of this one. Electra thinks of herself as the nightmare of the house, the incessant speaker of the unspeakable. However, Chrysothemis is actually the most terrifying figure in the house and in this version she has the last word. Chrysothemis is the awful voice that I know so well in my own head and that I think is present in so many women's heads. She is the one who says: "Who do you think you are anyway?"; "But whatever made you think *you* were important?"; "But you're just a girl, what do you know about anything of real consequence?" and so forth.

But Chrysothemis is also real, she isn't just a figment. She is the only functional member of this odd family. She is the only member of the family who isn't clinically insane, for starters. But she also has the strength and power of someone who is actually engaged in life. She sees everything and she maintains her family's crazy existence. Without her, nothing. She is graced with the irony that only those who are true survivors possess. Hers is an admittedly mundane and material existence. But that is actually the beauty of it. That is her power. She is no less intelligent or strong than her mother and sister, but she has chosen life, a certain kind of life, over heroism and myth. Therein lies her strangely tragic quality. She is actually the most difficult character for me to encounter because she enunciates the truths I fear the most. But her calm clear-sightedness in facing these things is deeply impressive to me at the same time that it is unbearable to me.

The easiest trap for the actor playing Chrysothemis is to perceive her as a cynic. She isn't. She is a realist. She lives in the noon light of an illusionless landscape. This is an impossible place for most human beings to live because it is too cold, too bright. Virtually nothing she has to say is anything anyone else can bear to hear. So she mostly watches and assesses her difficult charges.

All this is not to say that she doesn't have yearnings for scale and drama from time to time. She does wish desperately, I think, for memories, for the sense of consequence that a real, owned personal history would give her. But she has none of that. She knows what she is, the part she has always played. There has never been real love, nor its counterpart, hatred. Not for her.

ORESTES

Orestes is, first and foremost, a veteran. He is the embodiment of what they called in Vietnam the "thousand-mile stare." He has done things that he will never be able to live with. He has tried to turn himself into a monster and very nearly succeeded. But the monster he wanted to be, who could kill without feeling anything and who could do the one thing he was saved to do, is a monster he has never quite managed to become. He knows he is a tragic figure, but that has no appeal for him. He did not choose this. He would have preferred a far more ordinary life without this terrible tinge of drama and darkness. But of course that is unthinkable. This has been his condition ever since he can remember. And he can remember a lot—far too much. The crime he was forged upon and his duty in relation to it are as much a part of him as his hands and feet.

Aside from his identity as a veteran, his only other true identity is as an exile. He has been in exile all of his conscious life. But unlike most exiles, he has no home to remember with any joy. His return home is inevitable and terrible to contemplate since it will propel him out into a hostile world again, this time as a criminal as well as an exile.

As far as justice and history are concerned he is deeply ironic, as only a soldier of the First World War could be. There is no notion of honor and justice left after enduring such a spectacularly grotesque, absurd and futile war. But he has an unshakable notion of fate, and that is why he finally comes home to do its bidding. Exhaustion figures chiefly in my image of Orestes. He knows exactly what will become of all this, and he does know the world—all too well. The only tenderness he ever experienced was early on, not only from his sister, but from his mother. I think he remembers that.

Iphigenia in Tauris

This may be the quietest play I've ever written, and perhaps the strangest. But then the source, Euripides' play of the same name, is odd indeed. After the anguished, harrowing doings of *Electra*, it should seem that we are transported to an entirely different world, a sort of beautiful limbo, in fact, which is precisely what Euripides called for.

The chorus are all girls who, like Iphigenia, were saved from human sacrifice in some vague way, though Iphigenia's celebrity as the most famous example of such a dramatic personal reprieve obviously lends her prestige and special rights as a priestess in this realm. But they all share the same state now, which is to say that they are all frozen in privilege, preserved in a sort of fugue-state of adolescence. They will never get old. This has its advantages: they will never age, their beauty will never diminish, they will never again be in harm's way. And there is, as they point out, ostensibly nothing to complain about. It's all just plain lovely and never anything less, a Greek version of what some Christians hope heaven will offer. But that's just what doesn't recommend it. Unrelieved serenity and eternal idleness are frankly inhuman.

Even the nicest place imaginable palls after a time, and no one, certainly not someone so acutely curious as Iphigenia, would be content with living out only a fraction of her own life story. So it is with all these girls, exquisitely preserved in their first beauty though they all are.

This is a play about the perils and the costs of privilege, at least in part. I have known many such creatures and was myself a girl blessed with privilege, having been reared in relative financial and social comfort. The minor miseries of such specialness are such that it seems, even for those who suffer from them, tremendously unseemly to dwell on them, given the state of things for most of humanity. But being a girl, no matter how comfortably off, is never an easy thing, and I always look upon my students, caught in the gauntlet of late adolescence, with compassion, no matter how gently they were raised.

But *Iphigenia in Tauris* is not just about the obscure sorrows of a timeless adolescence; it is about two figures who are emblematic of what culture demands of the young of both sexes. The sibling relationship between Iphigenia and Orestes is at the heart of the play, and their recognition of a common, though sexually distinct, fate is what gives their encounter its subtle piquancy. Iphigenia's fate is rendered epic by her peculiar status, but it is a fate common to all girls—she is supposed to embody youth and beauty and ingenuous poignancy for all time. She is enjoined never to change, never to unsettle, never, in effect, to mature into particularity. Orestes, on the other hand, is cast unwittingly in the role of the avenger of wrongs he had no hand in, first as a soldier and then as a matricide. He bridles against this, but he knows he never had any real choice in the matter, any more than countless generations of young men have had, enlisted as they have been since time immemorial in the dark projects their elders write with the blood of others, the blood of youth.

The subversive plan the two siblings devise at the end of the piece is a peculiar event, but it is the final recourse these mythical characters have in resolving the perpetual cycle of their myth. They cannot escape from legend into obscurity in any ordinary way;

they have always been too special for that, too visible to the gods and posterity. A statue will have to be taken back to civilization. That is what legend demands as a means of releasing Orestes from his cycle of misery. Iphigenia, already translated to limbo by the workings of her saga, volunteers what is left of her humanness and distinctness to give her brother his means of escape. It is an act of self-sacrifice that is personally intentional as no other action of the play has been. In this way, the only two characters capable of a loving relationship in the entire play put their own terrible myth to rest and are quietly released at last into obscurity.

Setting

Iphigenia in Aulis and *Iphigenia in Tauris* are both set in something approaching the timeless, arid landscape of Greek myth. There is a kind of purity about them both that detaches them from ordinary, linear time. However, *Electra*, the centerpiece of this trilogy, has an entirely different quality for me. *Electra* takes place in a courtyard and in the midst of an actual, comprehendible day, a day unlike any other, but a day nonetheless in the lives of these three women. As I thought about it, I realized that I was seeing the play set in a Europe between the wars, perhaps just on the heels of the First World War. I suppose the reason I saw it this way had to do with the idea of the twilight of a certain type of aristocracy, but also it informed the notion of these women who spend their lives waiting for news of the great events of history, of the men in their lives and what has become of them. I heard somewhere that when the bombardments were taking place in France during the First World War, the teacups in Dover would shiver in their saucers. I suppose, if I had to nail it down, that was the image that generated *Electra*. It said so much about a particularly female relationship to history. So I came to think that Agamemnon's war, the Trojan War in the Greek version, translated roughly into the Boer War, which was perceived, at least in England, as the last satisfyingly exotic, remote and heroic war. Which would make Orestes, his son, a veteran of the First World War, a monstrously absurd and brutish war, fought far too close to home to be comfortingly misted in sentiment. Orestes is often perceived as the first modern hero in Greek literature. He has compunctions and ambiguities. He rails against his fate and doubts the authority and sanctity of the gods. He seemed to be easily translated into a veteran of the first modern war, a war that toppled the notion of heroism and ushered irony into the vocabulary of Western civilization.

The problem I present producers of this trilogy involves what to do about the apparent anachronisms, given the timeless Greek quality of the first and last plays and the modern references of *Electra*. As for the use of language—the prose of *Electra* versus the poetry of the Iphigenia plays—I don't think there should be much stylistic difference in terms of approach. The language is, to be sure, heightened in the first play and the last, but it is so throughout, just as there is a vernacular, ironic tone throughout, even at the gravest, toughest moments. The challenge for the director is to make the play into a seamless whole, so that the more conventionally Greek plays don't get too portentous and the *Electra* doesn't get too glib. That said, I think that the anachronisms in terms of the way eras collide, which are built into the text, are of use and important. Since the set will be, of necessity, relatively spare, given that it needs to serve all three plays, the burden of the anomalies needs to rest on the costumes, which should bear traces of the different eras. In *Iphigenia in Aulis*, Clytemnestra should look as if she's in a gorgeous, but not particularly specific, simple full-length gown. Iphigenia should be in the proverbial white dress, nothing fancy, a shift, for instance, made of beautiful material, but uncomplicated—the dress of an ancient princess. However, in *Electra*, Clytemnestra should have on something stripped down that looks like the clothing of a wealthy woman of 1919, while Chrysothemis should wear the sensible clothing of a woman of that era who does a lot of domestic work but likes to keep herself neat. Electra should be wearing what looks like a destroyed child's dress of the turn of the previous century (something that looks as if she's been wearing it for years without ever washing it or taking it off) and her father's Boer War army boot. And Orestes needs to walk in wearing something that smacks of a World War I uniform. The WW1 theme will then trail into *Tauris*, because, although Iphigenia is wearing exactly what we last saw her in (and the Chorus is in variations on that look), Orestes is still in the remnants of his WW1 uniform, if only the pants and boots. It's important that he still look like a relatively modern veteran, and that his presence be surprising and highly masculine in that paradisal context. He is, quite recognizably, a modern figure in an ancient world. The anomalies should be embraced, in other words, for the slightly jarring aesthetic shock they can provide.

The great saga of Greek mythology is the Trojan War. It is the saga toward which all the myths lead and it is the backdrop against which the largest number of mythic characters define themselves. The three plays that I have chosen to adapt here are all plays concerning women, and none of the characters in these plays ever sets foot in Troy. This is interesting to me. When you think of it though, the Trojan War lasts for ten years, the trip home can take quite a long time (in Odysseus' case, another ten years)—what *was* going on in those countries all that time the men were gone? Clytemnestra, for instance, runs her country for the duration of the war: she kills her husband within hours of his finally arriving home, then runs the country for another twenty years. That's at least thirty years during which she has reigned Mycenae at the start of *Electra*. These three plays address the margins of the epic, the footnotes to the great drama; they concern the lives lived outside the spotlight. Years and years go by. This strikes some essential truth about women's existence for me. While history is being made elsewhere, the shadow current of the subversive feminine narrative is always in the backwaters, waiting, waiting for its moment. It will come.

Production History

Iphigenia and Other Daughters was commissioned by The Actors' Gang (Tim Robbins, Artistic Director) in Los Angeles. The play premiered at New York City's Classic Stage Company (David Esbjornson, Artistic Director; Patricia Taylor, Managing Director) on January 31, 1995. The director was David Esbjornson, with scenic design by Narelle Sissons, costume design by Susan Hilferty, lighting design by Christopher Akerlind and original music and sound design by Gina Leishman; the movement consultant was Annie-B Parson and the production stage manager was Crystal Huntington. The cast was as follows:

IPHIGENIA IN AULIS

IPHIGENIA	Susan Heimbinder
CLYTEMNESTRA	Kathleen Chalfant

ELECTRA

ELECTRA	Sheila Tousey
CLYTEMNESTRA	Kathleen Chalfant
CHRYSOTHEMIS	Deborah Hedwall
ORESTES	Seth Gilliam

IPHIGENIA IN TAURIS

IPHIGENIA	Susan Heimbinder
ORESTES	Seth Gilliam
THE CHORUS	Jasmine Curry, Carley Dubicki, Cari Kosins, Karen Sackman, Jill Vinci

Characters

IPHIGENIA, a young woman just on the verge of maturity

CLYTEMNESTRA, a queen and no mistake

ELECTRA, an extremely problematic woman in her late twenties or early thirties

CHRYSOTHEMIS, an enigmatic, cool presence, a few years older than Electra

ORESTES, a young man who has seen too much to be young anymore

THE CHORUS, a minimum of five young women, colleagues and contemporaries of Iphigenia

Iphigenia in Aulis

Silence. Stillness. Brilliant noon light. Iphigenia sits, looking out.
Clytemnestra stands upstage of her, also looking out.

IPHIGENIA
In a windless place everything is eternal and bland
Nothing can be changed here
It all hums in terrible clarity
With no wind to transform, modify or shift anything
Feathers fall from a plucked chicken
And make a neat circle that stays and stays
There is a leaden singularity to each thing
Each color immobile
Everything has become too important here
Like something stared at too long
Until it might as well be anything
A person could go mad
As my mother combed my hair this morning
Each broken strand
Slunk down and coiled where it fell
Separate and smug as etched spirals on the floor
Bride
What is it to be a bride here?
In this windless place
A bleached column?
A sliver of standing bone?
But perhaps that will not happen
Nothing can happen here I think
It is a place of dead air.

CLYTEMNESTRA

We came down from the hot rock mountains. Everything
creaking on the backs of our animals and their flanks straining
to keep from falling. And as we descended, I was thinking—
a world of men, what kind of place am I taking my darling?
A place of idle soldiers—the most dangerous kind. Spears
over-sharpened by boys burning to kill for the first time.
A man. A man. And one of those boys, one of those eager,
beardless, ignorant hopped-up lonely bastards is waiting for her.
He will take her from me. Because he can. I looked back. There
she was behind me, squinting through the dust we kicked up,
looking down, waiting for something to see, something to make
sense. And she is taller than I remember. She is strong enough,
I suppose. So we kept on descending.

IPHIGENIA

Nothing more useless than ships
Miles—could it be miles—of them?
Lined up
Hauled up
Tilting
Impossible
Baking in the sun
Nosing the water which barely moves
As if the ocean were some bloated pond
That was what I saw first
So many useless ships
Bristling for such a distance along a flaccid shore
That was before my occupation became clear
My occupation as *something which is visible*
Because then we descended to walk among the men
Cities full
All of them watching me
What do they see, I wonder?
I am like Medusa, I change men to silent stone
Games stop, stories break at their start

And nothing stirs as I pass
Only their eyes, turning in their sockets
Such silence, such level dust
I am some phantom
No one in this dress
I am not here
I am just some spell that is cast
It is a powerless power
Like this wind which is only remarkable in its absence.

CLYTEMNESTRA
Achilles, well, one hears stories, of course. But where is the
man? How long have we been here? Yesterday and today. And
still no one sorts himself out of this murmuring, dirty mob to
present himself. "Watch for the armor," I am told. "His is
priceless. You will know it when you see it."
As if that meant anything. His armor.

IPHIGENIA
Helmets, lances, gold and iron skins they have
And me in this thin dress
It's a predicament.

CLYTEMNESTRA
"I'm a queen," I said, "and she's a princess," but these things
have no meaning here. The old man dropped a plate of shriveled
chicken on the wooden table and left without bowing.
Then I became afraid.

IPHIGENIA
They killed a deer yesterday
I saw it while it was still running
Stamping down the boughs
Cracking its forest
Spotting through the stricken trees
Suddenly so visible
All of them running after it, not losing sight

There I go, I thought, run fast
But they caught it
Of course
And when they brought it in
Limp and undignified, head lolling
I couldn't watch, I turned away
Because the eyes were open
And they saw me
Dead, they saw me
I shivered
You and me, I thought
We know each other
They offered me the heart
Nice of them, I guess
But I said something
And backed away
They watched me, of course
All the way to the tent
So many eyes glittering in the fire light
Fixed on me diminishing
Until the flap swallowed me and I became invisible again
And they could turn and eat
I hold the darkness to my face
As if it were food.

CLYTEMNESTRA

He finally appears out of the crowd, I recognize him by his armor.
My husband. Harried and odd in his movements. He knows
nothing, apparently. What is to be done on this windless shore
with an idle navy that he seems to be so busy? I ask him to leave.
He makes me nervous. He is happy to do so. Now I can't sleep.

IPHIGENIA

But something is wrong
My parents thrash at each other in the woods
Out of earshot

But there is screaming
Mother comes back, eyes swollen, face streaked
And smashes my head to her breast
Squeezing my ribs
I can't breathe I am so dear to her
Father stood in the tent for a while yesterday
He looks ill and won't meet my eyes
He won't touch me
Who is this husband?
What is this marriage?
Tonight the ritual knives are being sharpened on stone
Tonight there are figures circling the fire, all in black,
Telling hymns I don't know
What kind of marriage are we preparing?
I thought I would wear flowers
But nothing grows here
I thought there would be women
There are no women
Are there no other girls in the world?
Suddenly I am the last and only girl
And all these turning faces, all these anxious idle fingers
All these men to satisfy
This is the bride
The only bride

(Clytemnestra begins to pant, first slowly, then rapidly, under this next part of the speech.)

Morning comes and I am a white dress
Walking up the crumbling cliff as if I know where I am going
What I'm doing
To meet him
Whoever he might be
I am ascending to the altar
I look down from a great height to see how the ships still lie
Splayed like broken teeth

Today the light is merciless
And sound would travel if there was sound
But there are only my feet on the pebbles
That hurl themselves down to the ships as I pass
I come to the altar
But there is no one
Just the black-shrouded priests
And there my father
Who has made his face a stranger
Eyes locked in their sockets
Dull as coal
And a knife
But where are the animals?
Poor innocents
With the last cropped grass still in their moist mouths
But there is only me
And all the eyes are on me
Visible me
This is a terrible place
Something must be done

(Silence. Clytemnestra stops panting.)

Ah. I see.
I was right
Here is my husband
This ancient stone
And the quick shadow of the knife
I am to marry everyone
Every single one
This is what it is at last.

(Blackout. Sound of wind.)

END OF PART 1

Electra

Morning. Dim light. A courtyard. An unlovely place. This is not the fault of the gardener, but rather of the occupant, Electra, who has the same damaging effect on the place as any untrained dog. There is, perhaps, one elegant chair, out of place in the ruin.
Electra enters. She is exuberantly filthy and presumably smelly. She wears the remnants of a girl's dress, circa 1900. On her right foot she wears a man's large military boot, destroyed and caked with ancient blood. Her left foot is bare. She carries a stake and a rope.

ELECTRA
Look at me. Everyone else is asleep. But I am always awake. Rat scuttling in the wainscoting. In their heads, too. Even as they dream. I know, even there. Listen.

(Chrysothemis appears in a dream state, perhaps high above the audience on a revolving wall. It should seem magical and odd. Electra, smiling, crouches and listens, looking out.)

CHRYSOTHEMIS
What is that sound? Mama filing her nails. Polishing her teeth. Setting her tools down, click, click, picking them up, click, click, making her face.
What is that sound? A thumping, a scraping. Oh, it's Electra, digging up the garden, uprooting all the plants, making grave after empty grave for my father's absent corpse. The place looks like a bomb site now. Look at it. Gaping, misshapen holes, scalloped by her fingers, broken nails pawing, where flowers

once were, flowers I planted. She's dumped them with the
naked mud and they flail together, roots exposed, dying already,
while she squats in the mud, making more graves. The rain
begins to come down and she's working remarkably swiftly now,
mud streaked through her hair, her face, her arms, down her
dress. The holes fill and wink brown water. She scrambles up
the sides like a nimble pig. Suddenly she stops, only to look up
to make sure I am watching. She smiles at me. Oh. This is what
she wants. That I always be watching, from some high clean
place. This is my importance. I see. Oh God. My wrecked garden.

(Chrysothemis disappears. Electra cocks her head, still staring out.)

ELECTRA
And listen.

(Clytemnestra appears, like Chrysothemis, in a dream state.)

CLYTEMNESTRA
My father the swan has taught me how to give birth to perfect
things. I am heroic and extraordinary. I astonish myself. I stand
in a tree and reach between my legs and there—I have made an
egg. It is dove gray and smooth and its shape is the one true
thing in existence. I place it against my cheek. There is the
sound of a curved fingernail scratching. She unfurls herself like
a sweet pea blossom and stands beside me, tall and breathing.
We hold hands. Oh, wait. Another egg. I must let go of this
child, this wonder, to reach my hands again between my legs for
this sticky pink roundness. A slipshod copy of the first gray perfection. I tap it with my finger and a pale, good girl creeps out.
I did not need another. But she is here and already clinging.
What, another egg already cramping my belly? Is there no end
to this? I reach again, what is this horror? A misshapen oblong,
like a tortured walnut. A cracking like teeth on bone and it
emits itself, all bald eyes and scrabbling hands. Is it female?
What does it matter? It does nothing but stare and stare at me.
It is already injured. But a final, a fourth, has dropped uncaught

out of me. It cracks itself open on the ground far below. Perhaps it's dead. Good. What a long fall. But no. A boy. Looking up, armed and agile. Where is my girl, my gray-egg child, the only one I ever wanted? But she has flown forever, while these other mistakes grapple themselves to me, pulling me down. There is no trace of her in the sky and the boy begins his ascent up the tree, he is sure-footed, the tip of his spear flashing. He will come.

(Clytemnestra disappears.)

ELECTRA
(Exultant) You see? I am their condition.

(During the following, she stakes herself like a dog in the court-yard. One end of the rope is connected to her boot, the other to the stake, which she plunges into the center of the stage.
In the course of the coming scene, she will enter her daily routine, which is to patrol the garden at the circumference of her staked circle. She monitors her domain, sweeping like a second hand around a clock. There are points on the clock face where she will hang, leaning, tethered by her ankle, for instance, when she pauses to peer down the road or up into the house. This is presumably how she spends her days, and even today, which is not like any other day, she will occasionally fall into this routine reflexively, making it necessary for other characters to deal with the appara-tus, stepping over the rope, etc., when they want to engage with her. The rope should be short enough to allow her to hang taut from it and long enough to give her the proper range of movement. To ensure ease of movement, both the stake and the boot should be affixed with metal rings that can withstand the stress of this.)

I am their rabid dog who tethers herself in their garden.
Mongrel bitch.
Howling at moons, at suns, at stars.
At it all.

(She howls.)

That's what I do.
I am impossible.
Ask anyone.

I am the creation, battered on the anvil of this insanity, this
place smelling of blood, of slaughter, of helplessness. They
cannot get rid of me. I cannot get rid of me.
I make everything happen.

(Clytemnestra enters as Electra is in the midst of her routine.
She watches, disdainful, for a few moments. She wears a gorgeous
dressing gown and carries a dainty teacup. Electra notices her.
They stare at each other. Electra is cheerfully bitter.)

How did you sleep?

CLYTEMNESTRA
Badly. You again. You really nauseate me. Greasy and black.
You're like the ravens and crows that shit on the pediments and
shriek and dive at the windows. Unsightly, brutish mess. Let me
get upwind of you. You might at least bathe.

(She sits upwind of Electra, sipping tea.)

ELECTRA
And you. What are you anymore? You gave your face away. You
sold it on the butcher's block you call the family hearth. Look at
you. Propping your sagging carcass up, stinking of your rotting
beauty and even as you stink you stamp and flirt your pointless
feathers.

CLYTEMNESTRA
What have you done to the clocks? Two are stopped, three run
crazy in their circles and the rest won't stop chiming.

ELECTRA
They are reckoning the hour of your death, which is now and always. Nothing will ever work right until then. The house has been holding its breath for twenty years, waiting for judgment.

CLYTEMNESTRA
Then let them chime another twenty. Your brother, your dear fiction, will never return in my lifetime.

ELECTRA
Oh yes, in my lifetime and yours, although just barely in yours, rather near the end. And for me, life will just have begun.

CLYTEMNESTRA
Oh, you'll die before me. You don't have the strength for vengeance. I figured that out a long time ago. And you're useless otherwise. You'll die here having accomplished nothing. Not even a rat-faced child to mourn you. Merely an irritation first to last. Tick, tick, tick. You haven't got it in you to do anything by yourself.

ELECTRA
(Stung, but menacing) I am my mother's daughter. You should be terrified of me.

(She takes an ancient knife out of the bodice of her dress.)

This knife, rust or his blood on the blade, you tell me, this very knife, how did you hold it? My hands are so like yours. Show me the grip.

(Electra offers the knife to her mother, who takes it. Clytemnestra hasn't seen the knife in some time. She holds it with familiarity and then suddenly, viciously, raises it overhead in a convincingly murderous stance while still holding her teacup in her lap.)

CLYTEMNESTRA
Like this, girl. Like this. And brought it down twenty times at least on his old man's chest.

ELECTRA
And what did you scream?

CLYTEMNESTRA
"Liar! Filth! Butcher!"

(Clytemnestra hands the knife back to Electra in a sly challenge. Electra grabs it and tries to meet the challenge, holding the knife above her mother's chest. Clytemnestra looks at her critically, unconcerned. A pause.)

ELECTRA
Liar! Filth! Butcher!

CLYTEMNESTRA
Have you no originality? Raise your arm higher, girl. You'll need the force of a long swing. I did. His chest was wide. Higher. Don't you look silly. I hope I didn't look that silly. I don't think so. I could see what I looked like in his open eyes as I brought the blade down. Oh, give me back the knife, you're hopeless.

(Electra lowers the knife, stowing it again in her bodice, humiliated, and crawls away.)

ELECTRA
Hopeless. *(One final threat)* You shall get it back some day.

CLYTEMNESTRA
(Turning away from her) Oh, I'm so bored with you. I gave birth to a shrike. And she stiff-legged after me year after year, dropping dull feathers and muttering, always in the way, an embarrassment.

ELECTRA

You're right. I am warped and noisome. Spewed from the womb
of the crimes I've seen.

CLYTEMNESTRA

The crimes *you've* seen. Ha. A little blood. A bloated cipher of a
man you never knew. Creaking in rusty armor on the path from
the harbor. What do you know of him? Did he even touch you?
Did you even speak?

ELECTRA

He didn't have time. You killed him before I could know him.
I saw the flash of his teeth when he smiled. I saw how tired he was.

CLYTEMNESTRA

I knew him well. Let me tell you what he was. He was a pretty
boy and a bully. Rich and pampered. His men didn't trust him.
He knew that. He wanted their love more than anything else.
To be one of the boys. Pathetic. So that when it came to killing
his own child, his own daughter, he did it like a braggart,
grinned to them as he held up the bloody knife. And they
cheered for him obligingly, slightly stunned, faintly disgusted
but relieved. It was just a girl, they thought, still, it was his.
Well, it didn't bear thinking about, the wind was up and they
could go forth to the bloodletting. That was enough. And I
watched the sails heave and creak, swollen bellies disappearing
out to sea as I held her on the sand. Her warm body, new breasts
tight, her fingers long and hardening, the soft head swinging,
her neck open and undone. They say he vomited later, in whatever privacy a ship bristling with soldiers affords. Like a drunk-
ard into bushes, like the man he was. Who cares? That is the
father you weep for. Someone with a knife. His own daughter.
She could have been you. How often I've wished it was you he
called for. How different it would have been. If he had not asked
me for her, the best of me, the only perfect thing I have ever
made. My oldest, my only child.

ELECTRA

(Sensing her weakness) Ah, but then she would have been there, standing at my place next to the butcher's block. And she would have been here, instead of me, hating you.

CLYTEMNESTRA

I would never have killed him for your sake. I killed him for hers.

(Electra is stunned into silence.)

You see how the inevitable holds us in her hands. So here we are. My dead against your dead, my love against your love. My history against your history, in perpetuity.

ELECTRA

We wait. You have had your justice. I have yet to have mine.

(Chrysothemis enters. She wears sensible women's work attire of the 1900s. She carries gardening tools and a potted geranium. Her energy is entirely different from her sister's and her mother's. She embodies a curious combination of subversiveness and apparent placidity. She takes in the situation at once.)

CHRYSOTHEMIS

Hello, girls. What, at it so early? Lovely day, pink still. I've laid out a meal, not that anyone's interested. Dishes, plates, things to stop the mouth. But somehow I knew, not today. When I woke up this morning I thought, oh, something's wrong again. Today we won't be behaving like human beings. Today no one will sit down.

CLYTEMNESTRA

You've always had a flair for the mundane.

ELECTRA

(Quickening with hope) There is, she's right, something about today. Already I can smell it. Myrtle, is it? Death? Perhaps something will finally happen.

CHRYSOTHEMIS
(Gardening) No, nothing. Not in this life. This pallid little
female life we run out together. Everything of importance has
happened and happened long ago, elsewhere and without us.
We are not part of history. Women.
We three birds, circling empty air, cawing and jibing, hovering
over a plot of dirt, an unwanted circumference, a patch of mud.
There is nothing to be scrapped out of this place, this wasteland
we call home, but our own graves. And there we will tumble
soon enough and mingle our teeth with the roots and pebbles
and lie unmourned, unremembered and nasty as manure.
We were never part of the great drama. No one was ever looking.
All those years the gods were watching the fields of Troy, harbors,
camps and dark-haired figures on the pediments. The scraping
of chariots—wheels turning. Death and battle. Nothing happens
here. We are always at the edge of importance. We learn our
news from mud-spattered boys, days late, stammering rumors.
We wait out our lives. Waiting for action, waiting for judgment.
Houses of women.

*(Chrysothemis has cast a kind of spell. All the women look out, in
the thrall of the drama they were never part of. Clytemnestra
snaps out of it first.)*

CLYTEMNESTRA
(Viciously) Speak for yourself, girl. While you were doing finger
exercises at the piano, I was running a country. I have always
been at the center of the drama. And I have never waited for
anything. Except ripeness, the moment, the true beauty of the
crafted event. And then I did it.

ELECTRA
Until now. What is there left to do except wait, with us, for your
death? Isn't that right?
(Eyeing her mother keenly, sensing weakness) Did you shiver?
Just now?

CLYTEMNESTRA
No.

ELECTRA
(Cheerfully) Perhaps it's just some sort of palsy starting. You are getting on, we can begin to expect these things. First the body, then the mind. Or perhaps the other way around. *(To Chrysothemis)* Which do you think will go first? Shall we take bets?

CLYTEMNESTRA
(Murderous) I'll tell you what will go first. You.
There is something about this day, you're right. Actions can be taken on a day like today. Finally, something will be done.

(She exits into the house. Pause.)

ELECTRA
Don't you hate her?

CHRYSOTHEMIS
She's just a woman.

ELECTRA
A murderer.

CHRYSOTHEMIS
But I've always assumed she was crazy.

ELECTRA
And that makes it all right?

CHRYSOTHEMIS
It makes her pitiable. And dismissible. I don't have to figure her out. She is not like me.

ELECTRA

Then how do you deal with me?

CHRYSOTHEMIS

Oh, but I've always thought you were nuts, too. That's what makes you endurable.

ELECTRA

I see. So, you're the sane one. Such martyrdom. Trapped in this sagging mansion with two shrews screaming over your bowed head at the dinner table.

CHRYSOTHEMIS

Something like that.

ELECTRA

While you comb your hair, wash out your simple dresses, hum your tunes and carry on, shaking your head at the preposterous, sad shambles we have become. The pretty one.

CHRYSOTHEMIS

The one everyone likes. The one no one worries about. I am not frightening. I'm the good girl. Everyone pities me. I'm so reliable. I learned how to push my own pram the summer you wouldn't stop crying. Do you know that you cried for nearly three months straight? Nothing could be done with you. A jammed buzz saw. Life was impossible. So I crawled out of my pram unnoticed and pushed myself into the garden and stayed there. No one looked for me. Or sometimes I would close the door to my room and remain undiscovered for twenty-four hours. When I did come out, someone would sigh and hand me you, dripping and gabbling, or him, or something. I was, I am, unremarkable. *(In rueful sudden realization)* No one ever asked me a question. Not once in my life. No one has ever been curious about what I might be thinking or feeling. No one has ever said: "What did you see? Where were you when it happened? What do you remember? What did you feel?"

(Pause. Electra takes her sister in suddenly. She approaches her with real interest.)

ELECTRA
What did you see? What do you remember? What did you feel?

(Pause. Chrysothemis exhibits for the first time something like vulnerability, trying to remember.)

CHRYSOTHEMIS
(Finally, in defeat) I don't know. I don't remember. All I remember is what you and she have told me. Your stories. I remember your memories.

ELECTRA
(Slightly disgusted, but not surprised) Oh.

CHRYSOTHEMIS
(Her guard down) Was I there? Did I see it? Tell me.

ELECTRA
I don't know. All I know is that I did.

CHRYSOTHEMIS
Yes. And how could I not hate you for that? That you know you existed?

ELECTRA
(Brusque) Well, I don't remember you. So perhaps you didn't.

(Pause. They look at each other.)

CHRYSOTHEMIS
(Coolly bitter) No. I never did. I look at the family pictures and I'm always on the margin, smudged by your dirty fingerprints. It could be anyone in that pale dress. Your thumb across my face. Our little historian.

ELECTRA

(Back to her routine) Somebody had to be. Everyone else is dead or disappeared. And you. So placid. So stoic. Such a bore. What are you doing in a family like ours? You are utterly useless.

CHRYSOTHEMIS

(Astonished) Me? And what about *you?* You have done *nothing,* not one thing in all your life. You'd think we might get something out of you, having to put up with your insults and yammering year after year—a little light housekeeping, at least, an occasional botched dinner—but no. People ask and I think, well, she must do *some*thing, but I have no idea.

ELECTRA

(Irate) I remember. I remember. I REMEMBER. I have not chosen this. I would never have chosen this. To spend my life as a vessel for one impossible truth. But that is my condition. I have carried it like a dragon inside me. It is what is alive, not me. I feel it flip and slap its hard tail against me or slide its teeth along the tender pink walls of me. Its awful creature-song keeps me open-eyed and walking all night long. Do you think I would have chosen this?

CHRYSOTHEMIS

(Gently) But then how will you ever live differently? What can ever change this?

ELECTRA

Justice.

CHRYSOTHEMIS

But, my dear monster, there is no justice. Only life. You must finally wake up to that.

ELECTRA

He will come.

CHRYSOTHEMIS
He will never come.

ELECTRA
Then you must help me.

CHRYSOTHEMIS
Well, of course I won't.

ELECTRA
Because you're a coward.

CHRYSOTHEMIS
(Reasonably) Actually, I don't think I am a coward. You are.
I'm merely a pragmatist. I won't do it because it won't work.
We've discussed this. One more murder, one more corpse, and
then we are sucked back into the maw of history. Generation
after generation throwing up their bodies in the name of what?

ELECTRA
Justice.

CHRYSOTHEMIS
It is not for us to render that. What is justice anyway? Your idea,
nothing more. Perhaps there is nothing like justice in nature.

ELECTRA
Then nature is appalling. We can do better.

*(In the course of this, Chrysothemis goes to Electra and does a bit
of marginal grooming, such as smoothing the greasy hair from
her forehead and using a handkerchief to spit-clean dirt from
Electra's face. Electra submits, like a neglected child, to this minor
kindness from her older sister.)*

CHRYSOTHEMIS
I think you are naive. But then, of course you are. You were
never really forced to grow up. I was the only one who had to.

Our brother remains here, some phantom of a man-child we dream into an avenger. You are no less a phantom, no less a child, just taller, louder, but still there really, stuck at that hearthside, blood still wet on the stone, his screams still echoing in the air, you are still standing there, mouth open, hands empty. It's just that you walk around, dog our steps and eat sometimes so we forget that you're really just a ghost, that you never grew up. You know nothing about life. You just know your little corner of the history, and that you've fingered and fluttered in our faces until it's unreadable faint nonsense and probably wrong to begin with anyway.

ELECTRA

(Appalled, pulling violently away from Chrysothemis) What I know I know absolutely. It has made me. Everything I am is that knowledge.

CHRYSOTHEMIS

(Passionately reasonable) But what are you? A white-faced maniac. Someone who is welcome nowhere. Someone who has never actually lived. You have wasted your life, whatever life you could have had, with hatred, broken your only body in bitterness, ground a subtle, complicated mind down to nothing but a dull pebble of one memory, one notion, one impulse to action never taken. Have you thought of that? All this talk of justice and history and perhaps all you ever were was someone who hated life? Why not kill yourself?

ELECTRA

If I believed for a second what you believe, that there is no such thing as justice in this world, then I would kill myself. Certainly. What would be the point of me? But what I know is that I am the guardian of this truth and I am here to see it honored. The world will never forgive us if we do not make sense of it. What I have suffered has meaning only if I continue to suffer it. I am necessary. I believe that. My death would release me but bring down history in crashing ruin.

CHRYSOTHEMIS
(Tired of the argument) I wouldn't notice.

ELECTRA
No, you wouldn't. You'd merely sigh and go for the dustpan. But then you have become virtuosic in obliviousness.

CHRYSOTHEMIS
And I look at you, haggard and rank, and I think: the only thing she has ever accomplished is she has ruined her own life.

ELECTRA
That's not true. I've also ruined hers.

(She indicates Clytemnestra, who enters dressed for the day, looking menacing and imperious.)

CLYTEMNESTRA
(Coolly) I've been thinking.

ELECTRA
Oh, dear. Not again.

CLYTEMNESTRA
Considering your future, as a mother does. What do you think families like ours do with girls like you? Ignore them, hope that they won't embarrass them at parties? Dress them up as best they can, endure them privately, invent vague maladies, turn down their invitations out by saying, "Not feeling quite up to it," "Packing for a trip abroad," "Summer camp," "Swiss academy . . ." But you, you just kept growing, didn't you? And now you are this hulking, nearly middle-aged monstrosity who never did anything, went anywhere, only aged and aged and continued. You know what families like ours *really* do with girls like you, don't you? What we should have done long ago, what we will do now, at last. Wall you up in an attic or a basement somewhere.

Let your howling carom off walls with no one to hear you. Let
you shit yourself. There are people who don't know you, who
won't listen to you, who don't even speak your language who
will tend you. They'll throw you food from doorways, shut you
from light, turn away from your screaming to play cards with
each other, never think of you, never dream of you, never be
hurt by you. That is what people like us do with the wild girls
of families like ours. We have the money. We have the hatred.
I think in fact that would be the best thing all around. Don't
you? I'll take you there myself. This afternoon perhaps, after
I pick up the dry cleaning.
(As she exits) God, the smell out here.

(She is gone. Pause. Both women are in shock.)

ELECTRA
(With quiet clarity) And I will go. Why not? I will write on walls
with my blood. I will gnaw the bars and dull my teeth. I will
bang my lice-ridden head against the concrete floor and howl
and howl. Narrating my history to the air, telling my one story
again and again. It will all be the same to me. *(A new thought)*
And perhaps, if I am lucky, senility will loosen the past and
there will come a time when the faces will blur. I will confuse
yours with household dogs we once had and hers with fairy tale
monsters and his . . . and his with imaginary friends I once
played with, princes I dreamed about. And my father will seem
to be a tree perhaps, silent and high, gnarled and immortal,
shading some happy kingdom that I might visit in death. Ah.
You see. There is nothing she can do to me that would be worse
than what she has already done. She unstrung my life from the
beginning and nothing ever made sense again. What she doesn't
know is that I am stronger than she can ever hope to be. She
lives in fear. Me, what I am most afraid of has already happened.

*(Electra takes up her stake and exits. Silence. Chrysothemis looks
about her at the empty yard.)*

CHRYSOTHEMIS
The smell of burning is in the air.
Carried to us from the battlefields we can never see.
Ash of buildings, of bodies, of children
Finds us here.
Drops itself exhausted into the furrows of our fields
And spring is false again
We bear nothing, we bear all
We are blind to what is killing us
But we smell it in the wind.

I had a brother, so the story goes,
Another child in the household
Kicking his feet under the table, banging a spoon
Having ideas.
Dark he was and different from the rest of us
Only in his sex
We always knew that he at least would leave that table,
The four corners of the yard
Walk about
He read of boats and could picture himself on the prow
Eyes on the horizon
While we, the others, traced the pictured rigging with our
Fingers, yawned and wondered what would be for lunch.
It was not for us, the world.

We let him screech and run, flail a tin sword, make threats in
the nursery, jump from windows. We talked over him and
touched him in passing as he touched us in passing.
And so it was in the end.
We lost him to the world, as we lost all the men.
We never knew him at all, any more than we knew, or he knew,
his own father. A man: the crunch of boots on gravel as they go
down the path away from you. Badly written letters, smudged
by unimaginable hands and weather, to somebody they think
you are, from someone they think you might like them to be.

Men exit such places as this and never come again. Or if they do come back, like my father, they arrive, bearded and changed, distracted and absent even as they are here, stand a moment, blinking in the courtyard and then are quickly dispatched to the next world. My mother was right. He was an impossibility in a place such as this.

(She exits. Silence. Orestes enters. He is wearing a dusty, dirty uniform reminiscent of World War I. He is shattered, intelligent and ancient for all his youth. He has seen far too much.)

ORESTES

God, how depressing. A ghost town. Gaping with stillness. Occasional dog, chicken, duck . . . shutters closed, containing dust and teapots. Stifling. World of women. No color, no music, no sound. Every other house muffled in mourning, the obligatory plaque: "Gave of our best," "Precious son," "Beloved husband." Given for what? A moronic, terrified officer's gesture. A foot of foreign mud.

(He looks up at the house, slightly awed at having arrived at last.)

And here. A house that has given much, taken more, and all to achieve this grim garden, a roof that still leaks, another few years of tarnish on the unused silver. House of women. *(Speaking intimately to a hovering god)* What, yet more killing to be done? *(Looks at the house)* Their dead son, their darling murderer returns at last.

(He adjusts a black armband on his sleeve.
Electra enters, barefoot. Silence. Orestes is appalled to think that this might be his sister; he covers, immediately adopting a kind of military distance and correctness.)

Is this the house?

ELECTRA
What house are you looking for?

ORESTES
I bring terrible news.

ELECTRA
(Mirthlessly rueful) This is the house.

ORESTES
Orestes, son of this house, is dead. I was his companion.

(However Electra reacts to the terrible news—she may laugh terribly, for instance—it is odd and discomfiting to Orestes, for all his experience of the usual responses to grief.)

Here are his ashes.

ELECTRA
Do you have a gun?

ORESTES
No. I'm not a soldier anymore.

ELECTRA
Then what use are you? You might at least have killed me.

ORESTES
Who are you?

ELECTRA
No one now. I used to be someone's sister. First I was someone's daughter, but that was over a long time ago. Then I was a sister. That was enough to get me up in the morning. Years and years. Now I'm, what? *(Looks down at herself with a kind of speculative interest)* A thing of some sort, I suppose. Something you might

hang up in a field to frighten the crows, I guess. There must be some use for such a large thing. I'm sure they'll think of something.

ORESTES
Are you Electra?

ELECTRA
Well, I suppose we might as well name it. Pretty name.

ORESTES
I have his ashes.

ELECTRA
Oh, well, those will come in handy. Drainage for the tomatoes, filler for bad pie crust. *(Takes the urn matter-of-factly)* How light he is. No heavier than an idea. Which is all he ever was, I guess. Nothing. He has come to nothing after all. Ashes. Is that a tooth? I remember his smile. His hair, bright and long in the summer. How it must have curled and fizzed in the furnace. *(In anguished disbelief)* This was a man once?

ORESTES
Yes.

ELECTRA
Hardly seems possible. Look at this.
(Laughs quietly) He was such a funny child. He used to imitate me, how clumsy I was. He'd stalk about the parlor, muttering to himself, the way I do, pretend to trip, right himself, trip again. I can't explain it. He made me laugh. Did he make you laugh?

ORESTES
Oh, yes. I laughed at him all the time. He struck me as . . . somewhat ludicrous. He was something of an actor.

ELECTRA

(With genuine interest) Was he?

ORESTES

Taking on parts. Pretending to be people he wasn't.

ELECTRA

Did he imitate you?

ORESTES

Yes. And I imitated him. We were a riot.

(The longer the business of having to speak about himself in the third person continues, the more unsettling and revealing it becomes for Orestes, and the more Electra begins to grasp the truth of the situation.)

ELECTRA

Did you love him?

ORESTES

As much as he loved himself.

ELECTRA

Did you know him well?

ORESTES

No one did. He was always somewhat severed from his own life. An exile. It seemed he died many times. Perhaps, in a way, he was always dead.

ELECTRA

Did he ever speak of home? Of us? Of me?

ORESTES

He spoke of you. He spoke of duty and terror and guilt. He never spoke of home. Was this his home?

ELECTRA

No, not his. Mine either, for that matter. We, both of us, died in exile. What did he say about me?

ORESTES

That you were the one that saved him.

ELECTRA

Did he love me?

ORESTES

He didn't know much about love. He knew something about blood. He was fearless and cruel in battle. He could look coolly at sights that made other men scream or vomit and he could do things to people . . . that don't bear thinking about. We were afraid of him.

ELECTRA

You hated him.

ORESTES

A little. A lot. He seemed to be driven by a demon. He was utterly alone in the world and he never looked back. Because of that he was dangerous.

ELECTRA

He sounds very useful.

ORESTES

Efficient in battle. And he slept alone. He had terrible dreams.

ELECTRA

Nightmares.

ORESTES

They woke him screaming, teeth chattering, pants soiled.

ELECTRA
Did he tell you what he dreamed?

ORESTES
Something about being pushed down an endless, lightless tunnel
that got smaller and smaller, forced to crawl with a knife in his
teeth, pushed like rags into a gun barrel, and the walls getting
tighter and tighter around him.

ELECTRA
What was at the end of the tunnel?

ORESTES
Something warm and dark and soft and enormous that he
would have to climb inside of and slice and slice and . . . drown
in the blood or maybe slither out of, crawl away from, blinded
by blood, maddened by bats . . .

ELECTRA
What was it, did he say? What was it that was pushing him?

ORESTES
You.

ELECTRA
(She knows at last) Ah. Terrible dream.

ORESTES
It made him what he was. It was what he saw when he closed
his eyes. Always. *(Closes his eyes, winces)* Right there. *(Opens his
eyes and looks at her)*

ELECTRA
Who is this in my hand?

(Orestes takes her other hand and places it against his cheek.)

ORESTES
Your brother.

ELECTRA
So you say.

(She drops the urn and takes his face in her hands. She kisses him full on the mouth.)

Dark sunlight at last.
I have driven you mad.

ORESTES
(With sadness and affection) Yes. And I have driven you mad.

ELECTRA
(Delighted) Yes. And who better to kill her now than her two mad children? We will cavort and drool and shriek prophecies in gibberish. We will be happy and appalling. Free at last.

ORESTES
Oh, Electra. Your terrible eyes. *(He touches her)* They have been open too long.

ELECTRA
Like yours.

ORESTES
I'm tired of killing.

ELECTRA
I'm tired of waiting.

(During the following, he draws her down to him on the ground against her resistance. She gives in for a moment and they take a position familiar from childhood, like sleeping puppies.)

ORESTES

Let's just go sleep somewhere finally, let the years go by, let's
curl into each other the way we used to do, make new dreams.

ELECTRA

(Sitting up) Not yet. Your work is not over.

ORESTES

(Burrowing into her) Let me sleep.

ELECTRA

(Pulling away) No.

ORESTES

I can't raise my arm again.

ELECTRA

Only once more. That's all. *(Takes the knife out of her bodice and
places it in his hand)* Like this. High. High. *(Pulls his hand up,
showing him)*

ORESTES

You know how. You do it. *(Tries to give her back the knife)* God,
why haven't you done it? You've had time enough.

ELECTRA

(Desperate) I can't. It is for you.

ORESTES

You have the hatred. I'm past it. You can do it.

(He manages to get the knife back into her hand.)

ELECTRA

(Flinging the knife away) No! I can't!
If I could have done it, don't you think I would have done it
long ago? God. The misery I could have saved myself—all these

years waiting for you, who never came, never wrote. All these years, thinking of you out in the world, loose, knowing things, seeing people, looking at—something, anything other than this. I pictured you in Africa, standing in a marketplace, color all around you, languages buzzing, monkeys chattering and scrambling over while you drank something hot and sweet or bit into some strange fruit that dripped on the ground.

ORESTES
(Wearily) I was never in Africa.

ELECTRA
Or at sea somewhere, shirt sticking to your back, watching the sky go crimson and enormous.

ORESTES
(Steely, trying to get this through to her) It was never like that. Ditch to ditch, death to death, that's all.

ELECTRA
What you have done, what you have become, while I drag my skirt around the yard year after year becoming nothing, a middle-aged child eaten up by this, this nightmare.
(A naked plea) Please. Free me. You owe me. I gave you your life for this. Only for this.

ORESTES
(Bitterly, calmly) Yes. I know. For this. My life's pilot. Thank you. You have no idea what you have made me into.

ELECTRA
What do you think it has been for me? Yapping on the ground for twenty years like a severed head—nothing but eyes and tongue—waiting, *waiting* for my reluctant body to finally come back to me and *do something.* Here. *(She puts the knife in his hand once more and raises it)* My hand, my arm. Complete me.

(Pause. He takes the knife and stows it.)

ORESTES
Oh, Electra. We should have kept our eyes closed.

(Clytemnestra enters. It is impossible to guess what she surmises of the truth of the situation. Orestes snaps into impeccable military bearing.)

CLYTEMNESTRA
Sir?

ORESTES
I bring terrible news, madam. Your son is dead. Cut down in his glory. A great sacrifice. I'm sorry.

CLYTEMNESTRA
(Coolly curious) How?

ORESTES
While leading a charge he fell from his horse and was dragged out into no-man's-land. I crawled out that night to find him there tangled in the reins. It was a terrible death but heroic, lit by his valor.

(Slight pause.)

CLYTEMNESTRA
Sad. *(Assesses her own emotional state)* I'm taking it well, wouldn't you say? You look like a boy who knows his way around death and how people take it. My son. Huh. And his horse?

ORESTES
(Confused) I'm sorry?

CLYTEMNESTRA
What happened to the horse?

ORESTES
(Somewhat baffled) Well, the horse died, too.

CLYTEMNESTRA
Tragic. Dumb animals. The suffering of the innocent. Hardly
seems fair.

ORESTES
Sorry?

CLYTEMNESTRA
Getting animals mixed up in such a loathsome thing. War.
What do they know about it? What did they ever do to us? How
confusing and terrifying it must be for a horse, a creature like
that, all the noise, shouting of the dying, the cannons. Awful.
(She cries, genuinely moved) Why should they suffer as we do?
No justice. Excuse me.
(She recovers quickly, then stares at him with interest) You look
terrible. You must be tired, famished. People must eat. We must
have something in the house. Don't we? *(Turns to Electra)* Jell-O,
vodka, Ritz crackers . . . something? *(Electra looks glassy, trying
not to give anything away)* Hello, sunshine. Not a very good day
for you all 'round, I'd say. You look flushed. Nice to see some
color in your cheeks though. *(Little pause while she assesses
Electra)* Awfully quiet. *(To Orestes)* Uncharacteristic. Never
one to keep one in suspense about what she is feeling. *(Back to
Electra, who seems to be holding her breath)* Well, bright eyes?

ELECTRA
(Carefully) Let's give the man what he came for.

CLYTEMNESTRA
(Turning on Orestes, sunnily) Oh, by all means. Such a long
journey with such a lot of words in his mouth. Goodness. They
must have been heavy. Dead horses, valor and all. *(She is standing
too close to him for his comfort but he can't move)* May I touch you?

ORESTES

(Excruciatingly confused but still maintaining some semblance of military bearing) Sorry?

CLYTEMNESTRA

No need to be. No need. *(She touches his head gently, then cups the back of it with her hand)* Such a great round head. How it must have hurt your mother, butting through. I remember what I thought at the time. I screamed, I believe, well, one does. But I thought I was birthing the moon, you see. His head, a great pallid thing with a face that would watch me through all my nights and never really go away. *(She looks up)* See? *(Pointing)* Even now, the sun's still out and yet, yes, there it is, like a dim coin of some kind. You can't really ever get away from it. Well, perhaps tonight, hm? Come, my egg, *(She caresses his head again, then takes him by the hand)* let's see if we can find what you came for in this house.

(They exit, Orestes, in a haze, allowing Clytemnestra to lead him slowly into the house. Electra kneels in a kind of ecstasy. Chrysothemis has been watching all this from the margin of the stage. We should suddenly become aware of her presence and wonder how long she's been there. She knows exactly what's going on. She comes in farther.)

CHRYSOTHEMIS
(Pensively) What a strange day.

(Electra looks up, but doesn't turn to her.)

The weather can't make up its mind. Shall we rain? Shall we be pleasant? The sunlight has had a dull, metallic glint to it and the wind is upsetting the grass, running backwards.

ELECTRA
(Ominously) Earthquake weather.

CHRYSOTHEMIS
The teacups were all quivering in their saucers this morning and I thought, oh, it's just the war. But it's silent, have you noticed? Not a sound.

ELECTRA
(Listening hard for sounds in the house) I can't hear anything.

CHRYSOTHEMIS
Whatever it is, it's happening far, far away—out of earshot. Perhaps we'll hear about it on the news tonight. Isn't it odd? The way one goes through a day and nothing out of the ordinary happens and at the end of it one hears that, yes, during that day enormous events have taken place—stock markets crashing, landslides, train wrecks, handshakes—and one thinks, what was I doing at that time? Ironing? Planning dinner? Folding sheets? While millions died, while the world came to an end, what was I up to at the time? Making a sandwich?

ELECTRA
(Quietly insistent, trying to shut her sister out) Digging a grave—

CHRYSOTHEMIS
Humming a childhood song—

ELECTRA
Sharpening an ax—

CHRYSOTHEMIS
Yawning—

ELECTRA
Preparing the ground—

CHRYSOTHEMIS
Changing a lightbulb—

ELECTRA
Counting the seconds—

CHRYSOTHEMIS
Opening a can—

ELECTRA
MAKING IT HAPPEN.

CHRYSOTHEMIS
Looking in the wrong direction.

ELECTRA
(Explosively, to the world) MAKING IT HAPPEN. MAKING IT
HAPPEN. THERE. THAT'S WHERE I WAS. THERE. ME.
WITHOUT ME, NOTHING WOULD EVER HAVE HAP-
PENED.

CHRYSOTHEMIS
(Unruffled by her sister, still musing, looking out)
Winding the clocks.

*(Orestes stands in the threshold of the house, bloody. Neither
woman sees him; they look out.)*

Getting older.
Talking to the air.
Trying to remember a terrible dream.

*(The sound of wet wings, the Furies descending. Orestes looks up
slowly. The women look out.)*

END OF PART 2

Iphigenia in Tauris

Day. Iphigenia is in white and surrounded by five girls (the
Chorus), who are also dressed in white. Iphigenia is clearly the
leader of the group. The world they inhabit is achingly beautiful
and clean, a kind of natural paradise. They look out, pensive.

IPHIGENIA
I was never really a woman
And now I will never have the chance
I never really lived
And now I am immortal
They say I was spirited away at the moment of the knife
Some deer died in my place
But it looked like me to me at any rate
It was disorienting
I rose up out of myself
Looking down at the figure on the stone
She's so young, I thought
Beautiful in a way
But then I forgot about her
Because of the press of air and light
The fact of traveling at such a high speed
Intoxicating
This is death, I thought
Just another trip to an unknown place
To meet a stranger
And it seems I was right
Because this is a sort of heaven
The kind of place someone might have thought I would like

Safety, certainly, and a nice view
Who knew it would be so dull?
I am the keeper of a shrine on a wild island
I am surrounded by girls . . .

(Lines are split among the members of the Chorus.)

CHORUS
Who are all alike because we are all homesick for Greece,
Which is to say, life
No one to dress up for here
Just the unseen gods
No one to kiss
No crowds at the marketplace
No news
Nothing to talk about, really
I guess we should be happy
We are girls forever
And we are all rather pretty in white
And life is scorchingly uneventful
It's just that sometimes one dreams
And that can get you into trouble
Because we remember life in dreams
Noises, voices, cries
Colors that buzz up against each other
Things to touch:
The skin of oranges
The cheek of a lover
Books
Tools
Paper
There is nothing to touch here
Except each other
And we are all too sad for that
This is privilege

We can't help wondering what we might have become without it
If we'd been left alone.

IPHIGENIA
If I hadn't been so bloody special
I think I was fairly bright
Observant at least.

CHORUS
Maybe that was the problem.

IPHIGENIA
I can't help feeling that I was put away just when I threatened
to become interesting. Just when I started feeling things out of
the ordinary.

CHORUS
Bleeding
Getting angry
Talking too loud
Too fast
Too much.

IPHIGENIA
I hear my mother killed my father on account of me
I was impressed
I didn't know I rated so much vengeance
But Mom. Well, *she* was interesting
She lived long enough
I'm sure she's dead by now
No woman can afford to be *that* interesting
I wish I'd been that interesting
Now I am something made of stone
Handsome, bleached and perpetual.

CHORUS
We are stand-ins for Artemis

Who is too busy to be a stone
She's off hunting and conniving
Running
Being impressive
That would be fun
Knowing something
Feeling the muscle that pulls the bow taut
Judging distance
Accomplishing things
Like Greece.

IPHIGENIA
What did we know of Greece?

CHORUS
Or Life?
We think of Greece
And it is really all about what we didn't quite see, hear, touch
But what we sensed
We were girls there
Privileged girls
On the threshold of consciousness
Hurried past what was essential
We remember the cities and what we see are
Corners not walked around
Dark doorways
Like open mouths
We would not pass through
But wondered
Conversations held just barely out of earshot
So that we heard sound
Sibilance
Scattered syllables
But not the sense
Muted colors of a life seen through a veil
And now we are all still guessing

Just at a greater distance
At a terrible height.

IPHIGENIA

Oh, and here's the irony
If a man should reach us at this place
We are supposed to kill him.

CHORUS

But all we want to do is speak to him
Ask questions
Touch him.

IPHIGENIA

And I do
But only at the point of a knife
I feel their necks
From which would issue answers
But no.

CHORUS

We terrify them with our whiteness
Bind them in ropes
The way market wives bind vegetables.

IPHIGENIA

And then I say . . . something or other
And the knife comes down.

CHORUS

And we land ourselves in silence once more
The sea birds call
Rise and fall on currents of clean air
And we have served something
The silenced male body
Offered up to something.

IPHIGENIA
Just as I was offered
(With effort, trying to make sense of this)
It has a sort of
A circular
An inevitable
A sense to it, I suppose.

(They see Orestes offstage and look on with interest.)

CHORUS
Oh, there's a madman on the beach
Look at him
He seems to be attacked by phantoms
Birds is it?
How he screams
You can almost hear it
Covering his head and running
Rolling in the sand
To get away from what?

IPHIGENIA
Now would be the time to bind and bring him
Go.

(The Chorus leaves.)

What terrible suffering actual people endure
Look at life
A man trying to run away from his own head
I've heard of such things
What wars do to people
They cannot escape the moment
The horrifying moment, whatever it is
And they live inside of it forever
Even on a day like this

It's beautiful, of course
It always is
If he could only see it.

(The Chorus carries Orestes on, bound to a long pole like a kill from a hunt. They lay him before Iphigenia. A member of the Chorus hands her a knife. Then the Chorus leaves. Iphigenia looks down on Orestes with interest. The exchange between them, even before they recognize each other, has the quality of an exchange between colleagues. It is companionable from the first, gradually becoming something even deeper and far more powerful, an exchange between two siblings.)

ORESTES
(As if in the thrall of a nightmare)
Birds and more birds
Black or white
Black or white
They are all female.

IPHIGENIA
And what do the birds say?

ORESTES
(Beginning to come to consciousness)
"You have killed her. You cannot kill her."
"You have killed her. You cannot kill her."

IPHIGENIA
Who?

ORESTES
(Awake) My mother.

IPHIGENIA
(Genuinely interested) Well, why would you do that?

ORESTES

Oh, everyone told me to. A god told me to.

IPHIGENIA

And you always do what you are told?

ORESTES

(Simply) Yes. I was a soldier first and for a long time. Only lately a matricide.

IPHIGENIA

Ah, well. I'm a priestess. I'm equally gifted in compliance. And I'm also a girl. So.

ORESTES

(Rueful) Just my luck. Obedience meets obedience. We'll probably end up killing each other.

IPHIGENIA

Funny you should say so. That's why you were brought to me. I'm supposed to kill you.

ORESTES

(Merely curious) Why?

IPHIGENIA

It's what I have been told to do.

ORESTES

What god do you serve?

IPHIGENIA

Does it matter? Artemis.

ORESTES

Oh. And I serve Apollo. That's why I'm here.

IPHIGENIA

What did he want you to do here?

ORESTES

Steal the statue of Artemis. Bring it back to Greece.

IPHIGENIA

Why?

ORESTES

Who knows? I didn't ask. If I did it he said he would get the Furies off my back.

IPHIGENIA

(Half serious) We are all statues of Artemis. Take all of us with you. We are insane with homesickness.

ORESTES

But you're supposed to kill me.

IPHIGENIA

Oh, I know. I shouldn't even be talking to you. But you interest me. I miss the sound of men's voices. We don't hear them much and when we do, *(Shows him the knife)* not for long. You are a sacrifice, you see.

ORESTES

(Fatalistic and matter-of-fact) I was always a sacrifice. Since I was a child. Beaten into submission to the tune of fathers all my life. I was plunged into the arms of the military early on, world of boys. Muscled, fatted to sacrifice in the name of fathers, which is the name of states, countries, gods. Told to obey, to lay down my body, my spirit to him, to always him. Fathers. It was easy to kill her. I've done it so often. The quick quieting of limbs, dulling of eyes. Simple. What did I know about mothers? Everything I've learned about mothers is what

they have been screaming into my ears since the moment I did it. They strum my sinews like harps and sing about her. And in this song, this pain, this madness, I am taught that when I took my mother's life I made myself an exile from all nature. My crime, her blood, sears through the fabric of the world. *(To the gods)* What did I know about nature? *(To Iphigenia)* It was not in my training.

IPHIGENIA
I was schooled in sacrifice as well. Just of a different kind. The girl, the virgin. *(Searchingly)* It made a kind of sense, didn't it?

(An unacknowledged recognition begins.)

ORESTES
Oh, yes. The exchange. We knew it in our blood. We are the necessary payment of the people.

IPHIGENIA
The negotiation with the mystery.

ORESTES
The special ones. Were we special?

(She begins to untie him.)

IPHIGENIA
Oh, yes. Terribly special.

ORESTES
I come from a house eccentric in blood.

IPHIGENIA
Eccentric in suffering.

ORESTES
Lie upon lie.

IPHIGENIA
Generation upon generation.

ORESTES
Aberrant.

IPHIGENIA
Pariahs.

ORESTES
Netted up.

IPHIGENIA
Tight knots.

ORESTES
In fate.

IPHIGENIA
In fate.

ORESTES
I thought you looked familiar.

IPHIGENIA
And you.

ORESTES
Blood knits us.

IPHIGENIA
Blood and service of blood.

ORESTES
My poor sister.

IPHIGENIA
My poor brother.

ORESTES
Saved.

IPHIGENIA
Saved.

(They lean against each other. Now they are so intimately connected that they seem to be thinking as one. They look up.)

ORESTES
Everything is watching.

IPHIGENIA
What's up there.

ORESTES
Invisible.

IPHIGENIA
Terrible.

ORESTES
Hovering.

IPHIGENIA
We are performing a legend.

ORESTES
And the legend is performing us.

IPHIGENIA
For what?

ORESTES
In the name of what?

IPHIGENIA
Is it possible to become invisible at this late date?

ORESTES
Oh, to be unimportant.

IPHIGENIA
To live without a script.

ORESTES
Without duty.

IPHIGENIA
Oblivion.

ORESTES
Oblivion.

IPHIGENIA
So, who shall hold the knife now?

ORESTES
Which killing to echo? His of you? Mine of her?

IPHIGENIA
Or hers of him? Redress? Is it possible?
I can't remember the sequence anymore, just the deaths.

ORESTES
I do. I murdered her last. Mine was the last. If it's redress, you
should kill me.

IPHIGENIA
Oh, I know. But it's just death now. No sense.

ORESTES
No sacrifice.

IPHIGENIA
We have reached the threshold of futility.

ORESTES
The stone wall of history. End of sight.

(A pause as they try to think this through. She looks up, uncertain, holding the knife.)

IPHIGENIA
I have heard that a needle can be made to pass through stone.

ORESTES
A tiny hole, inconsequential to the structure.

IPHIGENIA
Just large enough for these two odd lives

ORESTES
To somehow thread their way through into a different air.

IPHIGENIA
A different light. Beyond bargains.

ORESTES
Beyond exchange. Blood feuds.

IPHIGENIA
Justice.

ORESTES
Justice.

(Pause. They are both looking up. They look at each other.)

IPHIGENIA
I am the statue you have come to find
Take me to the city
To the center of the city
Build noise and life around me
I will be silent and tall
I will remind them
I will seem to see everything
I will be female and slightly terrifying
I will be what I have always been
Visible and mute
You will place me at the center of something
And you will lay your tortured head upon my cold feet
And you will finally sleep
This is how the legend performs itself to an end.

ORESTES
I can do this for you.

IPHIGENIA
I can do this for you.

*(In the course of the following, Iphigenia will gradually strike a
pose like that of a statue, resolving herself into radical stillness.
Her eyes will go dead and her limbs harden such that by the last
line, Orestes will feel himself to be alone.)*

ORESTES
And this will be the part everyone will forget

IPHIGENIA
the needle through the wall of history

ORESTES
the part of justice which is merely

IPHIGENIA
personal

ORESTES
inelegant

IPHIGENIA
a quirk

ORESTES
a sliver of light

IPHIGENIA
that is only

ORESTES
and finally

IPHIGENIA
something like

ORESTES
love.

(Orestes looks up at his transformed sister. He has been left holding the knife. He places it before him. Silence. He curls up on the ground, laying his head upon his sister's feet. He closes his eyes.)

THE END

The Trojan Women

Introduction

In 1995, I received a grant from the Lila Wallace–Reader's Digest Fund for my work as a playwright. In addition to a personal grant, I received specific funding for three years for a project that I would come up with myself, involving a humanitarian group of my choice, and using theater in an unconventional way with a group of people who might not be exposed to it otherwise. I decided to work with recent immigrants and refugees from the war that was still raging in the Balkans. There was a relatively new but growing community of such people in New York, particularly in Queens. I determined to adapt a Greek play and have it performed as a staged reading by non-actors from the region. I was particularly interested in getting a group together that would represent all sides of the conflict: Serbs, Croatians, Muslims and Albanians. And I wanted to have the piece performed in all the dialects present in that constellation of people as well as in English. This was a rather formidable plan—in fact, I had no idea just *how* formidable it was when I dreamed it up. Nevertheless.

I had the great good fortune of meeting a social worker, Sara Kahn, who had just spent several months in Bosnia, working with traumatized women and children. Sara was uniquely suited in many ways to be a partner in this project, not just because of her enormous heart, felicitous set of capabilities and grace as a person, but also because her background was in theater. She had an appreciation of the potential of the medium and a real under-standing of what we would be attempting to accomplish.

We approached the Quaker human rights organization Amer-ican Friends Service Committee, which agreed to oversee and help administer the project, and then Classic Stage Company, which agreed to host the project in New York City. We started recruiting, a task which began with placing ads for the workshop in ethnic newspapers, putting up flyers and making phone calls, but which ultimately meant spending a great deal of time in var-ious bars in Queens just talking to people and trying to convince them to do this improbable thing. It was a fairly hard sell and I'm still surprised that we eventually were able to corral a substantial number of people to do it each year. Recent immigrants, even under the best of circumstances, are hardly in a position to make a commitment to any project not directly connected to putting together a coherent life. These people's lives were often a mass of obligations and uncertainty. If they were recent immigrants, they were struggling to find places to live, learn English, get jobs, and take care of their children, among other things. In addition, many of these people were severely traumatized by what they'd just been through.

All of them had lost family members and friends. Some were completely alone in the world, raw arrivals in an utterly alien cul-ture. Some of the men had been veterans; one woman had lost a leg to shrapnel during the siege of Sarajevo. At the very least, everyone had just endured the experience of fleeing a country that was in the process of self-destructing. We were asking each of them to give up quite a few nights and weekends to come into New York City and participate in a play with people they would normally cross the street to avoid. On top of all this, we were ask-ing them to act, which almost none of them had ever done, and which is scary enough in and of itself. And, of course, we could offer them no money for their pains. One might wonder why any of them did it at all. What we discovered was that many immi-grants had a terrific hunger to do something, anything, that engaged their minds and hearts. They made huge sacrifices to make this project possible and they overcame enormous fear in order to simply stand in witness to their own despair. I am still amazed by their generosity and their courage.

I had assumed I would adapt one of the Greek texts for this project because of my fondness for the power and simplicity of those plays and because they are removed in time and ethnicity from the immediacy of the conflict. I also felt that such texts would connect everyone in the project because we share in them equally as members of Western culture. They belong to no one and to everyone. The obvious text in this case seemed to me to be Euripides' *Trojan Women*. It is perhaps the greatest antiwar play ever written, certainly one of the oldest, and contains some of the most extraordinary roles for women in theatrical literature.

Not a single person I worked with over the years needed to be told the story of the Trojan War, much less who Euripides was. And the age range was from teenagers to people in their seventies. People who came from the largest cities participated, as well as people from tiny country villages who had been caught in the crossfire as the war ravaged the country. But none of the laborious work of teaching people the basic notions of Greek tragedy that would have been necessary for any comparable American group was required.

The basic premise every time we did the project was that the text would be performed in part in whatever languages the participants identified as their own, and that the translation of each role would always be done by the person performing it. This meant there were generally three languages to be heard in the course of the evening: English, Serbo-Croatian (in all of its different dialects) and Albanian. All the actors would have a chance to speak approximately half of the text in their own language, in their own translation. I felt that this was essential, however arduous the translation aspect of the rehearsal process, because it meant that each actor was performing, at least in part, his or her own words. It also meant that an audience member who didn't know English, as was the case with much of the audience, would be able to follow the play—as would a person like me, who knew only English.

I also planned that each part would be double- or triple-cast so that each part was represented by more than one voice, ethnicity, and experience. The challenges this presented to the participants can be imagined, since sharing a role is a difficult matter under the best of circumstances, but sharing a role with someone from whom you would ordinarily keep a wide distance requires a level of cooperation and collaboration that makes the mind reel. But when two people are genuinely attempting to move through the same gamut of emotion and thought, a remarkable synergy can take place and at any rate, there is nothing like stage fright to create alliances.

The night of the first performance, I went backstage beforehand and found the two Andromaches, a Bosnian Muslim and a Serb (remarkable young women who had been having a terrible time finding common ground over the course of the rehearsal), wrapped in each other's arms on the floor in the wings, the Serb rocking the Muslim woman like a baby and soothing her. These were women who had gone through unspeakable things, but the thought of going onstage was utterly daunting. They turned to each other to cope with it, and as partners they did. After every performance the relief and exuberance at overcoming those fears was always enormous and the parties would go long into the night, everyone celebrating their mutual triumph over the peculiar yet real hell that is performance anxiety. True bonds were formed between people who had no choice but to rely on their fellow actors to get through the night. Some of the most unlikely alliances created in this manner have endured over the ensuing years between people who met in the crisis and exhilaration of doing this performance.

The text that we came up with ultimately looked a bit like a musical score, with indications for choral speaking, dovetailings and overlaps. Each person wrote his or her own translation above the English lines in the script, so that each script was different but we were all working from the same basic blueprint.

For instance, this was the first page of the manuscript:

How to read this text:

The text is written in three different fonts:

This font = English
This font = Serbo-Croatian
This font = Albanian

A. When you see your lines written in a non-English font, that means you are going to have to write a translation above them. Sometimes lines are written like this:

NADA: My home.
    JASNA: My home.
        NEVENKA: My home. I am a mother there.

That means that the lines are said like a canon, or a round. In this case, Nada begins to speak in English, Jasna overlaps Nada on the word "home" in Serbo-Croatian, and Nevenka overlaps Jasna on the word "home" in Albanian.

B. When two actors are speaking and you see something like this:

Don't wake up, lady.   Don't wake up, lady.

that means that both actors will speak at the same time. In this case, Mario and Alexander will say the same line in two different languages. Sometimes you'll see the same words repeated four times on the same line. That means that four different actors will say the same thing, at the same time, in different languages.

And here is the text the actors started with for the first choral scene (each actor received a text with his or her part already highlighted):

I dream of a city.
I dream of a city.
I dream of a city.
My home.
   My home.
      My home. I am a mother there.
I am a mother there.
   I am a mother there.
   I am a mother there.
I am a sister.   I am a sister.   I am a sister.
I am a wife.
   I am a daughter.
I am a fine craftswoman.
I heal the sick.
I heal the sick.
I carry milk from my goats on the hills.
I carry milk from my goats on the hills.
I know everyone.
I know everyone.
I know everyone.
I know everyone. I know everyone. I know everyone.
I sell herbs.
   I sell herbs.
I am an artist. I paint fine drawings on slender vases.
   I am an artist.
I am a great beauty. I am a great beauty. I am a great beauty.
I am a great beauty.   I am a gossip.
      I am a gossip. I am a gossip.
I am a gossip.
So many stories to tell.
   So many stories to tell. So many stories to tell.
   So many stories to tell. So many stories to tell.
So many stories to tell.

I took various liberties with Euripides' text, most of them in an effort to make the text as economical as possible—it needed to be short, given the multilayered and choral nature of the piece. So I removed characters I deemed peripheral or blatantly villainous—such as Menelaus and Helen—lest members of the ensemble feel relegated to representing the aggressor or the feckless *casus belli*. It has always seemed to me that the Trojan War owes its mythic status as the quintessentially tragic war to the staggering waste it represents for both sides of the conflict. It seems more than usually true of the Trojan War that no one can really be said to have won it.

Everyone involved in the Balkan Theater Project, no matter what his or her ethnicity, knew something about the peculiar suffering wrought by war and the devastation it unleashed on a shared civilization. The project sought that common ground, which is at the heart of Euripides' play. The only human male character I retained for the Balkan Theater Project version (the grieving Poseidon still begins the play) is Talthybius, the Greek soldier who, under orders, kills Hector's child. I kept him because he strikes me as a uniquely moving character, full of compunction and ambiguity, despite his role as the enemy soldier. Ultimately, I think he has a real dignity and nobility as a man attempting to cope with an impossible human situation. Every time the project was performed, the character was played by two or three young Balkan men, occasionally former combatants. The choral nature of the part made for some of the most striking moments in the piece and some of the deepest connections between collaborators.

But the major focus of this version is on the notion of the loss of a great city. This idea is very much a part of the Euripides, but I made it the core of the work. I'd been listening to women talk with great pain about the cities and villages they'd grown up in that were now completely destroyed. Many in the group were from Sarajevo, which suffered such terrible physical devastation. But everyone had lost a city; a city, a civilization, doesn't have to be physically destroyed to be lost. The one thing everyone in the group had in common was a feeling of homesickness, not just for a physical place that no longer existed, but for an era that was no more. One evening at the start of rehearsal, we asked the group to sit in a circle, close their eyes and think of a place in a city or village they'd known as children and remembered with affection. Without opening our eyes, we then went around the circle, each person telling us about the particular place each stood, some speaking in English, some in Serbo-Croatian, some in Albanian. The result was dazzling to me, a kind of poetry: image after image of remembered cities, streets, corners, smells, marketplaces, arcades, and village squares. Many of the group wept as they remembered these beloved places they would never see again. I was struck anew by the deep link between this ancient text and the group's experience, but also by the hugeness of what we were asking these people to do.

Most rehearsal processes are designed to open the actors to the emotional content of the play. Ours was geared far more toward making it possible for the actors to stay on top of their emotions long enough just to speak the words. They had no problem relating to the tragedy of loss addressed by the material; the question was really whether they could get through the performance. Thinking ahead, we established a system: each actor chose another actor to whom she would hand her script in the event that she felt she couldn't continue. It was, if nothing else, a further acknowledgment of the cast's necessary interdependence and of the depth of emotional courage we were asking the actors to draw upon.

The version of the play presented here is the one I put together for Fordham University in 2003, a production directed by Rachel Dickstein. Rachel wondered if there might be a way to make the Balkan text accessible to American actors in a more conventional rehearsal process and production. She knew about the version I'd made for the Balkan Theater Project and liked the text, but asked me to expand it slightly and rethink it, given that there was no longer a need to do multiple casting or the choral treatment of the parts. I had by that time written *Helen* and was interested in that character's presence in this play, so I was happy to have the chance to revisit the text without the formal constraints we had been dealing with in the earlier project. I am indebted to Rachel and our colleague, the brilliant Morgan Jenness, for their suggestions about how to restructure the beginning of the play, something I would never have figured out alone. Rachel ended up casting all of the major parts with multiple actors, except Hecuba and Helen, because she became intrigued with the musical and theatrical possibilities. She also used canon techniques from the earlier script and incorporated different languages in the chorus sections, which worked well, lending an international, universal flavor to the piece. But I present the script here without such indications, hoping that future directors will make their own determinations of what works for their particular productions.

I should add that, despite the makeshift nature of the Balkan Theater Project, we always included live musicians in the productions, which I do think is vital for making the piece work as it should. The Fordham production was served well by Katie Downs's score and her presence onstage throughout as she performed it.

I would like to thank everyone involved in the Balkan Theater Project over the three years we worked on it, starting with the Lila Wallace–Reader's Digest Fund, an extraordinarily enlightened granting organization, which made it possible in the first place. Sara Kahn, as I mentioned, was essential to whatever went right and I will always be grateful to her. Elizabeth Enloe, who welcomed the idea of the project at American Friends Service Committee in New York, has my deepest respect and admiration. Jack Patterson, who worked intensely with us throughout each recruitment and rehearsal process and was our primary liaison at AFSC, provided invaluable aid and wise counsel; we couldn't possibly have done it without him. David Esbjornson was the artistic director of Classic Stage Company at the time of the project and his permission to use the theater as we did made all the difference. Classic Stage Company is one of the great sacred theater spaces in New York City and I can't imagine the project having had the kind of life it did anywhere else. A former playwriting student of mine, Jessica Zitzer, magically showed up and simply did whatever needed doing—for which I don't think I ever adequately thanked her. My dear friend Amy Stern volunteered her time as the stage manager for each production and was my cherished right hand. Jerry Kisslinger, Steve Kotanski, Candace Lautt and the people at Fellowship of Reconciliation were instrumental in helping recruit several of the participants, including several students at Chestnut Ridge High School who were recent immigrants and tremendously important to the project. Robert Anich at PAL Television East gave us video equipment when we needed it. Ivan Talijancic proved an invaluable support the first year and was generous enough to be my assistant director, though he is an established and accomplished director in his own right.

But of course the people I want most to thank are the participants in the project, who taught me so much about courage, greatness of spirit and the power of speaking the truth through art: Justina Aliaj, Svetlana Ardi, Magdalena Avramovich, Mario Bago, Elma Balic, Luan Begetti, Vorislav Besic, Sanja Blazekovic, Sonya Blazekovic, Maja Brajdic, Nives Deletis, Fatima Djekic, Gordana Dukovic, Azra Fazlic-Dujmovic, Ivan Firchie, Edin Hadzic, Emina Hadzic, Igor Hadzismajlovic, Sandra Hadzismajlovic, Ensar Halilovic, Taida Horozovic, Svetlana Jovanovic, Indira Kajosevic, Alexander Ljubicic, Sonia Ljubicic, Marko Maglich, Zeljka Majetic, Shqipe Malushi, Sandra Miocic, Jasmina Omerovic, Jelena Pejic, Nevenka Pobric, Darjan Pojovic, Jasna Pojovic, Edina Sarajlic, Nada Selimovic, Azra Sisic, Alma Subasic, Selma Subasic, Elza Zagreda, Andela Zivkovic, Lejla Zvizdic.

I've given my professional life to the theater, always in the belief that this medium has a unique ability to create ad hoc yet powerful communities, sometimes out of the most unlikely and arbitrary assortments of strangers. These expedient families are no less effective or miraculous for being temporary and contingent to a particular project. As a consequence, I have always felt that theater has a singular capability to teach us about the nature of community and how we can collaborate to transcend even the most terrible pain caused by human divisiveness and rancor. This project affirmed that belief beyond anything I could ever have imagined. It was humbling and awesome to see what this medium can accomplish given participants courageous enough to be open to it. Everyone who worked on the project endowed it with dignity and his or her own unique grace.

I will always be grateful.

Production History

The Trojan Women was developed through the Balkan Theater Project with support from the Lila Wallace–Reader's Digest Fund. It was presented in a staged reading at New York City's Classic Stage Company (David Esbjornson, Artistic Director; Patricia Taylor, Managing Director) in association with American Friends Service Committee on June 17, 1996. The director was Ellen McLaughlin, the co-director was Ivan Talijancic; Sarilee Kahn was collaborator, Jack Patterson was the administrator and Amy Stern was the stage manager. The cast was as follows:

POSEIDON	Ensar Halilovic, Marko Maglich
HECUBA	Justina Aliaj, Azra Fazlic-Dujmovic, Nada Selimovic
CASSANDRA	Taida Horozovic, Azra Sisic, Selma Subasic
ANDROMACHE	Svetlana Ardi, Elma Balic
TALTHYBIUS	Luan Begetti, Igor Hadzismajlovic
THE CHORUS	Maja Brajdic, Fatima Djekic, Sandra Hadzismajlovic, Sandra Miocic, Jasmina Omerovic, Edina Sarajlic, Elza Zagreda, Lejla Zvizdic

Characters

POSEIDON, a god, middle-aged

HECUBA, a queen, middle-aged

HELEN, a beauty, ageless

CASSANDRA, a prophet, twenties

ANDROMACHE, a mother, twenties/thirties

TALTHYBIUS, a Greek soldier, twenties/thirties

THE CHORUS, minimum of six women ranging in age from
   teenagers to elderly, the remnants of the citizens of Troy,
   including Hecuba's retinue

Setting

The shoreline below the conquered city of Troy.

*The stage is empty except for a group of Women asleep on the
ground. They are the last of the women of Troy, some of them in
the remnants of what were once ornate garments since they made
up the retinue of the queen. Some are in more modest clothing. All
are refugees. In the center is the queen, Hecuba. Poseidon enters.
He looks at the sleeping Women.*

POSEIDON
I am Poseidon. Stepped up from my element, the sea, to walk
one last time on the broken streets of the only city I ever loved.
Troy. What have they done to you?
Your gentle gates. Your tall trees. Your fine spires.
All gone. A ruin. A memory of a great city.   5
Another war has ended. When will the next begin?

*(In all the chorus sections, the Women split the lines among them.
The Women speak in their sleep. Care should be taken, particularly
in these early sleep-talking sections, that the choral voice be
seamless and musical, the speakers occasionally dovetailing
and overlapping each other so that the voices meld.)*

WOMEN
I dream of a city.
My home.
I am a mother there.
I am a sister.   10
I am a wife.
I am a daughter.

I am a fine craftswoman.
I heal the sick.
I carry milk from my goats on the hills.   15
I know everyone.
I sell herbs.
I am an artist.
I paint fine drawings on slender vases.
I am a great beauty.   20
I am a gossip.
So many stories to tell.

POSEIDON
And all these women, these sleeping mothers, wives and daughters,
Become trophies, spoils, baggage.

WOMEN
The smoke curls from morning fires.   25
The song of the fishmongers in the early light.
The scent of flowers on the ledge.
The streets.
The streets.
The streets.   30
Curving up the hills from the sea.
Echoing voices.
Laughter.
Talk.
Children's games.   35
Tradesmen's yells.
Dogs barking.
Cooking smells circling from all the hearth fires.
All the families.
All the children fed.   40
Such a city.
Such a city.
Such a city.
My home.

My home.   **45**
My home.
Every corner.
Every stone of every street.
I know it like the back of my hand.
Like the roof of my mouth.   **50**
Like the colors I find on the back of my closed eyelids.
It was mine.
It was mine.
It was mine.
I dream of a city.   **55**
My home.

POSEIDON
(Locating Hecuba) Even she, who was the queen.
Nothing now. A lot cast in the game of endings.
Odysseus, they say, drew her.
He who devised the Trojan horse,   **60**
That cunning and terrible trick.
He will drag the queen of Troy home in a saddlebag
To toss before his patient wife.
Don't wake up, lady.
Whatever you dream, even the most horrifying dream   **65**
Cannot be worse than what you will awake to.
Here is the end of meaning.
Here is loss beyond comprehension.

HECUBA
(Asleep) In a moment a stone will be thrown at the sleeping
crows. They will flap upwards, shocked from their home on   **70**
the ground. They will circle upon each other, screaming,
twisting the air like rope. At the center of this coil of wings,
I am the blackest crow, the mother of all the confused and
lost. It will be for me to make order from this chaos.
Our flight will be eternal, for sustenance we will eat the wind.   **75**
Stay the hand that throws the stone. One more moment. Just

one more moment let us weigh the soft, ordinary dirt with
our accustomed bodies.

POSEIDON
Oh, sleep.
Sleep a little longer.   80
From the moment you wake until your deaths
You will be exiles.

(Poseidon exits.
Helen appears. She walks among the sleeping bodies. She is exquisitely
dressed, in vivid contrast to the Women she steps around. Her long
hair is beautifully coiffed.)

HELEN
I too loved Troy.
Like you, soon I will stand at the back of a ship and watch
the smoking shore disappear from view, remembering the   85
beauty of the city I brought to ruin. The sound of her foun-
tains, the songbirds that graced her rustling, fragrant gardens,
the fruits that bobbed in the gentle breeze of her orchards. All
this I will think of as the sails belly us away and we drag a snake
of foam behind our sharp prows. Soon what's left of her will   90
be lost to the gray waves. All that will remain is the memory.
Such a city.
The city I came to destroy.

(Helen exits.
Hecuba wakes.)

HECUBA
My Troy!
Cross roads and shade trees!   95
Marketplaces and schools!
Graves of my ancestors!
Wake, my women!

Today is our death!
Lift up your heads!   100
Rise and be slaves.

(The Women wake and look around themselves.)

WOMEN
My queen, why do you wake us?
What's the matter?
Where are we?
Why are we here?   105
Is the queen upset?
Oh, the dream I had!
I remember they brought us here last night.
I'm shivering.
Is it cold or is it fright?   110
Where is my brother? . . . Oh, of course.
I remember now.
I remember now.
I remember now.
The war.   115
The war.
Our ruined city.
Our scattered families.
All the wounded.
All the maddened ones.   120
All the dead.
I thought I might have dreamed it.
Oh, the dream I had.
I thought it might have been a dream.
I keep thinking I'll wake up from it.   125
And then we wake to this.

HECUBA
Day is breaking and with it, our lives.
Today the fleet will leave and we will go with it to Greece.

Today we leave our home and each other
We scatter, each alone, to our fates   130
We will be strangers in a foreign land forever after.

WOMEN
I can't even imagine it.
Places I've only heard of.
Argos . . . The Islands . . . Sparta.

I once went to Greece. It was a long time ago. A great house at   135
the foot of Olympus, the holy mountain. It was really quite
beautiful. No one was poor or hungry. It was so warm. The
ground smelled good. Like bread.

It might not be so bad.
What do you mean? We will be slaves!   140
Prostitutes.
Spat on.
I don't know the languages, they'll laugh at me.
They'll kick you first.
No bruises; we are prizes.   145
Beauties.
Whores.
I will be homesick for the rest of my life.
I'm already homesick, my home doesn't exist anymore.
Perhaps we shall sail past Greece and west to Africa.   150
They say it never rains there and the earth has turned to sand.
And I've heard of Sicily.
The mountains are cool
It's covered with forests
And in the plains the grass grows up to your waist.   155
I think they would welcome us in Sicily.
They say if you wash your hair in their rivers it comes out gold.
Gold dust.
What are you talking about?
Don't be a fool.   160

Gold, they said.
What is that fire?
Look, a blaze!
What terrible brightness comes here?
Is the city on fire?   165

HECUBA
No, it is just a girl, but her mind is aflame.

CASSANDRA
(Offstage) Burn high! Burn strong!
Burn bright! Burn long!

HECUBA
Oh, look on her, and let her break your heart.
It is my mad daughter.   170
My beautiful Cassandra.

(Cassandra enters, dressed in white, garlanded, carrying a torch.)

CASSANDRA
Enter the bride! Happy, happy day!
Where are the dancers? Where are the singers?
Where are my maiden friends to swell the procession?
Dance me now, sing me now, to my bright burning bed.   175
I, lucky child, to be the Queen of Greece!
Lucky virgin, to trade my priestess veil for the wedding
    garland.
King Agamemnon calls for me!
The king himself!   180
Blood of my brothers washed from his hands
He calls the queen's mad daughter to his groaning bed.
In his bloated ship, laden with my city's jewels, pans and
    brooches
He calls to take me, mad me,   185

Across the sea to his neglected kingdom and his murderous wife.
That wife, that mother of his child
Whose throat he slit
To appease the goddess
To blow the winds   190
To set the sails
To bring the army to our walls
To sack the city
To kill my family
All those ten years ago.   195
That wife.
Home to her! With mad me in the crook of his arm!
Happy, happy day!
Raise the torch high!

HECUBA
Oh, my poor child. You don't know what you're saying. You are   200
still in the power of Apollo who loved you and cursed you at once.

CASSANDRA
Happy day!
Happy Trojans!

HECUBA
You can't mean what you're saying.

CASSANDRA
Ah, but I do. Poor blind Greeks.   205
Their general, so wise, killed his favorite daughter to come here,
to waste his best years, watching his men die on our beaches,
far from home. Their children that were babies when they left
grew up without them, learned how to walk, how to speak,
run, play, write and read (ten years is a long time) all without   210
them. And while the fathers threw themselves against the walls
of our city, as those years passed, sons and daughters forgot their
father's face, forgot their father's touch, his smell, the sound of

his voice, until they found they seldom thought of him—
almost never, in fact—and always without much feeling.   215
And they watch their mothers grow old and uncertain.
Not knowing if they are widows or not. The years go by.
The poor Greeks! Our conquerors! Homesick and tired,
eternally squabbling, mending their armor, stealing from
each other, squinting out from our beaches across the   220
water over which they came so long ago and for what?
Some wandered wife? Some faded adulteress? For whom
they lay down their lives for ten long years, sand in their
beds, meal after wretched army meal, days and months
and season after season. These are the men you fear?   225
Pity them!

And pity most of all the bridegroom general.
Agamemnon.
For when he carries me with him, he carries his death.
The ax is on him. And on mad me.   230
Oh, yes, I am there, naked beside him in the open grave.
I see us both.
But we shall both be dead.

(She kneels, knocks on the earth and listens.)

Are you there, my father? Are you there, my brothers?
I'm coming. I'm coming.   235
Where is the bridegroom? My stamping general?
Here is the bride! Here is the bride!

(Cassandra exits.)

HECUBA
Oh, Apollo! She was your favorite. Is this your ecstasy? Is
this your blessing? Raving and laughing as she goes to her
death? What can it mean to be a favorite of such a god?   240
Have all the gods gone mad? What kind of world is this?
Women, help me. Sing.

WOMEN
What shall we sing about?
Sing of the horse.
Yes, sing of the horse.   245
The way we saw it
So high and silent
Out on the beach in the early morning.
Dawn streaking its mighty flanks pink
How tall it was!   250
Higher than the walls of the city.
And its enormous glittering eyes.
The smile carved on its lips.
Its long black legs
Its ribs hooped like the hull of a ship   255
Its curving neck
Its massive head
Oh, we wanted it inside with us.
And as they dragged it in we sang
All the songs we hadn't sung since before the war   260
We danced around it in the square
Peace, we thought
With this beautiful wooden gift at the center
Bonfires burning all night long
All over the city   265
And instruments played that we'd almost forgotten how to play
It had been so long
The children were up so late
But how could you keep them in bed?
Everyone was so happy   270
At last.

And when sleep finally came
You slept to the fading sounds of a rejoicing city.
I thought: This is the first night we shall all sleep together
in peacetime. My husband beside me. I thought: Praise God,   275
he is still alive. We have survived the war intact. All of us.

Praise God. And I slept. Curled beside him. Smiling.
I woke when the children came to the bed. Their hands
were cold. They were trembling. "The Greeks," they
said, "The Greeks have come out of the horse!"   280

Who could believe it?
Who could believe it?
And the black wave of death swallowed the city
Coursed in rivers down the streets
Through open windows   285
Overturned all the cradles
Tipped all the spires
Cracked the walls
And we lost everything
Just when we thought we'd saved it forever.   290
Nothing more cruel
Nothing more terrible
Than hope
Hope
Followed by such darkness   295
A night we still wander in
Calling the names of our husbands
Our lovers
Our friends
Our children.   300

*(Helen enters. Silence. The Women move from her with
contempt.)*

HECUBA

Was it only yesterday you were still my subject? Only
yesterday when you still had to watch me from your place
at the long table and wait until I raised my glass before
you could begin to drink? How long ago it seems.
And how like you, coward that you are, to wait until we are   305
reduced to chattel, slaves at auction, before you dare to walk
among us.

HELEN

Slavery is new to you. No wonder you chafe at it. When you've
endured it as long as I have, years and years, you'll learn to
stand up to it without so much self-pity.   310
And then you'll know what I have had to bear.

HECUBA

What have you ever borne besides a lover's weight?

HELEN

The contempt of the world.
You'll know soon enough. When you rise from your raping
beds, wiping your eyes and smoothing your skirts down over   315
your thighs, now purple with your new masters' handprints,
perhaps you'll think of me. When you run from your
conquerors and find no mercy anywhere, only veiled eyes,
turned heads and snickering; when servants, children and
strangers on the street spit at you and call you a whore,   320
then, then, oh, I hope you think of me.

HECUBA

You actually expect sympathy from us? You, who never drew
a breath that didn't cause an innocent person pain?

HELEN

I gave up on sympathy long ago. How can anyone understand
what it is to live in the remorseless noon light of this endless 325
visibility? Always I've been watched and judged. Run through
by the gazes of gods and men. I have never known the cool
shadow of privacy, never known anything like ordinary kindness.

HECUBA

And you accuse me of self-pity.
What can your petty vanities mean here? Look at the cost   330
of your little drama and weigh your words.
We may be slaves, but we still have the freedom to take our
justice as we find it. What can keep us from having our revenge

now that you are finally helpless against our hatred and
without protection?   335

HELEN

When have I ever had protection?
This is so familiar.
And hatred?
It's all I've ever known.
Bought and bundled one bedroom to the next   340
To writhe beneath my many conquerors.

HECUBA

You had your choices.

HELEN

And you think I would choose this? To be loathed by the
entire world? To be the source of so much misery?
I never had a choice. I was the bride of force.   345
Behind every man who took me stood a goddess
Who steadied his hips and whispered in his ear.

HECUBA

The shame of your actions can't be blamed on a god. You
saw your chances, you sniffed the air and you went where the
pillows were softest, where the wine was sweetest. What has   350
it cost you? Nothing.

HELEN

I've lost everything.

HECUBA

What have you lost? What have you ever valued beyond
your own comfort? Your country? You abandoned them to
wretched turmoil only to drag them behind you in your   355
wake to us. Troy? You *love* Troy, perhaps? Fools that we were,
we opened our shining gates to you only to let you seed your
infection of woe in our perfect city.

HELEN
I went where I was taken.

HECUBA
When the war was feeding at our city's teats and our   360
husbands, sons and brothers were dying, the air shaking with
the keening of women bereft, still you walked the battlements
to flash your hateful beacon of beauty before the sea of troops
and make them writhe and toss into a fury at the sight of you.

HELEN
I was the cause. My place was there. It was my duty to bear   365
it in public.

HECUBA
I watched you. Not a flicker of remorse crossed that face of yours
as the massacre raged beneath you. No screams of pain ever
moved you. All our wrack and ruin was reflected in your unearthly
open eyes. Impassive as a bird of prey you looked down upon   370
the awful doings you had brought into the world and calmly
watched the balance of the scales dip and rise with every death.
Which side was winning was all you ever cared to know.

HELEN
I alone belonged to both sides of the battle. Have you never
thought of that? My face could not betray a preference.   375
There my own blood called, the land of my birth and
childhood, here my adopted country, the most beautiful city
in the world. Every death was a loss, one side or the other,
my heart was in ruins. There was no winning for me.
I was unique in that.   380
I could imagine no victory.

HECUBA
No victory? Nothing but victory. Either way you won.
Look at you. You came to us unharmed, at the height of your
power and beauty, and now you will be taken home intact.

HELEN

Of course. I am a piece of property. Something to be stolen,   **385**
hidden, rescued or restored. A statue. A symbol. Nothing more.

HECUBA

I cannot even kill you for the pleasure of that justice. That
is for your husband.

HELEN

You think he'll kill me? After ten years of fighting for me?
For all your wisdom, you know nothing of the truth of men.   **390**
He will take me back. It is what legend demands. What it
has always demanded. You know that.

HECUBA

I have wasted all my bitterness.

HELEN

It would seem. I did nothing to you.

(Long pause as they stare at each other.)

HECUBA

If this is the price of beauty, let beauty perish with   **395**
everything else. Take her and defile her.

(The Women grab Helen and begin to drag her off.)

HELEN

(As she is taken out) What I have was given to me by the gods.
It isn't yours to take from me. It belongs to no one, least of
all to me.
You are fools to hate me. There is no woman here to hate.   **400**
Only power. And that you cannot skin off of me.
Claw my face to ribbons.
Break these smooth limbs.

Shave my shining hair to stubble.
I will endure.   405

(Helen is dragged away. Hecuba is alone.)

HECUBA

What shall become of me? Old bee without a sting. I who
was the mother of a pride of warriors. Who walked my palace
floors on golden sandals amidst the bobbing of plumed fans.
Shall I watch at a master's door, or sit the night watch for his
coughing child? Might I hold a plate of figs for an idle Greek,   410
standing like a statue as the night wears on, listening to the
drunken talk spiral into babble as the wine takes hold? Wind
a prating girl's ringlet around my bony finger to curl her
hair? Crawl at my mistress's feet to hem her gown? Shall
I turn a spinning wheel or scramble down the dark slope   415
before dawn to carry water from the well? Shall I walk the dung
pile of a backyard, tossing cracked corn to skittering chickens, or
sling soapy water across another's floor? What won't be asked of
me? Curled with the dogs on dirty straw in my corner of the
yard, I will hug my rags around me at night and think of the   420
life I had, the city I lost. And perhaps some day, if I am lucky,
I will be past weeping for it. And the faces of my dead will
mottle and blur until they become indistinct, like stones
seen at the bottom of a rushing river bed.

*(Helen is brought back in. Her hair has been hacked off. She
wears a grimy sackcloth dress. Her arms have been strung on
a pole like a scarecrow; her face has been bloodied with scratches.)*

HELEN

(Laughing) So you think you're free of me now? As if what   425
I am were ever just some body you could shame. You still think
I am just some woman of flesh and bone with a single story?
Whoever I might have been was blasted to nothing long
ago in the transforming furnace of the gods' gaze. That girl

was just stick and dung, fuel to the consuming fire of my   430
fate. The girl you could have punished died long ago.

I became the Helen. The eating flame of beauty.
She happened to the world.
It had nothing to do with me.

HECUBA
Take her to her husband. Let him see her for what she is.   435
We are done with her. Let him take her. And kill her. We
shall not taint our sacred soil with her blood.

HELEN
Whatever you dream, you will always be dreaming of her.
Night after night, your city will fall for her. She is the fire
that hollowed you out. She leaves ash and silence and   440
moves on, having blinded. In your sightless eyes she
lingers.

Even as you breathe your last breath
The scent of her will fill your senses.
The shining beauty of her will flood you again.   445
Try to forget me.
You will fail.

(Some of the Women take her away.)

HECUBA
Give her back to her husband. His plucked chicken. His
stranger. Let him take his beauty home.
Andromache!   450

(Andromache enters with her infant son.)

ANDROMACHE
Mother! My queen!

HECUBA

My brave son's wife! Where are you going? What do you
take with you?

ANDROMACHE

I go to the Greeks. I take all I have. My son.
Was I a good wife?   455

HECUBA

He loved you deeply. He called you "his shield." There
never was a better wife.

ANDROMACHE

And that is to be the nature of my punishment. I am given
to the son of my husband's murderer. Achilles' own son
claims me. As his wife. I am to go to his bed. To let him put   460
his arms around me. I am to find comfort there. In the
arms, against the skin of his killer's son. I, who loved a
prince. And they say it is because I was so prized. There
was talk: "A gentle woman," "she who was most intimate
with the most powerful," "she who shared the bed of the   465
greatest hero," "saw him unmanned in sleep and guarded
his naked body with her own," "she will be the greatest
prize." I see the rest of my life, lived with this stranger,
contracted in sorrow and woe.
How can this be?   470
I am young! I have loved deeply! Shall I never be allowed
to feel anything other than hatred? Isn't that some sort
of crime? To waste a life in hatred? And yet, if I feel anything else, even an echo of the love and happiness I have
known, I will be betraying my family, my honor, my city,   475
my country.
Perhaps one can only hate a man so much. No matter who
he is. Perhaps there will be some light left for me in this
life, not just the watery dim light of duty and memory.
Perhaps I will forget.   480

HECUBA

You must never forget. You were blessed above all women.
You must never cease mourning. He was without peer. No
one can ever replace him.

ANDROMACHE

He's gone! He's gone! He left me here in this agony
and shame. I envy him! He feels no pain, he cannot be   **485**
disgraced. He is free. How am I to live?

HECUBA

You will live in gratitude and service to his memory.

ANDROMACHE

Without joy?

HECUBA

Without joy.

ANDROMACHE

Without hope?   **490**

HECUBA

Without hope.

ANDROMACHE

The dead ask too much of us. I cannot do it. I will find a
way to love life. Even in slavery. Even in bondage and
degradation. It is only my body that can be owned. My mind,
my spirit belongs to me.   **495**

HECUBA

You who were so blessed in that marriage.

ANDROMACHE

I was blessed before I ever saw him. I was blessed to be
given life. It is a gift. I cannot throw it back with disgust

because he was taken away from me. I must learn to love it.
Even in this horror. Even in this nightmare. Even without him.   **500**
Far from home. I will find a way.
Oh, Hector, I loved you!

HECUBA
You were a good wife and a sweetness in his life. And you
have given me my only grandchild. Be careful and raise him
well in his new home. Teach him to remember. Tell him   **505**
about his father. Murmur stories of us quietly into his ear when
he sleeps so he will dream of his father's city, shining again,
high on its parapets. And let him come back to the hollow
shell of this place and raise it again, long after all of us are
dead. Let him raise his father's city from the ashes and   **510**
neglect of history. Let him marry well and have many children
and let these walls echo with Trojan laughter once again.
(Looks at the child) Will you do that? For me? For your father?
Then we will live again.

WOMEN
Then we will live on.   **515**

(They cluster around the child.)

Yes, we will live on.
You will do this, little one.
In your memory, we will live.

(The Women turn. Talthybius, a Greek soldier, enters.)

TALTHYBIUS
Do not hate me.

HECUBA
You are only a Greek. Give me more reason.   **520**

TALTHYBIUS
I speak for others. They sent me here to do this thing, I can't say . . .

ANDROMACHE
What could you possibly do to us that is worse than what
has already been done? Kill us? We would sleep in surren-
der of our misery. Rape us? We are already tagged for parcel
to our different rapes. There is nothing we have left to fear.   525

TALTHYBIUS
I have come for the child.

HECUBA
Which child?

TALTHYBIUS
Dead Hector's child.

ANDROMACHE
Must he go to another master than the one I serve?

TALTHYBIUS
There is no way to say this—the council decreed . . .   530

ANDROMACHE
What? Must he be left behind in the ruined city, all alone?

TALTHYBIUS
Worse, terrible. I can't say it.

ANDROMACHE
What did the council decree?

TALTHYBIUS
That he must die.

HECUBA
How?   535

TALTHYBIUS
He must be hurled from the battlements of Troy. The top
of the city walls.

(Andromache clings to the child and moves as if to resist.)

(To Hecuba) You must reason with her. It will only be worse
if she resists.

HECUBA
You talk to her.   540

TALTHYBIUS
Lady. Please. Let it happen. No one can help you. No one
can save him now. There is no shame in submission at this
time. You've lost. Your city, your army, your protectors are gone.
It will be better for you, it will be better for him to just give
him over. He will not know. Do not let him hear his mother's   545
cry. He will not understand. And it will be quick. A moment
in the blinding air and then it will be over. Lady. Give over.

HECUBA
Let her speak to him. Let her have him alone, for the last time.

TALTHYBIUS
She has that right.

(Andromache cradles the child.)

ANDROMACHE
You smell so sweet. My dear baby. My dear baby.   550
You smell so sweet. I knew you were coming to me so long
before my belly swelled. I thought: My son! My son! He will
rule the world. And you arrived shining like a conqueror. And
through all my pain I looked at your face and laughed.
Great Hector's shining son!   555

Oh, let me smell your downy head once more. My darling
boy. Your arms, your belly, your feet, your eyes, your lips.
There is all the joy of life in you. All the hope. You are all
and only happiness.

(Talthybius takes the child and exits.)

Greeks! Savages! Murderers!   560
What has he done to you? That tiny child?
What are you afraid of? He's a baby!
I have no strength to save my only child.
It has come to this.
Oh, Zeus! Can you look down on this?   565
Can you look down on this?
Where are the gods who loved us?

My arms are empty.
I can walk now,
I am light now   570
Nothing to carry
I can walk down to the ships
And find the passage away from this cursed place.

(Andromache exits.)

WOMEN
They still tell the stories.
About the blessed city.   575
That when the gods walked the earth
They walked here in Troy.

HECUBA
I told you that story. I was raised on that story.

WOMEN
No city on earth as splendid as ours.
No city so beloved by the gods.   580

The palaces were built of gold.
The streets were wide and lovely.
When the harvest was good they said
Some god has breathed on our fields.
I was told that one of my ancestors was a god.   585
And I.
And I.
Even when they stormed the city
Even when the battlements were on fire
It was never hot inside the walls   590
There was always a cool breeze
And the scent of flowers.
We are blessed. Troy is blessed.
That's what I always thought.
That's what I was told.   595

HECUBA
That's what I was told.
Oh, gods!
I don't want to live through the moments that are coming.
I don't want to feel the suffering that is on its way.
Why do I still call on you?   600
I say your names still and feel protected
Just a childish habit
But still I call for you.

WOMEN
We have lost the way of pleasing God.
You cannot care for us anymore.   605
You watch us and do nothing.
We built you temples.
We burnt incense at your altars.
Sacrificed every day.
All the flowers I grew   610
And offered up to you.
The tree I planted

That gave apples every year.
All of what I viewed as sacred
You have betrayed.   **615**

(*Talthybius enters carrying the child on Hector's shield.*)

TALTHYBIUS
I washed the blood off in the river that still flows through
the city. And I found the shield. His father's shield. It was
a great war prize. But I took it and laid him on it. I will go
dig the grave and then we must go.

HECUBA
Such a little child still. So small.   **620**
And to think that I had planned your wedding already.
Saw it all so clearly. The flowers and shouts.
Because you would have been a king.
And when you died, late in life,
Your family and people around you,   **625**
You would lie in state
Mourned by half the world.
Find something to cover him.

WOMEN
Here.
I found something.   **630**
There's enough to wrap him in.
This will do.

(*The Women wrap the body in scraps of their own clothing.*)

HECUBA
Not that it matters to him.
His head is broken as an egg.
Oh, dark butcher Death.   **635**
You closed your eyes and swung wild.

I have seen the end of all my children.
Oh, my dear women, Troy was not meant to last.
All that we have loved has vanished from the quickening air.

WOMEN
The dead are safe in their nothingness.   640
It is we, captive in our own broken hearts,
Who must breathe and run, breathe and run.
Troy!
We will track your ashes throughout the world.
And when they ask us where we came from,   645
We will say "nowhere."
Nowhere.

HECUBA
Children of this city.
Now we are motherless.

WOMEN
Look! Look! What's that?   650
What are they doing?
Up there, up on the highest towers,
There are men with torches.
See the flame dance along the columns and arches!
All the houses are falling   655
Wall after wall flashes hot and crumbles
There is the city
Breathing her last
Screaming her death cry
Sighing as she falls   660
She is falling
She is falling
Troy is falling.

TALTHYBIUS
To the ships. It is over.

HECUBA

(Kneeling) You Trojan soil. You that I was laid upon as   665
a newborn baby. You that nursed my mother and her
mother's mother. You that nursed all my children. Hear
me! I call now to the dead. I beat the ground with my
hands. Listen! Listen!

(The Women kneel and beat the ground.)

WOMEN

Listen! Listen!   670
I call to my dead
I call to my love
I call to my husband
My children
My friends!   675

HECUBA
Troy! Troy! Troy!

WOMEN
Troy! Troy! Troy!

HECUBA
We will remember you!

WOMEN
We will remember you!

HECUBA
We will remember you!   680

WOMEN
We will remember you!

(A great crack, like thunder, is heard.)

What was that?
What was that?
Did you hear?
I heard the city fall.   685
She is gone.
She is gone.
She is gone.

HECUBA
I dreamed there was a city. Spires glinting in the sun.
Stones cool to the touch, even on the hottest day. A city of   690
such people, such faces, such hands, vivid with language,
with stories, with plans. I dreamed there was a city. My
home. And the sky arched blue above it as if to hold it in its
gaze. As if it would last forever. Great in its history. Famous
in its exploits. Known throughout the world for its fine   695
waters, high vistas and the smell of the sea.

TALTHYBIUS
It's over. We must go.

WOMEN
We must go.
We must go.

HECUBA
Yes. We must go.   700

(All exit.)

THE END

Helen

Introduction

Euripides' *Helen* is surely one of the strangest plays ever written. I have Brian Kulick to thank for turning my attention to it. Brian has always had an uncanny ability to steer me toward the most challenging and provocative texts. He was the person who suggested that I adapt *Electra* for a production The Actors' Gang in L.A. was putting together of *The Oresteia*. This production would instigate my trilogy, *Iphigenia and Other Daughters*, as well as Chuck Mee's *Orestes* and *Agamemnon 2.0*. Not bad for one dramaturgical idea. But then Brian has one of the great ears—he genuinely seems to listen to the particular playwright's voice, and that receptiveness to nuance and idiosyncrasy makes him capable of suggesting what a writer seems to want to grapple with, even when the writer herself does not know.

I must also thank Liz Engelman, a dramaturg of unparalleled faith and determination, who, because she simply wouldn't give up on me, basically *made* me write the play. I'd been asked to be part of the Women Playwrights Festival at ACT in Seattle, where Liz was then working—a festival that was shaped around the readings of four playwrights' newest work, followed by a retreat at Hedgebrook artists colony on Whidbey Island. This was all very well in theory, but I couldn't seem to write a play. I'd been through the crucible of the opening of my play *Tongue of a Bird* at The Public Theater to resoundingly dreadful reviews all around and I had consequently not been able to write so much as a postcard for nearly a year. When, in the winter of 1998, Liz asked me to consider doing this thing in May 1999, I'd thought, well, by then I'll either be writing again or I'll have to kill myself, so why not? But by April, though I still had a pulse, I was apparently incapable of even considering getting back in the shark-infested water that was the playwright's existence, as I saw it.

After weeks of staring into the remorseless blankness of my computer screen and my own mind, gibbering with frustration, I called Liz. For weeks, she'd been gently prodding me with emails about the need to see the play so they could cast it and so forth. Her cheerful tone had become somewhat strained as the days and weeks went by and I kept stalling, thinking I could write something or other before anyone had to know what a total washout I was. I finally had to admit that not only did I not have a play to send her, I didn't have an *idea* for a play. The only thing I could think to do at that late date was to back out and hope they could find some playwright who could take my place.

There was a pause and then Liz said, "If you wrote one page, we would produce it. We'll wait. See what you can do." So while I was wiping tears of amazement and gratitude from my face I recalled that Brian Kulick, who was the associate director at The Public when *Tongue of a Bird* was produced there, had said at the time that he thought I should take a look at Euripides' *Helen*, wherein Helen never goes to Troy at all, having been replaced by a simulacrum, made by the gods, who is taken to Troy in her place while the real Helen spends the entire war in Egypt, evading the wandering hands of the pharaoh's son and waiting for Menelaus to come pick her up after the war is over. Most peculiar.

Euripides wrote it, as far as we can make out, in 412 B.C., which was precisely the point at which the first reports were just coming back to Athens concerning the calamitous outcome of their expedition against Sicily. The city was in shock, beginning to take in just how disastrous that imperial venture had been. (Not a single boat came back. Of the Athenians who weren't killed outright, a vast number ended up working and dying as slaves in the quarries of Syracuse.) Rather than write something along the lines of

The Trojan Women, an outright *cri de coeur* against war and its horrors, of which the Athenians were all too aware at the moment, he wrote *Helen*, which is unlike anything else we have in the canon of classic plays.

Helen is what might be called a tragicomedy and the sense of it is somewhat surreal, at least to modern ears. The basic premise seems absurd and slightly amusing at the same time that there is something terrifically disturbing about the whole thing. As one might suspect, the play involves a number of recognition scenes—the Greek equivalent of double and triple takes—as Helen has to say, over and over again, that yes, it really is she and she's been here, in Egypt, of all places, all this time. Menelaus comes off as something of a buffoon and the ending devolves into hijinks as he and Helen try to figure out how they are going to escape and hie themselves back to Sparta without being stopped by the feckless new pharaoh, who, unlike his dead father, is something of a cad and has designs on Helen that don't need to be enumerated. But there are a few needle points of perplexity and despair that Euripides conceals in the froth of that demi-farce.

Early on in the play, Helen is confronted by a Greek soldier who, after finally being convinced that she is who she seems to be, lets out a howl of disbelief and horror at the thought that so many should have died for a mere phantom, for nothing, in fact. Helen herself is nonplussed by this, but then she would be. Later, when Menelaus has been led to the same improbable truth and she asks him to take her home, now that it's all over, he hesitates, just for a line or two, but it is enough to discomfit. If she wasn't there, in Troy, then she's not really the one who matters, not the one they fought the war over, he thinks, and taking her home won't make any sense of the whole senseless business of the war they all went through. But Euripides has the simulacrum vanish miraculously in a puff of smoke shortly after this conversation, and consequently Menelaus has no actual choice to make. He can either take the real Helen home or take home nothing. Euripides' Helen is far smarter than his Menelaus and handily persuades him past his slight wobble in resolve. Still, that moment interested me. And

I'm sure it didn't pass unnoticed by the audience at the first production either. To find that a ghastly war was fought under false pretenses makes the war almost unthinkably obscene—a truth Americans are all too familiar with at this moment in our history. Consequently, this play becomes one of the greatest, if strangest, antiwar plays ever written, and it continues to disturb centuries later.

I take greater liberties with this text than I have taken with any of the others, but I still feel that fundamentally, it is a fairly direct response to what the Euripides text invokes. This is a play that takes beauty quite seriously, as I think the Greeks did. The power of the phenomenon of human beauty still awes and mesmerizes us many centuries later, and we are still in the grip of a kind of psychotic addiction to it, certainly in this culture. There are Helens aplenty in the modern world, and I suppose always will be. My Helen is self-aware, conscious of the eerie powerless power she embodies, and no less in the thrall of it than any of her admirers are, since she's been one of its chief victims. She is an odd conflation of every modern notion of beauty bound to celebrity, from Jackie through Marilyn to Diana, as much as she is the quintessential Helen of myth. She is what Helen has become, what she has morphed into over time, but she is still what birthed the ideal. It is, not surprisingly, an overwhelming identity to maintain, as it has been for every Helen throughout human history.

I was first intrigued by the play because I'd always had such trouble summoning compassion for the mythical figure. Who can take her seriously? Not even Helen herself can manage to, it seems. But as I got a chance to work with the figure I found her quite compelling and complex. It is her very ambivalence about her power that interests. She certainly benefits from it—she gets through the bloodbath of the war fought in her name without so much as breaking a fingernail apparently, whether she spends the time in Troy or not. According to legend, unfazed by the mayhem she has unleashed, she then lives to simper charmingly with Menelaus in Sparta over the absurdity of it all when Telemachus visits the couple years later in *The Odyssey*. She was worshipped as a goddess in her home city, Sparta, and most myths imply that she sidled into the pantheon after her death and was rendered eternal in the bargain. No one, not even the Trojans she destroyed, could help worshipping her, but though she inspires awe, she never seems to inspire much affection. How could she, since everywhere she goes she wreaks havoc?

Still, she seems to *do* virtually nothing other than look like herself. Even the conventional story of the inception of the war seems to rob her of agency for her fate. She is always said to have been abducted by Paris, who ranks as the callow villain of the piece. She never has much say in the matter, either as to whether she wishes to go to Troy or whether she wishes to go home again once the damage is done. She goes, or is taken, where legend demands. Since she is never so much as nicked by the course of events and arrives wherever myth transports her looking as enchanting and flawless as she was when she started out, it's hard to see her as having any real character to speak of, which is to say dimension, a quality only mutability and agency can lend. I came to think that there was something poignant about a character of such awesome stature who has no legitimate claim to the authentic, tragic weight of most epic figures. This has something to do with the preternatural quality of beauty itself, which has nothing to do with character, justice or, indeed, truth. Beauty is simply endowed to her, as it is to all such entities, fictional or not, and it is their peculiar blessing and curse for as long as it lasts. Much of the play has to do with Helen's contemplation of this phenomenon—beauty—that she embodies. It is a contemplation she has been undertaking for all the years of her strange entrapment, and her partner in metaphysical discussion is, for the most part, the Servant.

The Servant is the most powerful figure in the play and the most elusive character for an actor to grasp. I was blessed in The Public Theater production to have the mighty and unique Marian Seldes interpret the role. She taught me a great deal about this character's sly subversiveness, her hidden grandeur, and her dry humor. The Servant has been Helen's sole intimate and confidant for seventeen years. She's also been the sole victim of her pettish rages and fits. Yet most importantly, she has been Helen's story-teller. Helen is addicted to narrative (having been deprived of her own) and the two of them have a ritual that has been enacted daily over the years, wherein the Servant tells Helen stories. But not just any stories—the Servant has been telling Helen stories that are all versions of her own myth—there are, after all, an infinite number. Why does she do this? For all these years, the Servant has been tracking her charge's progress toward enlightenment and prodding her along, using various techniques. But there is a sense that today is the day; today Helen must be brought to a recognition of her real story, her own story, of which she will have to acknowledge herself the author, and she must be brought to the understanding that the end of it is something she will have to write alone. Still, before she can do that, she will have to learn several things. Some she will learn from her visitors and some from the Servant herself, who will take their usual discussions to the next necessary step each time, nudging Helen toward conscious-ness of her capabilities and her ability to choose her fate rather than remain in passivity. But as much as the Servant is highly aware of everything that happens in the room, and is wise, even compassionate at times, these two people are heartily sick of each other as well, and their perpetual familiarity has bred a fair amount of weary bickering. The Servant is, as much as anything, preparing her mistress for the time when they will finally be free of each other. Nevertheless, there should be tenderness at times, particularly in the final section, when the Servant at long last tells Helen her own story. This is an act of compassion and high imag-inative verve and it should leave Helen poised on the very brink of the most important decision she will ever make.

I decided to bring Io in at the beginning of the play, though it makes no sense, as Helen points out, in terms of the chronology of myth. Io is one of the most ancient examples of the mortal girl raped by Zeus. And she pays a terrible price for his singling her out: she is transformed into a cow and persecuted for years by Hera's gadfly. But I liked the notion of these two icons of excep-tional female fate conversing with each other. They are bookends of a sort, the forerunner and the apotheosis of a kind of female singularity. And Io's narrative of exile and transmutation is important for Helen to hear, as is her forthright relationship to her own destiny. I also liked the idea of beginning the play with a character who is so genuinely benign, guileless and funny as a foil for Helen's tarter edge. She is also more worldly than Helen, having seen far more of the world than she ever wanted to, and her suffering has ennobled her rather than crushed her spirit. Helen, for all of her sophistication, is not particularly worldly, having been protected from all that by her special status, and it is appropriately startling and sobering for her to encounter this particular figure. The pairing of these two characters also gives me the opportunity to have two mortal women, colleagues, as it were, speak to each other about the odd trials and perils of being female. I wrote the part of Io for Johanna Day, who played it with the kind of depth and sharp pathos that only a really great comic actor can bring to such a part.

I chose Athena to be the herald of the news of what happened at Troy because, again, I thought this would be a fun conversation to overhear. I wanted the most male-identified female divinity (the goddess of war, after all) to encounter this ideal of the female, because the friction would be greatest and the conflict most fruitful. Helen is, to be sure, terrified, at least initially, by this goddess, much more than she would be by anyone else from the pantheon, male or female, and yet she needs to be able to hold her own with her, possessing as she does a mastery Athena never obtained. Though Athena is indisputably the more powerful of the two, Helen's self-possession and beauty rankle a bit and unsettle her. They should match each other, in other words, one paragon meeting another. As has been the case in all my writings about the Trojan War, the First World War, in all its lengthy absurdity and horror, is what Athena describes when she speaks of the Trojan War. This, more than anything, is what disorients Helen in the encounter. The poetry that's been skidding through her head all these years is impossible to assimilate into this nightmare of waste and futility.

Menelaus is not a buffoon, however befuddled he may be by the radically disorienting phenomenon he encounters as soon as he comes to consciousness. Indeed, he is a decent man who has been trying for years to make sense of his impossible predicament. I don't think there is any question about whether he loves his wife, and the choice he must make at the end is wrenching, given his feeling for her. But he is trying to do the right thing by all the victims of an apparently senseless war and he makes his choice accordingly. I don't think these characters ever touch in the scene; they are, in a strange way, past that. What we see at the very end of the scene is an old married couple, speaking as intimately and as tenderly as people ever speak. This makes his exit all the more devastating for them both.

Helen's day-to-day existence is strange indeed and it might be helpful to elaborate on it briefly. Though she is trapped in this tarted-up holding pen of a hotel room, she is not in anything like limbo. She does actually age and she can feel the time weighing on her. She doesn't in fact eat or sleep, as she says, but there is still the division of the years into days and nights, each one of which she manages to get through by use of a series of rituals. In this sense she bears a resemblance to Winnie in Beckett's *Happy Days*, whom I've always found strangely heroic in her ability to organize her time into a succession of meaningless rituals. Helen is rightfully proud of her fly swatting, a skill she has honed with her years of practice, and that gives her some tiny, if dwindling, satisfaction over the course of the day while it occupies the time. Since she dismantles her elaborate hairdo every night, she and the Servant must reconstruct it every morning, a fairly arduous task, at least for the Servant, who must also entertain her with a story. But this must be somewhat satisfying for both of them, the finished product being, of course, once again, absolutely perfect. Together, they are the custodians of this extraordinary thing—the Helen—and I don't think it ever ceases to amaze them once they create it. And then there is the poetry, all fragments from *The Iliad*, which Helen isn't in control of; it just occurs to her occasionally, out of the blue, and I don't think she has any idea where it comes from.

I've always been interested in the old notion that it was Helen herself who wrote *The Odyssey* and that she commissioned or compelled Homer to write *The Iliad*. The sense was that *The Odyssey* was so grounded in a female sensibility that no man could have written it. Odysseus is taught, painfully and over the course of the long years of his travel, everything he needs to know to reenter human society after the dehumanizing trauma of war. And each of his mentors, divine or mortal, is female. I liked the idea that Helen was, unwittingly or not, the author of the Trojan War, and that she might actually be the author of the story as well. So I had an aspect of her long process of self-discovery be the claiming of that story. This is partly my own notion of this odd business of being a writer. We are, most of us, ostensibly marginal to history, witnesses at the best of times, but often not even that. Our claim to our stories has less to do with our participation in narratives than it does with a deep preoccupation, an empathic dreaming into those truths. We earn the right to tell the stories because they matter to us. After a while, they live in us, getting into the bloodstream until the time they finally belong to us and teach us how to speak them. So my gift to Helen is to give her the opportunity, not to reenter the myth that outstripped her individual self so long ago, but to step outside of it and take her place in the margins, where writers stand. When it comes to true immortality, stories are all we mortals will ever know of the divine. They're what counts.

Production History

Helen premiered at The Public Theater (George C. Wolfe, Producer; Michael Hurst, Managing Director) in New York City on April 3, 2002. The director was Tony Kushner, with set design by Michael Yeargan, costume design by Susan Hilferty, lighting design by Scott Zielinski and sound design by Gina Leishman; the stage manager was C. A. Clark. The cast was as follows:

HELEN	Donna Murphy
SERVANT	Marian Seldes
IO	Johanna Day
ATHENA	Phylicia Rashad
MENELAUS	Denis O'Hare

Characters

HELEN, impossible to say how old she is; suffice it to say that seventeen years ago, she was in her absolute prime

SERVANT, about a decade older than Helen, hard to say

IO, about a decade younger than Helen

ATHENA, a goddess, yet Helen's age

MENELAUS, Helen's husband, a veteran, middle-aged

A hotel room in Egypt. It's a fairly upscale hotel, perhaps with a
dash of colonial Victorian detail, but there can be some slightly
kitschy elements in the decor as well as several touches that clue us
in to the fact that we are indeed in Egypt. There is a large television
set of the boxy, glowing, sixties type, complete with rabbit ears. It's
pointed away from the audience and toward the glum, if attrac-
tive, woman sitting on the bed. She is surrounded by a certain
amount of feminine debris—makeup, nail polish, clumps of
Kleenex, a waxing kit, that sort of thing. There might be a number
of aging bouquets of flowers. Her hair is down. She is wearing a
beautiful undergarment, a gown of some kind, covered by a
stunning robe. She holds a large, ornate flyswatter in readiness.
She stares out at the audience, listening.

HELEN

It's just a matter of time. It starts with one and then the next . . .
I spend the whole day killing them. One by one. Until they're
all dead. And then night comes. And it's finally silent. And that's
my doing. But then every morning it starts all over again when
the first one makes itself known. *(Listens)* This is the nature of
my existence. *(Turns her attention to us)* It's not . . . it's not a
punishment exactly, I mean I'm not in Hades . . . You know, that
poor sap Sisyphus, with the rock? No, for one thing, I'm not
dead, and this is . . . the whole setup *(She gestures around)* it's all
very . . . I mean, I have nothing to *complain* about, it's just . . .
it's just that nothing ever happens, I mean *nothing ever happens.*
No one comes, no one goes, except the help, if you could even
call her that—these Egyptian help, they need a lot of help, if

you know what I mean . . . And then there are flies. Not a lot. Just
enough. Enough to make you want to rip your face off, if you
could, and I can't, of course. If I could have done *that* . . . *(A moment
of depression; she shakes it off)* I've actually gotten rather good at
it. I mean, it's not *surprising* that you might excel at something
when it's the *only thing you do all day every day for seventeen
years.* But see, here's the thing, each slaughter is remarkably
like . . . an event. It makes the day, um, *occur* somehow. Here in
my sanctuary from all that *(She gestures outside)* I kill flies.

*(She hears a fly. She smiles and puts up a finger. Expertly she
stalks her prey and then—thwack—swats the night table. She lifts
the swatter to inspect the body, then darts the swatter beneath it
and carries it offstage, as if transporting a flapjack on a spatula.
We hear a toilet flush. She reenters.)*

Ah, the first little death of the day. I often think it's the best.
Except, of course, for the last.
Surprising isn't it? In this hotsy-totsy hotel. But that's Egypt for
you. Positively teeming with life. All that muck. River ooze.

As when flies in swarming myriads animate the spring
air—haunting the herdsman's stalls and spinning in
buzzing circles over the pails of new milk—in such vast
multitudes mustered the long-haired Greeks upon the
plain.

(A slightly perplexed moment.)

The war. Every now and then these snatches of poetry go
through my head. I can't explain it, and I never know when it's
going to happen. Maybe I make them up. Or maybe my unconscious mind is tuned to some frequency—WGR-EEK, or something, who knows? But it's the only news of the war I get.
God knows there's nothing worthwhile on *this* piece of crap.
(Smacks the television with her flyswatter) It's hardly worth

bothering. *(Turns the television on)* I mean, look at this.
Barbarian nursery rhymes, cooking shows, bowling, endless
foreign soap operas with tinny music and shiny polyester costumes. It's maddening. *I have no idea what's going on.* You go
looking for something with *relevance*, a larger sense of what is
happening, and the best you can do is The Weather Channel,
which . . . It's the only network with anything like *global
concern* and yet—look at it!—record highs, record lows. Spiral
clouds of color graphics that spin bumpily toward a coast and
stop, spin and stop . . . and there they are, there they always
are . . . those amiable people in sports jackets standing in front of
a livid map of some place you can't . . . quite . . . make . . . out . . .
and yes, they're gesturing with their pointers and they're
presumably talking about some sort of *front*, cold or hot, wet or
dry or *(Screams in frustration)* IS THIS NEWS? THIS IS ALL
SO *UNHELPFUL!* *(Bangs the top of the set with the flyswatter)*
There's a war going on, people, right underneath those cumulus
clouds! Could we maybe get a graphic of *that*? A little actual
journalism? How about a couple of reporters in safari gear
standing at the front AND TELLING US SOMETHING?
ANYTHING! IS THAT SO MUCH TO ASK? *(Changes the
channel)* MORE MAKEUP TIPS. WHO WATCHES THIS
SHIT? *(A Servant enters)* NO, I DON'T WANT A FACIAL. NO,
I DON'T WANT ANOTHER MANICURE. MY FINGERTIPS
ACHE AND THEY'RE TOO SHINY.

SERVANT
Cow to see you, madam.

HELEN
A what?

SERVANT
A cow. Anxious for an interview. *(Helen lifts an eyebrow)* She's
Greek.

HELEN
Send her up.

(Servant exits.)

First time in *years*. I mean (What am I talking about?) EVER.
FIRST TIME EVER anyone other than, you know, the *help*, has
entered this room . . . Oh, fabulous. *(Futzes with her clothing
happily)* A CONVERSATION. And with a *Greek*! Albeit a Greek
cow, but apparently a talking one. *(Puts a hand to her heart)*
I really must get a grip. Remember who I am and all that, but
oh, maybe she can tell me *what the heck has been going on!*

*(She hears and then sees a fly. She swats it efficiently and carries it
off to the toilet. We hear a flush. Io enters. She is in fact not a cow
anymore, though she has retained the white ears. Other than that,
she is quite human, attractive and a bit hyper. She wears a plush
white hotel robe—hieroglyphs indicating the hotel name on the
pocket—and hotel slippers. Helen reenters.)*

IO
Sorry to barge in like this. I just got to town and, my God, when
I heard there was someone on the top floor who spoke Greek,
I mean, I just *had* to talk to *someone*. I haven't talked to anyone
in ages, I mean I *literally* haven't talked to anyone in ages. I was
until recently a cow.

HELEN
(Nodding, getting the facts) You were a cow.

IO
Yeah. Four legs, tail, moo, milkable, the whole bit. Years like
that. Awful. But since I arrived in Egypt I've just been feeling so
much better. Practically back to normal. Except for the ears.

HELEN
I kind of like them.

IO

Some slight glitch. They keep telling me they'll work it out—

HELEN

They do nice things for your face.

IO

You really think so? Thanks. I'll be glad to get rid of them though. I've been working with such a limited color palette. I mean I have been a *slave* to white for years now. And you know how white spots. It's just impossible to keep clean when you're on the road. *(Pause)* You know who you look like?

HELEN

Yes.

IO

(Dawning realization) No, really, it's uncanny.

HELEN

Yes. I do.

IO

Oh my GOD. DO YOU KNOW WHO YOU ARE?

HELEN

Pretty much, yeah.

IO

What are you doing here? You're the queen! . . . Of Sparta! Shouldn't you be in . . . Sparta?

HELEN

I'm actually supposed to be in Troy at the moment.

IO

Troy?

HELEN

(Unsettled, not pleased she has to explain this) There was a whole kerfuffle with a sort of contest between the major goddesses, it was a big deal. And the upshot is that there's been this *huge* . . . 'cause everybody *thinks* that I'm in . . . *(Io is still clueless)* Gosh, you *are* out of touch . . . What happened was that this prince of Troy named Paris was for some reason the judge of the contest and Aphrodite promised me to him as a bribe so that he'd choose her as the most beautiful goddess. I guess it just kind of *slipped her mind* that I was already married. But hey, she's a goddess, what does she care? So Paris sails over to Sparta pronto for a visit and we just knock ourselves out for him. Endless banquets every night, tours of the capital, state functions, dances. House guests. You know the deal.

IO
Was he cute?

HELEN
Pretty dreamy. Coffee-colored skin, lots of hair, a way of sort of *taking you in* when he looked at you, like he was sort of *dying*. Real style—you know how foreign men are—top-notch fabrics, nice drape, no pockets, just . . . but not *too* . . . I mean, he had *taste* but he didn't make a big *thing* of it.

IO
Uh-huh.

HELEN
(Trying to remember) And he smelled like oranges . . . and . . . and crushed rosemary.

IO
Yummy.

HELEN

That's what I thought. Of course my husband, Menelaus, was
just completely clueless. Told one hunting story after another
while the two of us were playing footsie under the table. I'm not
proud of what I did, I'm just *saying* . . . The guy was a charmer,
you know, and I'd been doing the wife-of-the-great-man bit for,
like, *years*, nothing but Chanel suits and sensible shoes day in
day out. And as for the sex, it had been strictly missionary position from the git-go—years of staring at the ceiling while he
went at it. And, and, he *hummed*.

IO

Hummed?

HELEN

Yeah, all the time. I mean *all* the time. His eyes would glaze
over and he'd just . . . *(Hums tonelessly)*

IO

Yow.

HELEN

This is what I was up against. So when Menelaus leaves us alone
for a few days while he goes to visit his mother or something,
well . . .

IO

So, what? You eloped? Vanished into the night?

HELEN

So the story goes. One of the stories anyway.

IO

Weren't you, like, *there*?

HELEN

Well. No. Hera gets this bee in her bonnet about the whole thing—says I'm the reason she lost the contest basically, and she decides to replace me with some *copy* of me, I mean she looks just like me except that she isn't, you know . . . *me*. She's made out of *cloud* or something . . . So anyway she gets this *copy* to go to Troy with Paris and cause all this trouble while she spirits me, the *real* me, here. To Egypt. Where nobody knows me. And the TV reception stinks and the front desk will just NOT listen to my special needs and there doesn't seem to be a dry cleaner on the entire CONTINENT who can press a simple PLEAT to save his LIFE, for Pete's sake.

IO

Why did she do that?

HELEN

Hera? Who knows? It was probably all about preserving my virtue, whatever *that* means.

IO

Yeah, she's really into that.

HELEN

I just wish she could have let *me* make the call on that one.

IO

So, would you have done it? Gone with him? *(Slightly melodramatic)* Betrayed your husband, your people, your country for love?

HELEN

I honestly can't remember. It's been so long since I felt like I could make a decision of any kind . . . Who knows? I might have just made out with him for a while. He was pretty hot. It wouldn't have hurt anyone. It's not like I wanted anybody to *die* because of it, for goodness sake.

IO

Of course not.

HELEN

It would have been something my *own*. A little mistake, or a
little dalliance, something I could maybe *learn from*, you know?
In a personal-growth kind of way. *But they just don't give you a
chance.* It's like you are not *allowed* a private life, you know?

IO

Oh, I *know*. How long have you been here?

HELEN

Seventeen years, three months, nine days.

IO

(Slightly stunned, but covering) Huh. OK.
So how long is this supposed to go on?

HELEN

Well, the way the story is *supposed* to go, last I heard, is that
I wait out the war—

IO

The war?

HELEN

(Increasingly disoriented by Io's cluelessness) There's a war out
there, there *should* be a . . . See, the way my father set the whole
thing up was that whichever suitor married me—I had *loads* of
suitors—

IO

Like *thousands*—

HELEN

Exactly. The deal was that the other suitors had to agree to join an
alliance with the winner if anyone, you know, *abducted* me, or—

IO
Oh, I remember this—

HELEN
So, I'm basically assuming that—

IO
(Suddenly getting it) There's a WAR, being fought in YOUR
NAME—

HELEN
Precisely. Between the Trojans and the Greeks.

IO
Wow. No wonder you bailed.

HELEN
Bailed? Excuse me, darling, I was replicated and . . . dematerialized.

IO
Not before playing footsie for a while.

HELEN
Oh, that was nothing. I was just bored and . . . it wouldn't have . . .
(Irritated, she gives up and reverts to the point) So the idea is that
I wait out this war and Menelaus swings by and picks me up
after it's over. That's of course if the Greeks *win* it. And if
Menelaus isn't killed, or doesn't die on the journey home. And
then, on top of *that*, it's got to occur to him that the woman he's
got in the boat with him isn't me. And of course, the whole
thing depends on if he manages to stumble into this particular
Egyptian hotel.

IO
That's a lot of ifs.

HELEN
Tell me about it.

IO
In fact, the whole thing seems—excuse me for saying so—a little unlikely. Have you ever tried leaving?

HELEN
What do you mean?

IO
You know, getting in the elevator and . . . *(Makes a gesture of descending)*

HELEN
(Slightly put off) I don't think *that* would work.

IO
But the elevator's great, I just came up in it, no problem—

HELEN
That's not what I mean. I mean I'm supposed to wait here, in this room, until he comes. And he's supposed to take me home. That's the way it works.

IO
And if he doesn't?

HELEN
(Unsettled) I . . . It's . . . He has to come, eventually, it's just . . . *(Pause)* He'll be here. It's just a matter of time.

IO
(Unconvinced) Uh-huh. *(Pause)*
Well, this *is* a cushy setup, I have to say. Even if the reception's crummy. I mean, I'll trade you the last seventeen years of my life, no problem.

HELEN
It must have been awful.

IO
Crazy awful. *(Shudders)* Oh, that poor cow. Years and years,
I was just—

HELEN
Excuse me, before you . . . I mean, I do want to hear your whole,
you know, *saga* and everything, but I'm sorry, I just have to
ask—you mean you've heard *nothing* about a war?

IO
Um . . . I have to admit I kind of tuned everything out there for
a while. It's not like I could *ask* . . . And people don't tend to talk
to cows, as a rule. *(Tries to think)* I guess I knew there was a war.
But then there always seems to be a war, because there are
always refugees. There were so many of us. I wasn't alone. And
they're mostly women. I mean look. There we are.

HELEN
(Confused) That's just The Weather Channel.

IO
(Mesmerized by the image) No, it's us. It's the spinning masses
of refugees, swarming the globe like clouds of bees—swirling
in a twisting wash across the face of the earth. Unwelcome
everywhere. Stumbling from nightmare to nightmare, trying to
achieve invisibility. That is our great goal. It took me years. I don't
even know how I did it. I guess I just lasted long enough to cease
to be of interest. The gods looked elsewhere and gradually forgot
me. I still don't understand why it happened in the first place.
There I was, a vaguely happy shepherdess, minding my own
business, when suddenly a whirlwind descended and lifted me
from the lip of the hill. I felt myself being kneaded like dough,

like mud under a chariot wheel, and all the while the wind
sighed in my ear speaking to me in some warm language
I couldn't understand.

HELEN

(Nodding) The ravishment of Zeus. Mother told me all about it.

IO

But before whatever was about to happen could happen, everything stopped for a sickening moment and I could hear the
approach of something else, a screaming, sliding descent from a
vast distance. It sounded like an enormous bird, sharp beak
open, talons spread.

HELEN

Hera, of course. Breaking down the door. Trying to keep Zeus's
wick clean.

IO

You could feel the suck of air as she rushed down upon us. But
in the second before she arrived I lost my body . . . He took it
from me. Or really, it was more like being jammed into the cas-
ing of another body, stuffed like rags into an urn or something.
I looked down and saw my new self—a cow. This tent of a body
heaving and echoing like a drum. And all the while I could
sense the goddess hovering above me as an eagle hovers over its
prey. I tried to scream and that was when I realized the worst of
it. That I was mute now as well. All thought, all feeling locked
now in my wide, swinging head.
A cow. It's been a hell of a thing.

HELEN

You're Io, aren't you?
(Io nods)
That's a terrible story.

IO

Yeah. And this is the strangest part: it made a kind of awful
sense. Even then. Because I had only just arrived at the moment
when my body didn't seem to belong to me anymore. Like it
wasn't just *mine*. I could feel this distinct . . . I don't know . . .
like when I walked past a group of men . . . Suddenly there was
this girl, this other girl, the one they were looking at, who was . . .
well, *me*, I guess, but also, I mean she was, I was looking at her,
at me, *with* them and I felt what they felt for her which was a
kind of . . . *(She is disoriented and disturbed)* I don't know.
(Pause) You know?

HELEN

Yes.

IO

It's not that I wanted to be a cow. That was horrible. But it did
relieve me of the particular confusion of being a girl. Having to
live inside a body which was so desired and yet so detested.

HELEN

But that's what it is to be beautiful.

IO

Boy, they must really loathe you.

HELEN

(Flattered) That's a sweet thing to say. As it happens they do.
I've heard I'm the most hated woman in history.

IO

Really? Well done.
You know, I've got to admit, I've kind of hated you myself since
I was a girl, I mean, before the whole cow thing. Every magazine,
every movie, all those images of you. They were some of the
first ways I ever learned to feel bad about myself. But now that
I've met you, you know, up close, you're just someone else—I

mean, you're beautiful, don't get me wrong—but you look,
I don't know. You're not this impossible, perfect . . . *thing* to me.
Not anymore.

HELEN

You're free of her. I wonder what that would be like.

She is the dream to which we cling
That shining, shifting, darting thing
Her face is blinding as the sun
Her depths are sounded by no one
So we drift on her legend and drown there.

IO

Sad. Pretty, though.

HELEN

Well, that's me all over. I wonder what that's from.

IO

Gee, I don't know. I haven't been able to keep up, you know,
with the whole poetry scene . . .

HELEN

Maybe it's the gods. Messing with my head. Because they can.

(*Pause.*)

What do you think they want from us?

IO

The gods? All I know about the gods is what I learned from the
suffering of my own body. Hera set a gadfly on me and he drove
me in a dance of anguish across the face of the earth. He was
my halo, that gadfly, circling above me before landing, time and
again, to bow his sharpness to the tortured white. I was never
free of him. Oh, the landscapes we saw together. The length and

breadth of the known world. We crossed it all. There was one night when I kicked and howled, prancing unwilling down the Persian coast. The moon was twinned like a double cherry in its own reflection on the glassy sea. I watched it extract itself from itself and leave its ghost behind to stare up at it as it made its stately arc up the sky. *(Pause)* He showed me the world, my gadfly, and I finally learned to see it for what it is—just another hide stretched on pain. No different from my own tortured landscape of welts and weals. Every one of them a site of misery. My poor body. It was a terrible place and we made it together, my gadfly and I. It took years. Maybe we made it for God.

HELEN
For God?

IO
I don't know. I guess I have to believe my misery was sacred. After all, it's the only gift they ever gave me. *(Pause)* I'm sorry, it's just that I haven't spoken in so long—

HELEN
I haven't either. Really talked to anyone. It seems we've both been subject to . . . peculiar existences.

IO
I do think sometimes about the life I might have led if I'd never been noticed. If I'd lived out my days safe in the hollow of the one mountain, never out of earshot of the dull bells of my own herd.

HELEN
You could go home. Now that it's over.

IO
No. It isn't over. I'm still one of the refugees. We can never go home. We wouldn't recognize it. It wouldn't recognize us. That girl's life was not to happen.

(Pause.)

HELEN

(Abruptly) So what's up for you now? Off to the tourist attractions? Maybe do some shopping? See the sights?

IO

I don't know. I might just head back to my room and stretch out. I'm still a little zonked from all the traveling. I love my room. It has a door. And a lock. And hippopotami *everywhere*, even the bidet has these little *ears* . . . Do you use yours? I'm a little flummoxed as to how one is supposed to—

HELEN
My what?

IO
Your bidet?

HELEN
Oh, I don't use anything. Well, I mean, I use the toilet to flush the flies, but that's pretty much it.

IO
You don't use it to—? I'm sorry, I don't understand.

HELEN
I don't seem to have any bodily needs.

IO
(Flabbergasted) What? Like you don't eat or . . . you don't *eat?*

HELEN
No, I haven't eaten anything in years. Not even in the old days. I was always on a diet and I guess it just . . . *stuck.*

IO
God, you must be starving.

HELEN
I wouldn't know. It's hard to say *what's* going on in there.

(They both look at Helen's body.)

I'm probably exhausted too, but who knows?

IO
Wow. I wish I could do that. It's always been such a struggle for me to control my desire for, you know, food and stuff, I've just been such a—

HELEN
Cow?

IO
Exactly.

(They laugh.)

HELEN
No, you don't.

IO
What?

HELEN
Wish for this. It's terrible. Once you abandon your body you can never return and that means you can never really feel anything again. Hunger, fear, anger, delight, each is played on the only instrument you have, the body, your body, and if you can't hear it, feel it, you've lost hold of your very self. What is yours.

IO

Could you go back?

HELEN

What? Back inside my body somehow? At this late date?

IO

Might be worth a try. It's done wonders for me, I gotta say.

HELEN

(A little panicky) I don't think it's possible, I think, you know, the gods might—

IO

Well, it's up to you. *(Pause)* It's a nice room. I guess you could stay here . . . indefinitely.

HELEN

Do you know what they have in store for you?

IO

The gods? Not much, I hope. Infinite boredom? A sheer drop down to death? Lulled by television?

HELEN

Well, if that's your dream, you have indeed reached your heart's desire. I'm something of an expert at this point and this hotel simply *excels* in stultification and oblivion.

IO

How wonderful. I mean, after the last few decades, just the *idea* of a DO NOT DISTURB sign brings tears to the eyes.

HELEN

Oh, not to worry, you will be left alone for years and years. Enjoy.

(Io exits.)

(To the heavens) OK. What was *that* about? *(To the audience)* Of
course that makes no sense. That was Io. Io was *way* before my
time. I've heard that story since I was a kid. I was raised on that
story. She was one of the first of the endless hosts of Zeus'
unwitting, unwilling amours. My mother was one of them, and
she was long after Io. I mean, Io's part of a myth so old I know
like nine versions of it. And despite what she wishes, Zeus
hasn't forgotten her, even if Hera has. He's just biding his time.
And of course he *will* impregnate her soon enough, but this
time he does it by touching her gently—a ravishment so
uncharacteristically sweet she names the child born of it Epaphus:
"light touch of a hand." *(It just gets stranger and stranger the
more she puts it together)* And he becomes the king . . . of
Egypt . . . Ages ago. There are monuments all over the place.
(This is very disturbing) I don't understand. *(Attempts to shake
it off)* But then *(Shrugs)* that's Egypt for you.
Everybody ends up here sooner or later. Even the dead. Even the
fictitious. And they all carry their stories with them, like balls of
wool they wind and rewind over and over. Telling themselves
and all their variations, as if they'd never come to an end. As if
the echoes were never too faint to hear.
(Pause. Mounting anxiety) This is impossible. And still no word
of the war.

*(The Servant enters, wheeling a garment rack of several identical
gowns.)*

Any telegrams? *(Servant shakes her head)* Any letters? *(Servant
shakes her head)* Phone messages? *(Servant shakes her head)*

SERVANT
Are there ever?

HELEN

No. But I thought perhaps today . . . *(The Servant shakes her head, then gestures toward the rack à la Vanna White)* I can't decide. You pick.

(The Servant performs a little drama of deliberation, then yanks one of the dresses off the rack and begins to put it on Helen.)

Well, she was intelligent. For a cow. If uninformative. I mean, here she's traveled the entirety of the known world and she has absolutely bupkus to say about the biggest war that's ever taken place. Ever.

Two mighty armies poised in deadlock on the bitter stones of Ilium. They hold between them the pride of the world and their clangor will wake the woe of the ages.

Does that ring a bell?

SERVANT

(Shrugging cryptically) Greek poetry.

HELEN

(Noticing the dress she's wearing for the first time) Oh, why did you pick this one? I *hate* this one! *(The Servant rolls her eyes)* Do my hair.

(The servant begins to arrange an elaborate coiffure.)

You're *sure* there was nothing?

SERVANT

I was just at the front desk. There's nothing for you. Nothing at all.

HELEN

Tell me a story.

SERVANT

Let's see. Once upon a time there was an incident. What shall
we call it? An abduction? An elopement? The beginning of the
end of the world? *(Pause)* An incident. And forty-six household
servants—staff, secretaries and security personnel—flooded the
local police station. Quite a scene. And every one of them had a
story to tell.

One maid clutched a ring she said had been pressed into her
hand by the lady of the house as she'd been dragged weeping
down the hallway. "Tell my husband I love him," the lady had
gasped through her sobs, "and tell him he must find me!"
Touching. Yet the gardener said he'd heard the lady and the
visiting gentleman giggling together in the gazebo where
they had camped out like children, with a blanket and graham
crackers stolen from the scullery. In the spill of light from the
full moon, he could see them slapping each other's naked
buttocks and playing sordid games with their flashlights. On the
other hand, a secretary said that she'd seen her mistress, mink
coat shrugged over a negligee, run silently across the library to
throw open the French doors. The smell of freshly cut grass
flooded in as she ran barefoot down the long lawn that ended
at the harbor and a waiting ship.

There were as many stories as there were people to tell them.
Each one patiently taken down by nodding, tired men. The
night wore on. Then the real fun began. Because then the
detective sketch artists were brought in to do their work. Forty-
six remarkably similar renderings of an abductor were brought
forth but when it came to the abductee, well . . . there was no
consensus on any single detail, from the color of the eyes to the
length or even color of the hair. The sketch artists were wild
with frustration. They'd never done such insipid work; none of
the pictures satisfied them. They grew pettish, ripping up their
sketches and stalking out to the water cooler, such that the
witnesses themselves could be seen in the hallways, murmuring
encouragement, coaxing them to go back in and try again. Face
after face they drew, but each was strangely disappointing. Just

one more vapid beauty. Each one lovely to be sure but hardly
unique, hardly, well, what *was* it one expected of that face?
Something. Something no one had yet found a way of describing.
The police chief finally calls it a night and sends everyone
home. He rubs his aching eyes and yawns. He walks between
the desks, each one stacked high with conflicting narratives.
All he can hear is the sound of the sketch artists. They refuse to
go home. In the breaking dawn he listens to the swoop of the
pencils, the slough of the erasers, the low cursing, the quiet
agony as they work and rework, portrait after portrait, not one
of which will ever satisfy them.

(The hairdressing is complete.)

HELEN
(Quietly disturbed) I do worry about the world. This splitting of
image from being never bodes well. The first knockoff only begs
for another. Copy spews forth copy, an infinite proliferation, like
a nuclear reaction. Each replication spawning yet another generation of duplicates until she moves like a virus through a city,
facing you at every turn. Her name spelled out in the night sky.
Her pictures blown like debris to be trod underfoot and washed
into gutters. She is everywhere.

SERVANT
Hard to believe there ever was an actual Helen. Just some woman.
With breasts that swell or sag, hair that grows, menstrual cycles—

HELEN
THOUGHTS! THOUGHTS! SHE HAS AN INTERIOR LIFE!
SHE'S NOT JUST A BODY!

SERVANT
(Continuing unperturbed) Someone who belongs to herself and
not to the world.
See, there is the *image* of Helen and that does not belong to her.
It's ours. She is part of us, like our dreams, that Helen.

Something we see on the back of our closed eyelids when someone says, for instance, "The most beautiful woman in the world." We possess, it turns out, so much of her. Images of her crying at state funerals, sleek in black, the mist of a veil only adding to her beauty. Or we see her sitting on some podium, looking attentively at the back of her husband's head as he stands there pontificating, unheard. He knows she is there, blazing behind him. He knows no one is looking at him. Except her, of course. And that is enough.

We have tracked the nature of our times on her body. Eras of greed are displayed for us in her cycles of embarrassing weight gain, her mortifying battle with her demons. We pored over the least flattering shots, those furtive, ungainly escapes into limousines, her skirt rucked up over her thick haunches. Or there were the times she starved herself like a saint for us, when her dresses hung limp on her and her eyes sunk like bright stones in her bony face. Then we clucked our disapproval and shook our heads, feeling something we couldn't name—was it pity? *(Considers this, then rejects it)* No, just revulsion, really. I mean look at her. She never knew when to stop. Thank goodness. Because still we hungered for her. Image after image. We couldn't get enough. We made her sleep with the lights on, her window shades up, so that we could press our noses against the windowpane and watch her dreams slide over her face.

(Helen shudders, as if shaking off a nightmare.)

HELEN

I'll tell you the one I hated most. The simpering, vulnerable one. With skin like spun sugar so soft and sweet your jaws ached when you looked at her. Those wet eyes. That high breathy voice. The head always cocked to the side like a not-too-bright cocker spaniel who has to be told everything twice. *(Puts out a hand to have her nails buffed)* But that was only one role in an infinite repertoire. She was . . . spectacularly accommodating.

SERVANT
She was a child, and yet a whore.

HELEN
An angel, and yet a goddess of sex.

SERVANT
She slices, she dices . . .

HELEN
She walks, she talks, she's remarkable.

SERVANT
She *was* remarkable. How did she do all those things at once?

HELEN
Oh, I don't know. Sometimes I think it is impossible to pull it off, embody all those contradictions and still be so . . . vacant. No wonder she . . . disappeared. How could anyone keep it up? You just get worn out, sick to death of trying to slot into everybody's personal fantasies. Having to be so *visible* all the time . . . She never had a minute to herself. It was consuming her. It was terrible, it was— *(Pause)* That's enough! My cuticles are throbbing! Leave me alone!

(The Servant exits, taking the clothes rack with her.)

OH MY GOD, I CAN'T STAND IT ANYMORE. I NEED SOME INFORMATION. SOMETHING TO LIVE ON. IT'S LIKE SWALLOWING DUST FOR SEVENTEEN YEARS. *(To the heavens)* IF I DON'T GET TO *GO* TO TROY, COULD YOU AT LEAST SEND SOMEONE OVER HERE WHO CAN *TELL* ME ABOUT IT?

(Suddenly, amidst great fanfare, Athena enters in complete regalia, looking pissy.)

ATHENA

Would you simmer down, for goodness sake? They can hear you clear back to the ice machine.

HELEN

Athena? What are you doing here? You hate me.

ATHENA

Well, who doesn't, if it comes to that?

HELEN

Have you come to tell me about the war?

ATHENA

The war? Oh, that's been over for ages.

HELEN

Over? Who won?

ATHENA

We did.

HELEN

We did?

ATHENA

OK, so when you say *we*, you mean who exactly? Your big buddies the Greeks, whom you betrayed? Or your dear friends the Trojans whose civilization you're responsible for destroying?

HELEN

Um. Both I guess.

ATHENA

Well, then you won. And you lost. Horribly. But that's true of everyone. It was a very long war.

HELEN
Has the House of Priam fallen?

ATHENA
Oh, gosh yes. A smoldering ruin.

HELEN
Is everyone in the royal family gone?

ATHENA
(Trying to remember) Ummmmm, nnnnnnnnyes. Yup. Not a
soul left.

HELEN
All dead? Even the women?

ATHENA
As good as. Last I saw they were lining them up on the beach,
assigning them to various warriors as slaves.

HELEN
What about the queen?

ATHENA
Hecuba? Oh, she was given to Odysseus, not that he really wanted
the old bag. She was quite upset. Straw that broke the camel's
back kind of thing. It was the end of a really bad week for her.
Legendary bad. Oh, they'll be talking about her for years. I think
she threw herself off the boat or something. Or maybe they
stoned her on the beach. I can't remember. Anyway, she's dead.

HELEN
I'm . . . that's terrible. Queen Hecuba. I've been thinking about
her all these years, imagining her. It's like I knew her, though
I never . . . I loved her, I think.

ATHENA

Well, she was never exactly over the moon about you, I can tell you that.

HELEN

No, I suppose she wouldn't have been.

ATHENA

She called you: "The gift that keeps taking."

HELEN

I see.

ATHENA

Tough old bitch. I liked her.

HELEN

What about the Greeks? Did many die?

ATHENA

Oh, yes. Thousands. The best of them. *(Yawns)* It was a nightmare, really.

HELEN

You sound like you're bearing up pretty well.

ATHENA

Well, it's not like it wasn't very *sad* and *tragic* and *momentous* and everything, it's just that it *took so long. Ten years.* I mean, really, who can stay interested?
Of course the first few weeks were just plain thrilling. We could see waves of soldiers skidding across the landscape—it was delirious, like watching a sheet being flapped in the wind, lines of men curving and snapping. And, oh, the horses, glorious. None of the gods could get anything done. We just dropped everything. We'd be down on the mountains, cheering them on,

or leaning on the clouds, propped up for the show. Marvelous
stuff. What a disappointment when everything bogged down
and all the boys went underground. For months all you could
hear was the sound of spades, the rasp of miles of barbed wire
being uncoiled. There was really nothing much of interest after
that. You'd catch yourself nodding off, head lolling on the
clouds, even during the long bombardments. Very little enter-
tainment value in a siege. Pretty soon we were stifling yawns
and slinking back to our hobbies: archery, jewelry-making,
trying to train birds. And still the war went on, unnoticed.
For nothing and no one.

HELEN
For me.

ATHENA
Not even for you. For some *idea* of you. Whole populations,
whole cities wiped out, and all for a *concept*. Not even a *good*
concept. Some chick. A *rumor* of a chick. A rumor of a chick
pretty much everyone despised, including the husband who was
trying to get her back, including the guy who took her in the
first place. All that mayhem in the name of *what?* I mean, look
at you. You're just some blond. And the big joke of course is that
you weren't even there.

HELEN
What was the point?

ATHENA
Oh, it seemed like a good idea at the time. Something about glory.
You know we've been around for a while, watching you people.
The interest was beginning to wear thin. After a while we just
wanted something truly epic. All those piddling little sacrifices,
a bull here, a deer there. No, no, we wanted *you.* The human
race itself on the altar, twisting like worms on pavement after
a rainstorm.

HELEN
You *wanted* that?

ATHENA
We thought we did. But I began to have my doubts.
I remember looking down at the pocked mud—the burnt daggers
that once were trees, the dun-colored creatures struggling about,
tanks tipped and lodged in mud, horses screaming—you could
almost hear them. I remember thinking: Perhaps there was
little in the way of glory to be gleaned from this.

(They lapse into silence, staring out.)

I notice you haven't asked.

HELEN
About what?

ATHENA
Your hubby.

HELEN
Ah, yes. Him. Is he all right?

ATHENA
Just fabulous. Got through the whole thing without a scratch.

HELEN
(Without enthusiasm) Great. *(Pause)* So where is he?

ATHENA
Oh, he's wandering in circles around the Aegean. Honestly, that
guy, he couldn't find his prick if you gave him a map.

HELEN
You know, for a goddess who is supposedly staunchly pro-Greek—

ATHENA

Well, of course I am. I was. But they pissed me off at the end
of the war. Poseidon and I decided to make their journey home
really interesting. We blew them all *over* the fucking place.
Menelaus has spent seven years tacking against the wind and
puking over the side of his boat only to be blown back to the
wrong coast time after time. It's been fun, what can I say?

HELEN

Does he know he's looking for me?

ATHENA

Are you kidding? The *hummer*? We could have put a dress on a
dog's squeaky chew toy and he would have bought it. Really.

HELEN

What's she like?

ATHENA

Who? You?

HELEN

Yeah. Her.

ATHENA

Sweet, really. If you like that sort of thing. All melting looks
and breathless giggles. Good tempered but not saintly. Knowing
but innocent.

HELEN

Sounds familiar. So she did her perfectly.

ATHENA

There was a kind of perfection involved.

HELEN

I remember. Once I stood at the center of history. It roared
around me, whipping at my clothes, howling and breathing its

terrible breath on me. But I would turn a face like marble to the
world. A face unmarred by thought, serene and closed-up tight
as a vault. A face that could hold itself still and unblinking as it
was battered by the gazes of the millions. Nothing animated it.
It was a mask of perfection. Shining and reflective as a pond. So
that when they peered into me, I showed them their own dream
of themselves staring back at them, lips parted, inaccessible and
spellbound. Beauty. It's a hell of a thing.

ATHENA

You couldn't have kept it up. That's why we had to replace you.
You were losing your edge.

HELEN

(Incensed) What are you talking about? I never slipped up for
a second. I could walk through a crowd of screaming fans and
hear nothing. They could claw at me, each one trying to get a
fistful of me, and I would merely smile and keep moving. I was
beyond good. They would look at me and . . . no, I wasn't there.
I had retreated back from my eyes, curled my entire soul into
the size of something unremarkable and tiny, like a walnut.
I would lodge in my throat and stay there for days, safe in my
own darkness, far from view.

ATHENA

I'm not saying you weren't good. I'm just saying you were losing
it. Your eyes. There was something you started betraying.
A distinctness of feeling. Your own. Nobody wanted that.

HELEN

OF COURSE THEY DID! They LOVED my feeling! They
couldn't get enough of it! One time I got some grit under a
contact lens when I was sitting in the theater and I teared up a
little. The paparazzi were on me like piranhas, blinding me with
flashbulbs. The next day every supermarket tabloid was screaming: HELEN WEEPS FOR HERACLES! It was pathetic.

ATHENA

They wanted you *weeping*. They didn't want you *feeling*. Not
you. Personally. Feeling. Not at all. Feeling your own feelings,
thinking your own thoughts? Absolutely not. It's all supposed to
be written on the body. Right out front where they can see it
and own it. Otherwise you're no use to them. You're just another
woman, full to the brim with tediously idiosyncratic and impen-
etrable secrets and needs. You think you were "loved?" Please.
They just endowed you with whatever qualities they were
hankering for at the moment and made up everything else.
Nobody was ever particularly interested in *you*. Human love.
What a joke.

HELEN

What do you want from us?

ATHENA

The gods? *(Helen nods)* What do the *gods* want from *you*?
(Laughs) You guys. You crack us up. I swear. *(Pause while she
chuckles)*

HELEN

Well?

ATHENA

You're too much, kid. *(Pinches Helen's cheek)* You know what we
love about you people? You die. And that means you've all got
stories. That's why we came up with you. Even the dullest
mortal life has a beginning, middle and an end. It's so fucking
poignant. It could be that the whole Trojan War was just a big
fat dramaturgical mistake on our part. Way too tidy. Our desire
to wrap everything up with a single enormous blowout just
ended up diluting all the stories down to one unsatisfying
truncated shrug of a narrative. I mean, it's not like it's your
fault, but we lost respect for you guys. You just looked like so
many panicked beetles scrambling around on that dunghill. Or

maybe it was the monotony of the deaths that got to us. Not that
there wasn't a lot of *variety*—we could watch people get blown
to bits by bombs, cut down like wheat by machine-gun fire
slicing across rows of stumbling men; or, of course, there were
those endless agonizing deaths, all the boys lined up in their
cots, oozing through their swaddling in the tent hospitals—oh,
there were *variations* . . . But really when all was said and done,
it was just a whole heck of a lot of death. And it turns out that
death makes human *life* interesting. But that death *itself* isn't
particularly interesting. Because you all die the same way.
Looking surprised. It's amazing. Here you are the only creature
on earth who knows you're going to die—it colors your entire
existence from your earliest moments of consciousness. You can
even spend years on a battlefield, watching *other* people die left
and right of you, but when your *own* death comes, *as you always
knew it would*, you're still like, "What? ME? Surely you don't
mean ME!" *(Amused)* It kills us.

HELEN

You know, sometimes I think *we* came up with *you*.

ATHENA

(Ominously calm) Is that right? And why would you do that?

HELEN

So that we could have someone to blame for everything that goes
wrong, some way to explain everything we don't understand.

ATHENA

You watch yourself, missy. I think you've had a bit too much
time on your hands. It just makes you brood. Why don't you take
up weaving or something? It passes the time. While you wait.

HELEN

What exactly am I waiting *for* do you think?

ATHENA

(Smiles) The end of the story, doll. If nothing else, there will be your death. And I, for one, am *really* looking forward to that.

HELEN

But I'm a story now. I'll never die.

ATHENA

Oh, don't kid yourself, honey. You'll die. Your *story* will go on and on. But it'll have precious little to do with you.
Not that it ever did. I mean, you're *pretty* and everything, but let's face it: *no*body's *that* pretty.
I gotta run. *(Starts to exit)* Give my regards to that hubby of yours when you see him.

HELEN

Wait! *(Athena turns)* Do you think he'll find me?

ATHENA

Stranger things have happened. You of all people should know.

(Athena exits, with appropriate fanfare.)

HELEN

(Profoundly disoriented) It's over. It's been over all this time.
I missed everything.

(The Servant enters, dragging a bouquet of racetrack magnitude.)

SERVANT

More flowers.

HELEN

Who are they from?

SERVANT

Who are they ever from?

HELEN
No card? No telegram?

SERVANT
Just the flowers.

HELEN
It *reeks*. God, my allergies. Get it out of here.

SERVANT
And take it where?

HELEN
I don't know! Dump it in the nearest pyramid, I don't care! My
sinuses are going bonkers!

*(The Servant drags the flowers out as Helen reflexively and futilely
lifts the receiver of the ornate little bedside phone for what must
be the umpteenth time.)*

AND I STILL DON'T HAVE A DIAL TONE!

*(She dumps the phone on the floor, then grabs the remote and
begins to channel-surf agitatedly. We hear a ping from the elevator
in the hall and the Servant reenters.)*

SERVANT
I left them on the elevator. Going down.

HELEN
That's nice. *(They watch television)* Maybe they'll get all the
way down to the underworld. Make some dead person's day.
I wouldn't be at all surprised if Egyptian elevators had a direct
line to Hades. Your whole country just seems to be mad for dead
people.
*(Cruising from channel to channel) Arts 'n' Crafts with Pampas
Grass*, the Sideways Sex Station, *Painting Landscapes Without*

Looking at Landscapes, The Make Your Own Mummy Show . . .
Why am I even watching this anymore? *(Turns off the television)*
Nothing I thought I was looking for was ever there for me to
find. My war. I lost it.

> For ten years, 'twixt the black ships and the river of Xanthus,
> the watch fires of the armies glitter through the nights. As if
> the countless stars, burning above in fathomless space, were
> mirrored below in a sea gone glass still, so many and so
> bright were the multitudes of those great armies.

That war is lost.
Tell me a story.

SERVANT
There's a girl who is imprisoned in a high tower, or a ring of
fire, or she's chained to a rock above the thrashing sea, or she
sleeps in a glass box, a coffin made of ice in the center of a forest
of thorns. She is frozen. Stranded in the perpetual stillness of
her most beautiful moment. There is no animation there where
she waits because life cannot continue in the face of such
perfection. It's a spell she casts, such a girl, such a beauty, and
we skirt death when we look at her. She stops the breath. Nature
shudders to a halt to gaze upon her and the world freezes slowly
around her, like a lake around its coldest island.

HELEN
Is she dead?

SERVANT
Almost. The next best thing. She's perfect. Meaning symmetrical,
as nothing in this rocking asymmetrical mess of a world is. She
waits in a kind of impossible balance, straddling the two worlds,
between life and death. Completely alone.

HELEN
It's awful. What is it about beauty that is so . . . killing?

SERVANT

It shames the world. This slovenly, pulsing world, limping toward its own ruin, charging around some hot star like a dog chasing its tail. Perfection is an affront in such a place.

HELEN

She's cold.

SERVANT

You think?

HELEN

No, worse. She's numb. She's fallen asleep in blankness and she'll never wake up.

SERVANT

We'll see.

HELEN

Does anyone know she's there?

SERVANT

Oh, there's someone looking for her. A man. There always is.

HELEN

Will he find her?

SERVANT

That's certainly the idea. Someday.

HELEN

What if he doesn't?

SERVANT

Then I guess it's up to her.

HELEN

But how can she do anything? She's practically dead.

SERVANT

Not quite.

HELEN

But she doesn't even know who she is!

SERVANT

Oh, really? But this was all her idea.

HELEN

It was not! It was done to her! She couldn't help what they did
to her!

SERVANT

Nobody had a gun to her head.

HELEN

It was that old witch with an apple! I remember this. Some old
lady poisoned her.

SERVANT

Far as I can tell she climbed into that coffin all by herself—

HELEN

There was a witch!—

SERVANT

without any help from anyone—

HELEN

You're telling it wrong!—

SERVANT

and she pulled the lid down after her.

HELEN
You know that's not what happened!—

SERVANT
And that's where she's been for a long time now, pretending to sleep.

HELEN
You're lying! I hate this story. This is a terrible story.

SERVANT
(With calm, bitter finality) Yes it is.

(A nasty pause. Helen hears a fly and begins swatting about her ferociously yet unsuccessfully.)

Did it ever occur to you that you might have a choice where the flies are concerned?

HELEN
(Distracted, still whacking away) What are you blathering about now?

SERVANT
Yes, you can kill them, of course. But they are in fact only creatures desperate to escape this place. (And who can blame them?) They're not *trying* to irritate you. They're screaming, that's all. They're begging you *(Does a fly voice)*, "Let me out! Let me out! Let me out!"

HELEN
(Still flailing) SO? What are you proposing?

SERVANT
You could pity them.

(Helen turns on the Servant and glares at her.)

HELEN
I really loathe you at the moment.

SERVANT
Foot massage?

HELEN
(Defeated) Oh . . . why not?

(The Servant sits on the bed. Helen lies on the floor and puts her feet in the Servant's lap. The Servant massages her feet.)

Seven years. Seven years since all the fires burned down to embers. Seven years since the first vultures circled the ruins of the city, wobbling in the smoky air, dizzy with the feast of death beneath them. Seven years it's been over.

SERVANT
Oh, it's far from over. They're still sorting everything out on the banks of the river which courses through the basement of the world. The whole operation has been backed up for ever so long. One can hear the complaints of Charon, the harried ferryman of the dead. Even up here, at the top of the elevator shaft. The size of the slaughter was awesome. Men in every uniform imaginable line the bank as far as the eye can see. Waiting to cross.
This is so familiar, they think. Yet another riverbank, yet another maneuver gone wrong. Countless men to be shifted and not enough boats. It must be the usual idiocy: some git in the rear must have failed to fill out a form. And here they all are, crammed together on the muddy bank, waiting for a single boat, manned by a wheezing old coot, to carry every mother's son of them to the opposite shore. It will take forever. But happily, forever is exactly what they have now, their only remaining possession.

They settle and wait, scratch themselves, write letters with
blunt pencils or pop the white lice eggs which are strung like
tiny pearls along the seams of their pants. Or they simply stare
open-mouthed into a middle distance where the fog leans down
to meet the iron silence of the river water.
Boat after boat he loads with them, each shipload packing itself
with an admirable efficiency. Charon never has to say a word.
They are so used to making themselves small, these men. They
hug their knees to their tight chests and array themselves snugly
as teeth in a jawbone along the long swag of the gunwale. The
boat fills silently again and again. Charon turns it around and
grunts as he stamps the pole once more on the silty river bottom
and heaves his weight against it. The tin helmets chime against
each other with every push. But other than that the boat is
silent. Even Charon is unnerved by such quiet docility. He shivers
in the stillness, lonely in the midst of countless men. He finds
his only solace in watching each boy shed his brief history in
the crossing. He sees the mist rise off the water and wreathe
itself around the faces of these ancient children. In the course
of the slow journey across he can see the coils of each life story
loosen and fall, leaving the creases smooth and the fists
unclenched as forgetfulness washes over them like a summer
rain. The blessing is so complete that by the time the boat
nudges the opposite shore, they dazedly tumble out, often leaving
their guns and jangling kits behind. No more organized than
skittering seabirds, their heads lift as they wander up the dim
shore. Lit by a vague curiosity, they patter aimlessly into the
next world.

(Helen lifts her feet off the Servant's lap and rolls on her side.)

HELEN
(Staring out) I wonder where he is.

SERVANT
(Gently) He's just lost.

HELEN

Just lost. The poor dope.

Are you sure there wasn't a telegram? A phone message? A letter?

SERVANT

I'll go down and check again.

(The Servant exits.)

HELEN

Perhaps I've been unkind. It's been so easy to be cruel about him
in the abstract. It's just been such a long time. And he had the
great misfortune of playing the fool. Someone had to.
I never thought about what it must have cost him. It must have
been awful. Coming into that empty room, the rumpled bed, the
traces of hurried packing, a jumble of shoes strewn on the floor,
a perfume bottle shattered in the bathroom sink. I see him
standing in the wake of our flight, window open to the dark. He
blinks, his head is heavy, his mind is blank. He is staring at the
pattern of the bedroom rug. He's like a bull in the bullring as
the afternoon closes in and his death approaches. He's trying—it's
terrible, his head is buzzing—he's trying to make sense of it all.
There are two wives, he thinks. The one he loved and the one
who could do this. Or perhaps there never was the one he
thought he loved, only the second one, or perhaps . . . But the
more he tries to figure it out the less it makes sense. All he
knows for certain is the hollow roar of shame at the center of
his chest. And this is only the beginning. There are humiliations
unimaginable in store. News cameras and microphones jammed
in his face, the cool silence followed by the audible contempt as
he passes a crowd, any crowd. He has never been more famous.
Famous for this. A cuckold, a rube, a chump. He walks the
empty house at night, muttering to himself, snapping with rage,
but then, exhausted, he winds himself in my dressing gown,
which is still hanging where I left it. He stands there, a blind
cylinder, anchored to the closet door, smelling the wife who left

him and weeping for the love of her.
I think he did love me. And perhaps I loved him.
I try to remember sometimes. But it was so long ago.
What he must think of me now . . . I can only imagine.

(The door to the hallway slowly opens and Menelaus, in the wet remnants of a World War I army uniform, slides unconscious to the floor. It is as if he had fallen asleep in the act of knocking.)

Well, what do you know.

(She goes to where he lies and reaches out to touch him, but he scares her off by plunging suddenly into a nightmare.)

MENELAUS
(Still unconscious) Heads down, boys! Heads down! She's coming in, she's . . . Oh, God . . . Where's my whistle? Where's my . . . ?

(He braces, curling himself into a ball in anticipation of a bomb. It "hits" but he is unharmed and he relaxes a bit. Helen touches his face gently.)

HELEN
Ah, but the happy gods did not forget you after all, long-suffering warrior. Even she, the iron goddess, pitied you, and waved the darting arrow from your heart as a mother waves a fly away from her dearly sleeping child.

(Menelaus' eyes snap open, and though he doesn't see Helen, he sees the room. He is disturbed.)

MENELAUS
This isn't my suite.

HELEN
Isn't it?

MENELAUS
I must be on the wrong floor. *(Pause)* Literally.

(As he begins to get up, he sees Helen for the first time—he is shocked. He attempts to cover.)

I'm so sorry.

(He scrambles to get up and pull himself together, utterly disoriented.)

HELEN
It's all right. It's confusing.

MENELAUS
I was shipwrecked. I haven't had much sleep.

HELEN
It's all right.

MENELAUS
Is it?

HELEN
Yes. You've had a bad time. I can tell.

MENELAUS
It's only the last in a long sequence of . . . You don't want to know.

HELEN
I do though.

MENELAUS
No, I don't think I could even begin to . . . It's too . . . I'd be . . .
(Pause) Do you know my wife?

ABERDEEN COLLEGE
GORDON LIBRARY

HELEN
Yes.

MENELAUS
It's funny. From the moment . . . And you speak Greek. I can't
tell you what a . . . Huh.

HELEN
Where is she?

MENELAUS
Who?

HELEN
Your wife.

MENELAUS
She's already . . . You're . . . *(A monumental effort to understand
this thing)* Hang on, is this 28B?

HELEN
29B.

MENELAUS
Ah. The difference of a story.

HELEN
Exactly. Where is your wife?

MENELAUS
(Slight hesitation as he tries to remember) I killed her.

HELEN
Did you?

MENELAUS
Yyyes.

HELEN
Just now?

MENELAUS
No, no, years ago. The sack of Troy.

HELEN
You didn't though.

MENELAUS
Didn't I?

HELEN
It just felt like it.

MENELAUS
(Slaps his forehead in a gesture of remembrance) No, of course, of course. You're right. Of course. She's . . . she's *here*, right *here* . . .

HELEN
Yes, she is.

MENELAUS
She went straight up. Something about a hot bath, she's . . . she's fine. She's always fine. She's quite . . . remarkable.

HELEN
So I've heard.

MENELAUS
(Exhausted and disbelieving, he looks at her) She's . . . something else.

HELEN
You hate her.

(He shrugs.)

You wanted to kill her.

(He nods without much passion.)

Why?

MENELAUS
I could take it, everything, everything she did to me, until the horse.

HELEN
The horse?

MENELAUS
The Trojan horse. Odysseus' crazy idea. It was our last ditch to break the siege. We pretend to sail away, the whole army, like we just gave up, but we leave this enormous wooden horse on wheels outside the city, just looking at the gates, like a pet dog waiting to be let in. I was inside it with the others. We spent the whole day in there, wearing all our armor, trying to hold still so we don't clank, you know? We're in there from dawn to dusk listening to everybody trying to decide what to do with this thing. Somebody wants to *burn* it, somebody wants to stab *javelins* into the belly, we're *worried*, OK? But lucky for us, it's a beautiful piece of work, this thing, and nobody wants to nick it up. Somebody, thank you God, has the bright idea to drag it into the city and after that, we're pretty much home free if we can just wait it out until everybody goes to sleep. But that's, like, *a long time*. First they *dance* around us, then they *sing* for a while, then there's a substantial amount of, like, *drinking*, but it's finally dying down around two in the morning. We're actually beginning to relax. It really looks like we're going to manage to get *out* of the fucking thing, and I know I am not alone in saying that I personally would have risked death at that point just to take a whiz—fuck the sacking of the city, you know?

HELEN
Then what happened?

MENELAUS
She comes up. You can hear the little jingling of the bangles
around her ankles. She's really quiet. But you just knew. There
she was. And then she starts stroking the side of the horse and
sort of, um, *chuckling.* I don't know how to describe it. But it was
like she was making love to it, us, *all of us.* And she was *good,*
you know? These guys, we hadn't seen our wives for ten years,
and you can practically *feel* her hands stroking, just sooo . . . But
that wasn't the worst of it. Then she starts calling our names,
not *loud,* but like the way you call a lover back to bed, you know,
each name of us. And this is the thing—she calls each man
using his *wife's voice.* I don't know how she—but it's worse than
that even, she's calling them by the pet names the wives used.
Names they haven't heard in all this time. It was unbearable.
These guys, they are, like, losing it, grown men weeping, trying
not to make sound, but tears are just streaming down their faces
and everybody's sort of shaking, clanking a little bit. And then
she does this thing. She calls to Antichus, this one kid, sweetest
guy in the world, right? He'd left for Troy only a week after getting married. His wife is this skinny girl he's known since they
were kids together and he's just like totally nuts about her, talks
about her all the time, dreams about her every night. He's just
so homesick for her he's going crazy. Then Helen, she puts her
mouth right underneath where Antichus is sitting and she says,
"Darling Bear, why did you never come home to me?" How she
knew that's what his wife called him, I have no idea, but he's
just freaking out at this point. Odysseus is sitting behind him
and he puts his fist in Antichus' mouth to try to stifle the sound
of his crying and he might have made it but she says, "If you
don't tell me you love me now, I'll hang myself." Antichus is
making little animal sounds like a dog dying, he can't help it:
"Do you love me? Tell me! Tell me!" And that's when he tries to
throw off Odysseus and call to her. But Odysseus is too quick for

that, he can see it coming. So he strangles the guy. Right there. This sweetheart of a kid. We all listen to the air choking out of him and then watch as Odysseus rests the body against his chest, then tips the head back so he can close the eyes, which are popping out of his face. That's when you could hear the little jingle of her, her bare feet running away across the city square. But that's not all you could hear. You could also hear her laughing. Then dead quiet. So we came out of the horse like bees swarming out of a hollow oak. And we went to work. There was no mercy.

HELEN
So why didn't you kill her?

MENELAUS
Because it wouldn't work.
It'd be like slashing a movie screen to kill the film star. From the first time I saw her, I knew I'd never be free of her. If I killed her, it wouldn't make any difference at all.
And I never lost her to Troy. She's plastered all over the walls on the inside of my head. I close my eyes and I see her. I look up at the sky at night and her face knits the stars up.
I spent ten years trying to get a woman back I never lost and when I finally got her back I still didn't have her. Not really. I can hold her naked body next to me all night long but she's still . . . it's not . . .
I've never really been with her. Not once since the beginning. But I've never been without her. Not once since the beginning. (Looks at her) It's a hell of a thing.

(Long pause.)

HELEN
Where is your wife?

MENELAUS
I don't know anymore.

HELEN
Who is your wife?

MENELAUS
I don't know anymore.

HELEN
Do you know who I am?

MENELAUS
Yes.

HELEN
Who am I?

MENELAUS
(Trying not to answer, begging her) Please . . . Don't make me . . .

HELEN
Who am I?

MENELAUS
It doesn't make sense.

HELEN
No, it doesn't. But who am I?

MENELAUS
It can't be.

HELEN
But it is. I've been here all this time.

MENELAUS
See, I used to dream of this. Because I hated you so much but
I couldn't stop loving you. Years went by. I would walk the

beaches all night long. I would look up at the high walls and see the yellow lights coming from the windows of the palace and I'd torture myself. I'd try to pick out which one of those rooms might be yours, which one of them was where he was pawing you, where you were straddling him, riding his hips and laughing the way you did. I drove myself crazy. Until the only way I could put the pain to rest was to think the whole thing must be some sort of hoax. Just another cruel joke of the gods. That maybe you weren't even there at all. That there was some phantom in your place, some girl tricked up to look like you and all the while you were safe somewhere, waiting for me to come get you.

HELEN
But that's the truth!

MENELAUS
But don't you see, it's too late.

HELEN
Of course it's not! It's what you wanted! You just said—

MENELAUS
It's too late.

HELEN
But you just said!

MENELAUS
TOO MANY PEOPLE HAVE DIED.

HELEN
What does that have to do with me?

MENELAUS
They died in your name!

HELEN

BUT I WASN'T THERE.

MENELAUS

IT DOESN'T MATTER. THEY DIED FOR YOU.

(Long pause.)

HELEN

But you took her, you took me back. You didn't kill me. Her.

MENELAUS

I couldn't do it. We'd fought a war for her. You. I had to take her home. That was the whole point.

HELEN

Take me back.

MENELAUS

It's not you they want. They want her.

HELEN

I've been waiting seventeen years. I want to go home.

MENELAUS

I can't. It's not fair.

HELEN

What? To *her*?

MENELAUS

TO THEM! TO THEM! CAN'T YOU GET IT THROUGH YOUR HEAD WHAT'S HAPPENED? A generation of men threw down their lives in that hellhole for the sake of you. My God, the dead. They rise up in terrible armies every night in my dreams. They stalk around my bed on their hacked limbs, moaning of homesickness, the families they never saw again. They carry their severed heads in their arms—and the heads scream and scream. They died for you.

HELEN

They died for the *idea* of me. The gods did this. Not me. It's not my fault.

MENELAUS

IT DOESN'T MATTER WHETHER IT'S YOUR FAULT OR NOT.

HELEN

How can that not matter?

MENELAUS

IF YOU WEREN'T THERE, THEY DIED FOR NOTHING.

HELEN

BUT THEY DID!

MENELAUS

(His hands to his ears) It's unbearable.

HELEN

THEY DIED FOR NOTHING. IT'S THE TRUTH.

(Menelaus is in agony.)

MENELAUS

It's unbearable. All those boys. I must have written ten thousand letters. Ten thousand reorderings of the same tepid lies: "He left this world shining in the wake of his glory," not, "Your son died as he was trying to stuff his entrails back into his belly." Or, "He gave up his body with characteristic nobility of spirit," not, "His head was shattered like a pumpkin under his own wheels."

All for some schmuck of a husband whose whore of a wife
threw her dress up over her head for a houseguest.

HELEN

But that didn't happen.

MENELAUS

What does it matter when everything else did?

(Pause.)

HELEN

Take me home.

MENELAUS

I can't. You're not the woman all those people died for. You're
not the woman a city fell for. She is.

HELEN

Let me be her then. Leave her here. I'll play her.

MENELAUS

But don't you see? You'd never be able to *stop* performing her.
Not once for the rest of your life would you be able to retreat
into the privacy of the truth. There would be no end to lying.
You couldn't manage it. No one could.

HELEN

I'm good. Don't you remember how good I am?

MENELAUS

(With tenderness and finality) That was a long time ago. We're
old now. You couldn't keep it up. *She can.*

HELEN

Look at me. *(He does)* Do you feel love for me anymore? *(He
shakes his head. Pause. He nods. Pause. He shakes his head)* Do

you love her? *(He nods. Pause. He shakes his head. Pause. He nods)* I see.

MENELAUS
I should go.

HELEN
Yes.

(Menelaus exits.
Silence. Helen is disoriented and devastated. She speaks quietly, with bitter clarity.)

I shall die having accomplished nothing.
I saw nothing. I heard nothing.
My single achievement: I did nothing wrong.
I was saved from that.
I made no mistakes. I was perfect.

(The Servant enters.)

SERVANT
Time for bed.

HELEN
Yes.

(The Servant begins undoing Helen's elaborate coiffure, brushing out her hair.)

Tell me a story.

SERVANT
Once upon a time there was a woman. She was loved, if you can call it that, or at any rate considered so extraordinary that thousands of copies are made of her, every one of them more

durable than the original. Some are put in museums in good or mottled light. Some are in village squares, where dogs lift their legs at them or women dance around them. Some are sold to investors who keep them in their dens and do God-knows-what to them. With every copy comes another rumor, another narrative spawned. The most famous copy goes on a long voyage and animates a city. She breeds herself there and her image is simultaneously in several places: cat walking the battlements in an iridescent dress to make the soldiers below sick with lust and hatred. Or moving like smoke through the streets at night, tumbling from bed to bed, house to house, slipping into the dreams of men and women alike. She is impartial and perva-sive, this cipher, this phantom. And the strange thing is that all this time, the copy has been thinking of her original self, the real Helen, who has lived in seclusion, protected from every-thing, even narrative.

Literally nothing has happened to that woman. Except that she's aged. As her replicas have not.

And during all the years she spent waiting to meet herself, her own story, on its long way home, what has she done?

She has dreamed.

She has dreamed of a war. A great epic. And a terrible one. A war fought for nothing and costing everything. A war that churned around an emptiness, a hollow, like the navel at the center of the world. Battles reeled and spun, treading centuries of civilization under their bloody wheels. Like corn under a millstone they are all ground to dust. Until at last all beauty vanishes from the earth and only that emptiness remains, perfumed by death.

What can she do with the awesome weight of this story?

Her own story.

She has a choice, it turns out. She can do one of two things: Either she can maintain her costumes and that body she never knew, keep herself in readiness as best she can for some distant day, almost unimaginable now, when she might tread the boards again in the guise of that sex goddess she has been impersonat-

ing since time immemorial; or she could eschew all that, leave it
to the other girls, the copies, who do that kind of work so much
better than she could ever manage it, being objects to begin
with and thus immortal, if dead. Because she might instead do
something quite surprising. Something no one sees her do. She
might open her eyes. She might lift the lid of her own casket
and climb out, then slip through the thicket of thorns in the
dead of night into utter invisibility.

And no one would ever hear from her again.

Years go by and though her image in all its unearthly beauty
still breeds and transfixes on billboards and movie screens,
prolific as ever, the world loses track of the woman herself.
There are rumors, of course, sightings in the oddest places,
though the figure glimpsed is always silent. Tramps say they
met her hopping freights up North, sleeping with her shoes on,
a newspaper shielding her eyes. Some woman says she sees her
every Wednesday walking the empty seashore and tossing
Saltines to the gulls. Some physicist claims that she attended
his lecture, sitting in the back with her knitting, nodding and
chuckling when he got to the tricky stuff.

But this is what I think:

There's a diner in the high desert. It's winter and she is sitting
at the counter one afternoon when the blind old man on the
stool next to her starts to tell her about himself. (Everyone she
meets tells her about themselves, she notices.) He's a storyteller,
you see, has been doing it all his life. He can memorize anything
he's told after hearing it only once. It's a gift, you see.

"Everybody's got a story," he says, "did you ever notice that?"
She's smiling now, this ancient woman, crumbling crackers in
the old man's soup for him. He can't see her, of course, but he
can tell she was probably beautiful once; it's like a scent that
comes off her. But they're so old, these two, that they look like
twins. It's hard to say who's the woman and who's the man—
that's how ancient they are.

A silence comes over the place. It's late in the afternoon, no
one's in there but the two of them, sitting at the counter. It's

snowing outside and the steam rises from their bowls and makes
her eyes shine. And then as she hands him his spoon, he catches
her hand, the blind poet, and he says the thing she's been
waiting all her life to hear. He says: "Tell me a story."
And she opens her mouth at last. And she does.

*(Helen's hair is down. The women stare out together.
The door opens. Sound of crickets. Long pause in stillness.)*

THE END

Lysistrata

Introduction

This script was compiled specifically for the March 3, 2003, reading of *Lysistrata* at Brooklyn Academy of Music's Harvey Theater. This was one reading among thousands done as part of the Lysistrata Project, which was a worldwide protest against the burgeoning war in Iraq. I was proud to participate in this unprecedented event. This version was born of a collective desire to make a short and sweet version of the Aristophanes play, which was truly funny, as opposed to so many of the translations which are just not. It should run less than an hour. The cast consisted of thirteen actors (four men, nine women) playing the twenty characters. You can, of course, use more actors, but probably not fewer. The evening was designed as a festive event, involving a broad range of performance, including acrobats, musicians, aerialists and political cabaret artists. There was an elaborate pre-show involving female acrobats and musicians, while stilt walkers, musicians and acrobats were in the lobby and on the street, entertaining the people lined up for tickets. I do recommend this approach, since this sort of event tends to end up being very much a matter of the whole being greater than the sum of its parts. And I also believe this particular brand of ancient comedy has its counterparts in new vaudeville clowns, circus and cabaret far more than in conventional drama.

Whether you choose such an ambitious and complex approach, I do think that having a band onstage to provide transitional music, a few sound effects, and the final climactic and celebratory number is a very good idea. And using a balloon-manipulating clown onstage in order to create those indispensable, erect phalluses is well-nigh essential. I just don't think anything else is nearly as funny. We were fortunate in having a female clown at BAM, an attractive woman who came out at the beginning of the show and made absurdly large (two to three foot) colorful phallus balloons. (They were tied to a circular hoop of another long balloon, thus making a sort of hip belt—with a spectacular accessory—which a man could step into and pull up when the time came for his entrance.) Bill Irwin, a seasoned clown, was already onstage introducing the band and making the speech cautioning the audience to turn off their cell phones, etc., when the balloon artist marched in, wearing a marvelous womanly outfit, sat down, placed an air pump between her legs and began rapidly pumping up long balloons and twisting them efficiently into unmistakable shapes. Bill's speech began to disintegrate as he became increasingly distracted by the balloon-making activities stage left. (Far more phalluses were made than were used, but this meant that, when the time came, the actors could choose from a wide array of "props" their creator proudly displayed for them.) In this way one establishes the balloon convention from the very beginning so that they don't come as an abrupt surprise device when they appear three-quarters of the way into the play. There is something to be gained by making evident from the git-go the nature of the enterprise—this is a sex comedy of a particular sort—and also in having the emcee develop a relationship with the balloon mistress. (In our case, Bill blew up a small heart-shaped balloon, which he gave to the balloon mistress at the beginning of the show, but which didn't quite do the trick—she was too fiercely focused on her task to give him much attention. But after the curtain call, as the cast walked out, Bill stayed behind hopefully and she shyly blew up a balloon heart for *him* and they walked off together arm in arm.)

However you choose to make use of this version of an ancient antiwar play, enjoy.

Production History

Lysistrata was presented in conjunction with the Lysistrata Project ("A Theatrical Act of Dissent"), a multiple reading of the classic text, which took place in more than 800 theaters, throughout 52 countries and within all 50 U.S. states, as a show of protest to the upcoming Iraq war. The co-founders of the project were Kathryn Blume and Sharron Bower. This script, adapted by Ellen McLaughlin, was presented at Brooklyn Academy of Music on March 3, 2003. The director of the reading was Ellen McLaughlin, the assistant director was Lisa Rothe, the aerialist was Montana Miller, the acrobats were members of Cirque Boom, music was performed by Raining Grace, the Amy Kohn Band and Lava, and the stage managers were Erica Schwartz and Janet Clancy. The cast was as follows:

LYSISTRATA	Mercedes Ruehl
CALONICE	Johanna Day
LAMPITO	Vernice Miller
MYRRHINE	Kyra Sedgwick
DIPSAS	Kathryn Grody
ISMENIA	Lori Singer
MAGISTRATE	F. Murray Abraham
BELPHRAGIA	Lori Singer
FISHERWOMAN	Kathryn Grody
CINESIAS	Kevin Bacon
ATHENIAN CHORUS LEADER 1	Delphi Harrington
ATHENIAN CHORUS LEADER 2	Kathleen Chalfant

GEEZER 1	Bill Irwin
GEEZER 2	Johnny Lee Davenport
GEEZER 3	David Strathairn
OLD WOMAN 1	Delphi Harrington
OLD WOMAN 2	Kathleen Chalfant
OLD WOMAN 3	Kathryn Grody
SPARTAN ENVOY	Johnny Lee Davenport
SPARTAN DELEGATE	David Strathairn

Characters

LYSISTRATA, an Athenian woman

CALONICE, her neighbor

LAMPITO, woman from Sparta, a beauty

MYRRHINE, woman from Anagyra

DIPSAS, woman from Corinth

ISMENIA, woman from Boetia

MAGISTRATE, head man in Athens at the moment

BELPHRAGIA, woman from Athens

FISHERWOMAN, woman from Athens

CINESIAS, man from Athens

ATHENIAN CHORUS LEADERS 1 AND 2, middle-aged women

GEEZERS 1, 2 AND 3, men from Athens

OLD WOMEN 1, 2 AND 3, women from Athens

SPARTAN ENVOY

SPARTAN DELEGATE

An affluent neighborhood in Athens. Lysistrata is pacing back and forth, muttering irritably to herself. The Athenian Chorus Leaders run on and address the audience.

ATHENIAN CHORUS LEADER 1
OK. So, we're, like, the chorus, and we're going to have to figure out how to tell you this whole story in, what?

ATHENIAN CHORUS LEADER 2
Forty-five minutes.

ATHENIAN CHORUS LEADER 1
Forty-five minutes? I thought we had the place for an hour and a half.

ATHENIAN CHORUS LEADER 2
I don't know, there's a lot of acrobatics and stuff they've got to fit in. It's a whole, you know, *event* . . .

ATHENIAN CHORUS LEADER 1
Yow. OK, just the high points.
So. Let's see. It's 411. A very bad year to be an Athenian.

ATHENIAN CHORUS LEADER 2
Just plain sucky.

ATHENIAN CHORUS LEADER 1
We've been at war with Sparta for twenty years.

ATHENIAN CHORUS LEADER 2
It's this endless, stupid Peloponnesian War you may have heard about.

ATHENIAN CHORUS LEADER 1
We started it, basically because we could, you know, we were the big cheese after the Persian wars, loads of subject states.

ATHENIAN CHORUS LEADER 2
(Rolling her eyes) Our "allies."

ATHENIAN CHORUS LEADER 1
Right, though they hated our guts because we kept bleeding them for tributes and bullying them around.

ATHENIAN CHORUS LEADER 2
But of course regular people never wanted to go to war in the first place. Why in the world would they? But they got shouted down by the politicos and told to shut up about peace.

ATHENIAN CHORUS LEADER 1
Yeah, *peace.* What a silly idea.

ATHENIAN CHORUS LEADER 2
How *naive* . . .

ATHENIAN CHORUS LEADER 1
Right. Plus, everyone kept assuring them that it would all be over in a few months.

ATHENIAN CHORUS LEADER 2
Ha! Twenty years go by. Our treasury is bankrupt from paying for a whole lot of warships that keep getting lost or sunk. And Athens is surrounded by an occupying Spartan army.

ATHENIAN CHORUS LEADER 1
It's a disaster. Assassination plots and right-wing conspiracies are afoot to undermine what's left of our democratic constitution.

ATHENIAN CHORUS LEADER 2
Meanwhile, the war grinds on.

ATHENIAN CHORUS LEADER 1
And every two minutes one of our generals has the bright idea to charge off and invade someplace else.

ATHENIAN CHORUS LEADER 2
Sicily was the last one.

ATHENIAN CHORUS LEADER 1
Yowsa. What a fiasco.

ATHENIAN CHORUS LEADER 2
How many thousands of Athenians died?

ATHENIAN CHORUS LEADER 1
Boy, did they kick our sorry butts.

(Pause.)

ATHENIAN CHORUS LEADER 2
Well, look on the bright side. We have done one thing.

ATHENIAN CHORUS LEADER 1
What's that?

ATHENIAN CHORUS LEADER 2
We've united the rest of Greece.

ATHENIAN CHORUS LEADER 1
Huh?

ATHENIAN CHORUS LEADER 2

It's kind of a miracle. Greeks can never agree about anything, right? But we've done the impossible—*everyone* hates us! They all seem to be in perfect agreement about that!

ATHENIAN CHORUS LEADER 1

That's true. Spartans and Thracians are talking to each other for the first time in centuries. Of course they're basically talking about what assholes *we* are but still . . .

ATHENIAN CHORUS LEADER 2

It's an accomplishment. *(Looks at her watch)* OO! We've got to get this show on the road!

ATHENIAN CHORUS LEADER 1

Anyway, that's Lysistrata.

(They point to Lysistrata, still pacing behind them.)

ATHENIAN CHORUS LEADER 2

That's who the play is named after.

ATHENIAN CHORUS LEADER 1

You'll see why later. She's upset. Not only because it's 411 and it's sucky to be an Athenian, but also because she called a conference for all the important women of Greece. It was scheduled for dawn—

ATHENIAN CHORUS LEADER 2

Today—

ATHENIAN CHORUS LEADER 1

Right here. And nobody's shown up.

ATHENIAN CHORUS LEADER 2

Yet.

ATHENIAN CHORUS LEADER 1
Not even us.

(They realize they shouldn't be onstage and run off.)

LYSISTRATA
(Pacing back and forth; furious) I hate women! Everything men
say about us is true! Women are late to everything! Sometimes
they don't even show up! Totally unreliable! Impossible!
WHERE IS EVERYONE? This is just so embarrassing. Here
I call a meeting of all women from every city in Greece—PAN-
HELLENIC WOMEN'S CONFERENCE TO DISCUSS THE
MOST IMPORTANT ISSUES OF THE DAY—and who shows
up? Nobody. That's political consciousness for you. I hate women!

(Calonice, her neighbor, enters.)

CALONICE
What are you bitching about?

LYSISTRATA
I call this huge historic meeting and nobody shows up.

CALONICE
Well, it's *dawn*, for goodness sake. Who throws a party at dawn?

LYSISTRATA
It's not a party, it's a, it's a . . . IT'S THE BIRTH OF A NEW
ERA! CIVILIZATION WILL BE REDEFINED THIS MORNING!
I invited every important woman in Greece!

CALONICE
Gee, and me in my bathrobe. How embarrassing.
So where's the food? These thousands of women are going to
come from the four corners of the earth, and after all that trouble
they get, what?, not even a handful of raisins? What kind of
hostess are you?

LYSISTRATA

I'M NOT A HOSTESS! I'M A POLITICAL LEADER! THIS
ISN'T ABOUT CHIPS AND DIP! THIS IS ABOUT THE
FUTURE OF OUR COUNTRY!
(She looks offstage) Oo, oo, oo! Look! Women! I knew it! I knew
it! They're coming! It's Myrrhine from Anagyra, Ismenia from
Boetia . . . Dipsas from Corinth. Oh, and Lampito with some
Spartan women! I'M A GENIUS!

CALONICE

A *Spartan?* You invited a Spartan here? Have you lost your mind?

*(A large, bedraggled group of women enters, looking hungry and
pissy.)*

LYSISTRATA

It's all part of my cunning plan. You'll see.
Myrrhine. Nice to see you. Lampito. You're looking annoyingly
beautiful.

LAMPITO

I try.

LYSISTRATA

No, really. I don't know how you get through the day. Men must
regularly throw themselves down at your feet and just sort of howl.

LAMPITO

The dears. One just steps over them.

LYSISTRATA

I'd hate you on principle if it wasn't that your very beauty will
be the linchpin of what I like to call LBP, which is short for
Lysistrata's Brilliant Plan, a little something which I flatter
myself may just change the course of human history. I mean, if
we play our cards right, LBP might—

MYRRHINE
Is there anything to eat?

LAMPITO
Really. I'm starving.

LYSISTRATA
Don't you want to know what it is?

MYRRHINE
(Searching her clothing) I thought I had a couple of figs on me somewhere.

LAMPITO
I had a piece of toast, but that was like three hours ago.

LYSISTRATA
Lysistrata's Brilliant Plan?

MYRRHINE
See, I'm on this new diet, all fruit. Tons of figs.

CALONICE
Does it work?

MYRRHINE
Well, I've lost a few pounds, but I feel so bloated all the time—

LYSISTRATA
Isn't anyone curious?

LAMPITO
Well, you look great.

MYRRHINE
(Flattered) You think so?

LYSISTRATA
Will everyone please just shut up for a minute about FOOD!
God! Men are right! It's all women ever talk about!

(Bad little pause.)

LAMPITO
(Calmly) I see. So what you're saying is that, having answered
your unintelligible call to women everywhere, we now find
ourselves here at dawn, miles from home, worn out, and yes,
hungry, and it is at this moment that we learn we have traveled
all this way only to be—what?—YELLED AT? BY SOME
LUNATIC ATHENIAN WOMAN WHO ONLY HAD TO
ROLL OUT OF BED TO GET HERE? How uncouth of us to
mention food. I, in fact, am now so humiliated that I feel I must
remove myself, perhaps all the way to the market where I can
only hope to console myself for my lack of tact with some thinly
sliced lamb and a carafe of red wine.

DIPSAS
Gosh, I'm feeling pretty humiliated, too. Maybe some coffee?

ISMENIA
Me, too. Just so ashamed. Or a little hot bread?

MYRRHINE
You know how ashamed I am? I'm ashamed enough to go off
my diet . . .

LYSISTRATA
All right, all right, all right. I get your point. I'm sorry I snapped.
I'd like to apologize.

LAMPITO
Go right ahead.

LYSISTRATA
Go right ahead and what?

MYRRHINE
Apologize.

LYSISTRATA
Didn't I just do that?

ISMENIA
No, you said you'd *like* to.

LYSISTRATA
But, I— Didn't I—? I thought I said . . .

(They all shake their heads.)

LAMPITO
Pathetic.

MYRRHINE
(To Lampito) Sad, really. Just like a man.

LYSISTRATA
Look. *(Quickly)* I'm sorry I made you mad because I need you all in order to make my plan work. (It really is brilliant.) I hope that you'll help me because I can't do it alone.

LAMPITO
Ladies? Shall we stay?

(Pause. They decide to stay.)

MYRRHINE
All right. Tell us.

LYSISTRATA

First, let me just ask a question. How many of you ladies have husbands at home right now? Raise your hands.

(No one raises a hand.)

All of your husbands are away, right? How many of you have husbands fighting in some godforsaken place, away for weeks, months, years at a time?

(They all raise their hands.)

Your husbands are probably all off right this minute fighting with each other, isn't that right?

(They nod.)

You probably all spend your days the way I do, bored and scared at the same time, just numb, staring at the walls, too unhappy to even leave the house sometimes, praying that the war will end. And you spend your nights tossing and turning, worried sick that your husband is lying in a battlefield somewhere, wounded, dying, calling your name . . .

(The women start to cry.)

How many of you are SICK OF WAR?

(They all put up their hands.)

How many of you would give up anything for peace?

(They all put up their hands.)

Repeat after me: I WOULD GIVE UP ANYTHING FOR PEACE!

WOMEN
I WOULD GIVE UP ANYTHING FOR PEACE!

LYSISTRATA
I WOULD GIVE UP MY YOUTH!

WOMEN
I WOULD GIVE UP MY YOUTH!

LYSISTRATA
I WOULD GIVE UP MY SIGHT!

WOMEN
I WOULD GIVE UP MY SIGHT!

LYSISTRATA
I WOULD GIVE UP MY HEARING!

WOMEN
I WOULD GIVE UP MY HEARING!

LYSISTRATA
I WOULD GIVE UP MY BEAUTY!

WOMEN
I WOULD GIVE UP MY BEAUTY!

LYSISTRATA
I WOULD GIVE UP ANYTHING AT ALL!

WOMEN
I WOULD GIVE UP ANYTHING AT ALL!

LYSISTRATA
I WOULD EVEN GIVE UP SEX!

(The chorus of women, which has reached an ecstatic fervor, completely disintegrates.)

Come on, ladies! I WOULD EVEN GIVE UP SEX!

ISMENIA
What are you, nuts?

DIPSAS
We may be unhappy but we're not idiots.

LAMPITO
Why do you think we miss our husbands so much?

CALONICE
Absolutely. Sex is what makes life worth living.

MYRRHINE
It's the ONLY thing that makes life bearable sometimes.

DIPSAS
Nothing could make me give it up.

(The chorus of women shouts agreement.)

LYSISTRATA
But that's the reason my plan is so brilliant!

LAMPITO
What, because it's insane?

LYSISTRATA
No, no, don't you realize that as much as you miss your husbands, they miss you just as much?

DIPSAS
So what? We're all miserable. What's your point?

LYSISTRATA
If we say that we won't have sex with them until they all declare peace, they'll *have* to settle their differences. Don't you see?

ISMENIA
You mean the next time they come home for a few days for a little nooky, we just SAY NO?

LYSISTRATA
Absolutely. It's very simple.

LAMPITO
It's impossible is what it is.

LYSISTRATA
Oh, come on, it's for such a good cause.

MYRRHINE
Maybe you can do it, but I'm not giving up the only pleasure I've got left.

LYSISTRATA
But it won't work if we don't all do it. That's the point.

DIPSAS
It's a lot to ask. Particularly now that I've finally taught him all the best tricks I know to make me happy.

CALONICE
I know! It took ages! Who wants to go through all that again?

MYRRHINE
Who has the energy? Also, I like the way his hair curls on the back of his neck.

ISMENIA
Mine's got the most wonderful mole, right under his rib cage.

DIPSAS
Mine's got this way of hooking his leg over my hip and—

LYSISTRATA
Enough! I'm sure they're all fabulous fellows. Let's not descend
to dewy-eyed idiocy. Focus, ladies! Think of it! We could end
war forever.

CALONICE
Think of it. Lovemaking every single night.

MYRRHINE
No more lonely days.

ISMENIA
No more dying of fright every time I see a messenger coming to
the door.

LYSISTRATA
Think of it.

LAMPITO
Think of it. *(Pause)* All right, I'll do it.

LYSISTRATA
Oh, you Spartan queen! If we have you with us, then we've got
nothing to worry about!

(They embrace.)

DIPSAS
Well, I'm not going to be outdone by a Spartan. I'll do it.

LYSISTRATA
Oh, wonderful!

CALONICE

We Athenians can do just as well as any other Greeks. All right, Lysistrata, I'll give up sex, too. Even if it kills me.

LYSISTRATA

I take back everything terrible I ever said about you. *(They embrace)* And that's a lot.

LAMPITO

One little thing: I'll spread the word through the women of Sparta, and I think we can rely on all of the rest of the ladies present to get their country's girls together on this. But I'm not entirely confident that you can make your war-mad Athenians put down their swords. Your men are just plain loco when it comes to starting fights. And then there's the problem of the gold in your acropolis. Until that's in the hands of women, Athenians are never going to stop killing anyone who comes within sniffing distance of it.

LYSISTRATA

My dear Lampito, you are as brainy as you are beautiful. And I agree with every word you said. Men are fools for battle everywhere, but nowhere more than in Athens, where the boys are born with teeth, I think, and stab each other in the playpens before they can even pee standing up. That's why, while we've been talking here, a group of older women, widows all, who know the cost of war better than anyone, have taken the acropolis from the geezers who were left to guard it. They went there at first light, supposedly to do their usual prayers, bent over and muttering, all in black, looking like the innocent old crones everybody thinks they are. But when they got to the gates of the acropolis they hiked up their skirts and ran in, bopped the old men on the head with their canes, dragged them out and closed the doors behind them. They're up there waiting for the women of Athens now. And the geezers are rubbing their heads outside the gates, surprised as all get-out. So, while you ladies are back home organizing, we Athenian gals will hole up in the acropolis together, and we'll just bide our time until our men get wind of what's happened and come back home. I can see it now. They'll be pawing the ground, begging us to open our gates and then . . . to open our gates.

CALONICE
But we won't, right?

LYSISTRATA
Not until we see a delegation of men from all over Greece standing before us, hands over their swollen peckers, humbly pledging themselves to peace.

MYRRHINE
This IS a brilliant plan!

LYSISTRATA
I thought you'd like it.

LAMPITO
Let's swear to it, girls!

(The women, in a circle, place their right hands together.)

KEEP IT ZIPPED 'TIL THEY FLIP!

WOMEN
KEEP IT ZIPPED 'TIL THEY FLIP!

DIPSAS
CROSS YOUR LEGS OR HOPE TO DIE!

WOMEN
CROSS YOUR LEGS OR HOPE TO DIE!

MYRRHINE

DON'T GIVE THEM A PIECE OF ASS, UNTIL THEY GIVE US A PEACE THAT LASTS!

WOMEN

DON'T GIVE THEM A PIECE OF ASS, UNTIL THEY GIVE US A PEACE THAT LASTS!

CALONICE

MAKE LOVE, NOT WAR!

WOMEN

MAKE LOVE, NOT WAR!

DIPSAS

That sounds so familiar.

ISMENIA

Doesn't it?

CALONICE

I just made it up!

ISMENIA

It's nice. Catchy.

CALONICE

Thanks. Oo, hang on, I feel another one coming on . . . WAR IS NOT HEALTHY FOR CHILDREN OR OTHER LIVING THINGS!

DIPSAS

Nah, too long.

CALONICE

Wait, wait, um . . . STOP IN THE NAME OF NOOKY . . .

LAMPITO
Quit while you're ahead, doll.

(The women, ignoring Calonice entirely, are discussing strategies, shaking hands, and leaving.)

CALONICE
REACH OUT AND TOUCH SOMEBODY'S HAND, I mean, *DON'T* . . . REACH OUT AND TOUCH SOMEBODY'S HAND . . . um, hang on . . . *(Realizes she is alone onstage)* . . . Hey, wait up, you guys! *(She exits)*

(The Athenian Chorus Leaders rush back on.)

ATHENIAN CHORUS LEADERS 1 AND 2
Meanwhile . . .

ATHENIAN CHORUS LEADER 1
Excuse me?

ATHENIAN CHORUS LEADER 2
Do you mind? I've just always wanted to say: "*Meanwhile* . . ."

ATHENIAN CHORUS LEADER 1
Oh, *fine.* Just get on with it.

ATHENIAN CHORUS LEADER 2
Meanwhile . . . over at the acropolis. Word gets out that the women have taken over the treasury, and the local police force mobilizes itself.

ATHENIAN CHORUS LEADER 1
Only problem is that the flower of Athens is off fighting everybody in the world—

ATHENIAN CHORUS LEADER 2
Yeah, so the average age of the geezers available to take on the women is, like, eighty-six and change.

ATHENIAN CHORUS LEADER 1
Talk about your thin blue lines.

ATHENIAN CHORUS LEADER 2
And they have the bright idea that they're going to burn down the acropolis to save it.

ATHENIAN CHORUS LEADER 1
Or something like that.

ATHENIAN CHORUS LEADER 2
Well, here they come, they can tell you themselves.

(The Athenian Chorus Leaders exit. Geezers teeter in slowly, coughing and flicking butane lighters. An unprepossessing lot.)

GEEZER 1
Hup! Hup! Hup! Come on fellas! We'll show them what it takes!

GEEZER 2
(Coughing) Slow down, for Pete's sake, I've got a pebble in my sandal that's killing me.

GEEZER 3
A pebble! Cry me a river, bub, my toga's been twisted funny around my armpits since we began this forced march. This maniac here wouldn't let me stop and fix it. Two minutes I ask for, but no. Now I'm black and blue from the chafing.

GEEZER 1
Bunch of sissies. Bunch of pantywaists. You don't deserve to call yourselves Athenians. The fate of the city's at stake and all you can think about is your withered carcasses!

GEEZER 2
(Hopping as he tries to free the pebble from his sandal) Or maybe it's a bit of glass—is that blood? I'm *bleeding*!

GEEZER 1

When I think of our former glory—

GEEZER 3

(Struggling with his toga) Since my wife left me I just haven't
been able to get the hang of this thing—

GEEZER 1

The way we stood shoulder to shoulder against the barbarian
horde at Marathon—

GEEZER 3

It's a mystery, this thing, there's some sort of extra tuck or roll
I neglect to do—

GEEZER 1

All for one and one for all—

GEEZER 2

I think that's actually blood! My blood!—

GEEZER 1

Those were the days! That's when Athens had greatness!

GEEZER 2

Now on top of impetigo, cataracts and this new allergy to root
vegetables, I'll be crippled for life.

GEEZER 1

That it has come to this! Unmanned by *women*! The indignity of
it! *(Notices that no one is paying attention to him)* Will you quit
bellyaching and LISTEN UP? *(They do)* This is the situation,
men. Our gold is being held hostage by a bunch of old biddies—
it's downright humiliating. We're locked out here shaking our
fists at the air while they're lolling around in there on the
money bags, filing their nails and doing crosswords.

GEEZER 3
For shame!

GEEZER 2
For shame!

GEEZER 1
Why, it makes my blood boil.

GEEZER 2
I am vexed indeed.

GEEZER 3
(Agreeing) Irked and vexed. Mightily.

GEEZER 1
Shall we do it, gentlemen?

GEEZERS 2 AND 3
You betcha! Yes sirree bob! By cracky we will! *(And so forth. Pause)* Do what?

GEEZER 1
Smoke the hellcats out!

GEEZERS 2 AND 3
SMOKE THE HELLCATS OUT!

(Geezer 2 starts wandering around flicking his lighter menacingly.)

GEEZER 2
Let me at 'em! Where do we light up?

GEEZER 3
There'll be no holding this firebrand back!

GEEZER 2
Try and stop me! Try and stop me!

GEEZER 1
That's the spirit, fellas. Now we're talking!

(The Old Women come in unnoticed by the men. They hold squirt bottles.)

OLD WOMAN 1
Well, well, well, what have we here?

OLD WOMAN 2
Looks like a bunch of John Philip Sousa groupies. What's with the lighters, boys?

OLD WOMAN 3
Where's the fire? Or rather, where isn't it?

GEEZER 1
There's one of the shameless hussies now.

GEEZER 2
Running loose like some wildcat on a prowl.

GEEZER 3
Singe her heathen eyebrows off. *(Flicks his lighter menacingly)*

OLD WOMAN 1
Just try it, old man, and you'll be walking funny for the rest of your life.

OLD WOMAN 2
Which amounts to . . . gee, anyone have a stopwatch?

OLD WOMAN 3
I don't give any of them more than twenty minutes tops.

GEEZER 1

You think I won't take you on? I'll take you on!

GEEZER 2

Yeah. If you think we're gentlemen who don't dare to rough girls up, you've got another think coming.

OLD WOMAN 1

Oh, I'd never have leapt to that assumption.

OLD WOMAN 2

(Reacting to the smell of the men) No, no, it'd be impossible to make *that* mistake. When did you last take a bath, leaky-pants?

OLD WOMAN 3

Let's at least get upwind of them.

GEEZER 1

Mess with us, Sister, and you're throwing caution to the wind.

GEEZER 2

We're trouble with a capital T.

OLD WOMAN 1

And that rhymes with B.

OLD WOMAN 2

And that stands for—

OLD WOMEN 1, 2 AND 3

BULLSHIT!

GEEZER 1

(With regret and determination) All right, that tears it. Fall in, men. Hup, hup. Let's teach these she-devils a lesson.

(The men line up, prepared to implement their lighters.)

To arms! Ready! Light!

(They brandish the lighters.)

OLD WOMAN 1
Ladies?

(With a minimum of fuss, the women squirt the men with water.)

GEEZER 2
Well, that was just so . . .

GEEZER 3
Totally . . .

GEEZER 1
Uncalled for!

GEEZER 2
Yes! Uncalled for! Underhanded, really.

GEEZER 3
(British accent) Not quite pukka.

GEEZER 2
Hardly.

GEEZER 1
Are we going to let them get away with that?

GEEZER 2
Not on your tintype.

GEEZER 3
Not on my nickel, bub.

GEEZER 1
Stand aside, fellas, it's not going to be pretty.

OLD WOMAN 1
Aw, can the balloon juice, grandpa. If you so much as wheeze in my direction you'll be singing soprano.

GEEZER 1
Oh yeah?

OLD WOMAN 2
Yeah.

GEEZER 1
Says who?

OLD WOMAN 2
Says me.

GEEZER 1
Says you?

OLD WOMAN 2
That's right.

GEEZER 1
And who's going to stop me?

OLD WOMAN 2
Me.

GEEZER 1
Oh yeah?

OLD WOMAN 2
Yeah.

GEEZER 1
Is that so?

OLD WOMAN 2
You're cruising for a bruising, old man.

GEEZER 1
Give me one good reason I shouldn't knock you into next week,
ya toothless old freak-job.

OLD WOMAN 2
(Making a fist) I'll give you five good reasons, prune-breath.

GEEZER 1
You and what army?

(They square off. Pause.)

Are you as turned on as I am?

OLD WOMAN 2
At least.

GEEZER 1
I guess we've still got some snap in our garters after all.

OLD WOMAN 2
Apparently. And there's a lot to be said for toothlessness when it
comes to you-know-what.

GEEZER 1
(Confused) Do I? *(Thinking it through)* Oh, you filthy minx.

(The men and women are still squared off. The Magistrate enters.)

MAGISTRATE
What the heck is going on here?

GEEZER 2

Just a little dust-up, Your Specialness, sir.

GEEZER 3

Everything's under control.

MAGISTRATE

Excuse me, "under control"? The Athenian treasury is in the hands of a rabble of women. I can't get into the vault of *my own city* and my entire police force consists of a trio of wheezing nitwits who can be held at bay by a handful of menopausal geriatrics with spray bottles? UNDER CONTROL?

GEEZER 1

I don't think you fully appreciate just how formidable and, well, *perfidious* these females can be, sir—

GEEZER 2

They're tricky—

GEEZER 1

Very crafty, particularly this one—

GEEZER 3

It's the wily, instinctual mind of the she-cat—

GEEZER 2

The lynx, the lioness. You're not dealing with a rational being here—

GEEZER 1

By no means. It's a sort of animal cunning, really, beyond our ken, shadowy, slippery, untamable, alien to the sunlit reaches of our masculine intelligence—

MAGISTRATE

Oh, SHUT UP! I'm surrounded by imbeciles. Coots and schmendricks to a man. And now the women, who seem to have lost what little sense they ever had, have started pulling these ludicrous hijinks. I'm the laughingstock of the Delian League. Is there anyone on this acropolis who isn't a complete jackass?

LYSISTRATA
(Entering) What seems to be the matter?

MAGISTRATE
So you're the ringleader, are you?

LYSISTRATA
I suppose so.

MAGISTRATE
The little lady we have to thank for all this bullshit.

LYSISTRATA
You're welcome. It was really a pleasure. And much easier than I could ever have imagined. If I'd known all it took was a modicum of intelligence and a bit of determination I'd have shut up this slaughterhouse long ago.

MAGISTRATE
Slaughterhouse? It's the treasury.

LYSISTRATA
Slaughterhouse, treasury, what's the difference? It's all men can ever think to do with money—fund their wars. There's a truly criminal lack of imagination in evidence.

MAGISTRATE
I suppose you, with your vast housewife's knowledge of money, could do better?

LYSISTRATA
Housewives know a few truths you exalted politicians seem to forget. For instance, we spend our money on our children too,

but we hand them meals and books unlike you who hand them swords and daggers. It's the same money, just different principles.

MAGISTRATE
This is typical emotional blackmail. But then that's all you girls can ever resort to.

LYSISTRATA
Perhaps you're right. Perhaps we do feel it more. After all we're the ones who have to stay in, closed behind shutters in our houses of mourning, listening for the lost echoes when our loved ones have died in your wars.

MAGISTRATE
I can't expect you to understand the higher principles at stake, what we are defending. Your sphere is too tiny to appreciate what we do for you.

LYSISTRATA
Yes, you really knock yourselves out for us, and you get so little thanks in return. It's hardly fair. We should really send you bouquets of black flowers for every wasted year, every hollow hour, every shudder of fear when a messenger knocks. Garlands, wreaths and chaplets of blackness would pile your halls, lie like black snowdrifts along your marble corridors, so that every day you would have to trudge through the rotting stinking wasted vastness of our gratitude for all, all that you have taken from us, our lost youth, our spent and useless love, all that we have lost at your hands. Thank you. I speak for mothers and wives every-where. Thank you.

MAGISTRATE
Well, if you're just going to get morbid there's no talking to you.

LYSISTRATA
God forbid I should talk about death to a warmonger. How uncouth of me! Like mentioning sex to a whore.

MAGISTRATE

I was talking about money.

LYSISTRATA

As does any good whore. You prove my point. Indeed, let's talk about money. Why not?

MAGISTRATE

Will you be reasonable and give me the keys to the city's vault?

LYSISTRATA

I will be reasonable and keep them. You have exhibited all too clearly that you can't be trusted with the keys. You've squandered my great city's fortune on the machinery of death and the fuel for your nightmare factories. It's time you went on a diet. No more gold, no more blank checks. All your shiny ships have sunk to the bottom of the wine-dark sea with half our dear ones in them. We have other plans for our riches.

MAGISTRATE

I can't believe I'm even bothering to discuss this with you. You know nothing of politics. You have all the sanctimonious stubbornness of the utterly ignorant. You have a brain the size of a flea turd and you dare to stand on your hind legs and scold me about how I conduct affairs of state? It's preposterous. This is a national emergency. There is more at stake than your little soap opera. I need the money for battleships. We're under siege, or perhaps you've forgotten. We are in the middle of a war, woman, stand aside and behave yourself.

LYSISTRATA

Yes, that's your favorite tune. I've heard it all my life: Shut up and don't ask questions, we're trying to win a war here. Every woman has had to bite her tongue a thousand times when men come home from a long day of gassing about *when* but never *whether* to attack some hapless new enemy or other. When we

ask if such unchecked aggression is wise we are told: "Now is
not the time." It never is the time to listen to any voice other
than your own. Until now. You'll have to listen to us because
it turns out we do have something you want. It simply never
occurred to us that we had a choice as to whether to let you have
it. But we do. And we refuse to bring any more children into the
world to be fodder for your wars. That's what it comes down to.
It's up to you.

MAGISTRATE
This is utterly unnatural.

LYSISTRATA
Is it? Unnatural to prize life over death? Peace over conquest and
havoc? Plenty and joy over deprivation and fear? No, sir, the system
you have imposed on us all these years is what is unnatural. Left
to their own devices people would never choose your mayhem
and sorrow. All any people have ever wanted is the chance to
love and work to the best of their abilities. It's the same
everywhere. We are not unique in our hopes.

MAGISTRATE
By all means, ally yourself with the mud-spattered doltish masses.
They are your natural kin. But I choose to think that our
Athenian destiny is special. I'm proud to breathe the rarefied air
of this most exalted of nations. Our singular fate brings with it
a singular burden of responsibility.

LYSISTRATA
It may very well be that at my washtub I don't snuff the same
heady air as you do. But from what I've seen, people don't differ
too much, place to place. Some aren't as lucky, that's for sure,
but we've got no monopoly on either virtue or evil. There are
assholes everywhere (they're thick on the ground in these parts
certainly), but also people worth knowing and loving at the
other end of every drawn sword. If Athenians were as special as

you make out we wouldn't hold other people's lives so cheap.
We'd be more enlightened than that. And perhaps if we could
master our own egotism we might find that the only people
singing our praises weren't just other Athenians. But that's
somewhere down a very long road. In the meantime, we'll be
keeping ALL the vaults shut up tight, and all the assets frozen.

*(Lysistrata and the Magistrate exit. The Athenian Chorus
Leaders enter.)*

ATHENIAN CHORUS LEADER 1
So you can imagine how happy that made them.

ATHENIAN CHORUS LEADER 2
But what could they do? We held the acropolis for weeks while
the old coots fumed and stamped around the base of it muttering
threats.

ATHENIAN CHORUS LEADER 1
But that was nothing compared to the ordeal going on inside.

ATHENIAN CHORUS LEADER 2
Lysistrata had her hands full getting the women to stick to their
no-nooky oath.

ATHENIAN CHORUS LEADER 1
It was nip and tuck there whether the girls were going to manage
to keep their legs crossed.

(The Athenian Chorus Leaders exit. Lysistrata enters, irked.)

LYSISTRATA
Have I said how much I hate women? Keeping these rabid
alewives in line is like trying to herd cats. Scratch the surface
and there isn't one who isn't basically feckless and sex-mad.
I haven't slept in weeks. I've got to watch the barricades all
night long to make sure one of them doesn't slip her leash and

slope home to throw her dress up over her head. Here's one now. Watch this.

(Belphragia, an Athenian woman, is attempting to sneak past.)

Belphragia, my dear.

BELPHRAGIA
Oh, hello, Lysistrata, I didn't see you there.

LYSISTRATA
Yes, well, here I am. Heading someplace?

BELPHRAGIA
Yes, I'm afraid I need to go. I just got an urgent message from home.

LYSISTRATA
Oh really? From whom?

BELPHRAGIA
Well, luckily my husband being home on leave now was able to alert me to the fact that, um . . . *moths* have, um . . . *attacked* some wool I was trying to untangle when I got the call to the Pan-Hellenic Women's Congress. I just dropped it and ran and, well, now it's just *lying* there . . . at the mercy of . . . *moths* . . .

LYSISTRATA
And this is such a crisis?

BELPHRAGIA
Yes! I mean, *no*, it'll only take a minute. I just need to spread it on the bed and air it out for a while. I'll be right back.

LYSISTRATA
Uh-huh. Forget it.

BELPHRAGIA
Oh, but Lysistrata, if you only knew what a pathetic, sorry snarl of moth-eaten wool it is now. And it's really quite lovely when you pat it down and smooth it out. So calm and bright eyed, so well rested and cheerful once she's had a little attention.

LYSISTRATA
I have no doubt. But then we're all a bit frayed at the moment. The fact of the matter is that until peace breaks out your sorry snarl will just have to cope.

(A Fisherwoman tries to get past.)

And who is this? Not so fast, missy.

FISHERWOMAN
You cannot keep me from my livelihood!

LYSISTRATA
What's that?

FISHERWOMAN
I am a gardener of the sea.

LYSISTRATA
I knew something smelled fishy around here.

FISHERWOMAN
And it's neap tide. The beds are calling me.

LYSISTRATA
I bet they are.

FISHERWOMAN
The clam beds need digging
The mussel beds need plucking
And the *oyster* beds, the oyster beds need . . .

LYSISTRATA
Shucking?

FISHERWOMAN
Well, yes.

LYSISTRATA
Dream on, sunshine, no one's doing any shucking until peace is declared.

(The Fisherwoman exits. Calonice enters, apparently, but unconvincingly, pregnant.)

CALONICE
A midwife, what ho! A midwife!

LYSISTRATA
Calonice!

CALONICE
I'm sorry but I must leave you girls to carry on the siege alone. My sacred motherly duty calls. I am poised on that awesome threshold . . . the divine mystery of childbirth.

LYSISTRATA
Funny, you weren't pregnant yesterday.

CALONICE
It's a miracle!

LYSISTRATA
You're carrying high.

(She raps on Calonice's belly with her knuckles; it makes an unmistakable metallic clank. Bad little pause.)

CALONICE
It's a boy!

LYSISTRATA

Yes, well, that would explain the helmet.

CALONICE

He's a true Athenian warrior! Born armed!

LYSISTRATA

How convenient. So you can skip the diapering.

CALONICE

(Breaking down and begging) Oh, Lysistrata, I'm on my knees. My husband's home on leave for the first time in ages and I've *got* to see him. I'm not brave and strong like you. Pleeeeeeease let me go home, just for a toss, I'll be back in no time. He's going crazy, staggering around the acropolis with all the other poor schmucks, moaning like unmilked cows, it's just so pathetic.

(Moans from offstage.)

Listen to them all. I HEAR YA, BABY!

LYSISTRATA

That's exactly where we want them. Don't you see that this is working at last? If we can just hold out a few more days, we'll be sitting on velvet, it's just a matter of—

(Cinesias, nursing a hard-on, wanders onstage doing a Stanley Kowalski. The women all look at him sympathetically, though he doesn't see them.)

CINESIAS

MYRRHINE! MYRRHINE!

LYSISTRATA

Myrrhine dear, there seems to be someone here to see you.

(Myrrhine enters and sees Cinesias.)

MYRRHINE
Oh, look at him, the poor little bugger.

BELPHRAGIA
It's not that little.

MYRRHINE
It just makes me go all gooey to look at him like that. I just want to go over and—

LYSISTRATA
Steady on, Myrrhine, there's no going back now. We're on the brink of success. Will you hold out just a little longer? Will you drive him to distraction? Take him right up to the edge and then turn him down?

MYRRHINE
But look at him Lysistrata, he's in agony, you could hang a hat on that thing.

LYSISTRATA
Which is precisely why you can't submit.

MYRRHINE
But, but—

LYSISTRATA
Stop frothing at the mouth and get a grip! The fate of Greece is in your hands. Will you do it for Athens? For the sake of all our children and our children's children?

MYRRHINE
All right. All right. All right . . . Sheesh. I'll keep a lid on it this once. But it's going to be tricky.

LYSISTRATA
Brave girl. I'll get him warmed up for you.

(All the women except Lysistrata exit.)

CINESIAS
MYRHINNE! BABY! MYRHINNE!

LYSISTRATA
And who might you be here to see?

CINESIAS
(Confused) Um, Myrrhine?

LYSISTRATA
Well, I'll let her know that there's a gentleman to see her. And your name would be?

CINESIAS
Cinesias?

LYSISTRATA
Cinesias, well, well, well, you're all she talks about.

CINESIAS
Really?

LYSISTRATA
Oh yes, it's a broken record. Cinesias this, Cinesias that. *Everything* reminds her of you. She showed us a very amusing trick with a peeled banana the other night that had us all in stitches. Oh, she's quite a scamp. And *so* devoted.

CINESIAS
You think?

LYSISTRATA
Oh absolutely. Why just last night she was toying with a sausage we had for dinner and she let on as to what a fine cook you are.

"This is nothing compared to my Cinesias' sausage," is how I think she put it.

(Cinesias grunts in some distress.)

I'll just go see if she's available, shall I?

(Lysistrata exits past Myrrhine on her entrance.)

Just cross your legs and think of Greece.

MYRRHINE
Never fear. I just sat on an icicle. *(Approaches Cinesias)* Hello, Nuptial Unit, what's up? I mean, how are things?

CINESIAS
How do you think they are? I'm miserable! I'm having difficulty stringing sentences together.

MYRRHINE
Gee, that is unfortunate. What seems to be the problem?

CINESIAS
I'm beside myself. If you don't come home soon, I'm going to do myself damage. It's not *healthy*.

MYRRHINE
Well, you certainly look in the pink.

CINESIAS
I'm in the purple! I'm verging on blue! Baby, have mercy. Give me a squeeze or I'll keel over in a faint.

MYRRHINE
What, *here*?

CINESIAS
Sure here, there, anywhere. What does it matter at this point?

MYRRHINE
(Referring to the audience) In front of all of them?

CINESIAS
What do they care?

MYRRHINE
They came here for a refined evening in the theater.

CINESIAS
Refined? It's a sex comedy.

MYRRHINE
It's by Aristophanes!

CINESIAS
Come on, it's a bunch of Ancient Greek dick jokes with some
acrobatics thrown in to fill out the evening.

MYRRHINE
You seem to be very unclear on the nature of this whole endeavor.

CINESIAS
I'm unclear on EVERYTHING at the moment. I'm blinded by
desire. All the blood's left my head, I can't think anymore.

MYRRHINE
You poor dear. Let me feel your forehead.

(She does.)

CINESIAS
Oh, honey, oh, baby . . .

MYRRHINE
You do seem a mite warm.

CINESIAS
You don't know the half of it.

MYRRHINE
Let me go see if I can rustle up something to help you with that.

CINESIAS
(Hanging on to her) Everything I need is right here.

MYRRHINE
Let me take your pulse.

CINESIAS
Take anything you want but just don't go away.

MYRRHINE
It's racing.

CINESIAS
No kidding.

MYRRHINE
Stick out your tongue.

CINESIAS
(Somewhat incoherently) Gladly.

MYRRHINE
Yes, it does seem to be a bit coated.

CINESIAS
(Still agape) It's been hanging out a lot with all the panting.

MYRRHINE
The what?

CINESIAS
Panting! Panting! *(Illustrates)*

MYRRHINE
Well, you'll have to stop doing that.

CINESIAS
I'd gladly stop, and you're the girl to help me.

MYRRHINE
And your eyes are a little glazed.

CINESIAS
I'm surprised I'm not cross-eyed by now.

MYRRHINE
(Getting very close to him) There's a kind of sheen to your skin
that concerns me, and a smell—what is that smell?

CINESIAS
I don't know, you better keep sniffing.

MYRRHINE
The key to the diagnosis of several diseases is olfactory.

CINESIAS
(Losing it with her proximity) Ola . . . ole . . . oh la la . . .

MYRRHINE
This is very serious indeed. I may have to take drastic measures.

CINESIAS
(Desperately hopeful) Mouth to mouth? Mouth to mouth?

MYRRHINE
If I give you mouth to mouth will you work for peace?

CINESIAS

If you give me mouth to mouth I'll set up a little shrine in your honor in the backyard and worship at it daily.

MYRRHINE

That's nice but not what I need at the moment. I want a treaty.

CINESIAS

A treaty? Just for some nooky? We'll talk about it later, give me a kiss.

(He puckers up. She leans in. Pause.)

MYRRHINE

Gee, you know, I just can't get in the mood when there's a war on. Give me a holler when you come home for good.

(She runs away.)

CINESIAS

What, you're leaving me like this?

MYRRHINE

(From offstage) I'll be waaaiiting . . .

*(Cinesias moans in despair.
The Athenian Chorus Leaders enter. They look at Cinesias sympathetically.)*

CINESIAS

Ow.

ATHENIAN CHORUS LEADER 1

So she left you high and dry, huh?

ATHENIAN CHORUS LEADER 2

That's quite a large problem you got there, buddy.

CINESIAS
Tell me about it.

ATHENIAN CHORUS LEADER 1
Do you think you can handle it alone?

CINESIAS
I've been handling it alone so much I think I hurt myself.
Maybe you could help me?

ATHENIAN CHORUS LEADER 1
Sorry, I don't freelance.

ATHENIAN CHORUS LEADER 2
And besides, we took the oath:

ATHENIAN CHORUS LEADERS 1 AND 2
You don't get a piece until *we* get a peace.

CINESIAS
Well, fuck. Where's the nearest brothel?

ATHENIAN CHORUS LEADER 2
No dice, bub, the whores are all on strike, too.

CINESIAS
I guess it's back to going steady with my own right hand.

ATHENIAN CHORUS LEADER 1
You know what we women say:

ATHENIAN CHORUS LEADERS 1 AND 2
If you're sick of self-abuse
Now's the time to make a truce.

CINESIAS
But I'm just one poor schmuck with a hard-on, what can I do?

ATHENIAN CHORUS LEADER 1
Ah, but you are one of *many* poor schmucks with hard-ons.
That's the beauty of it.

ATHENIAN CHORUS LEADER 2
Yes! I mean, look!

(A group of Spartans trudge on in sexual distress.)

ATHENIAN CHORUS LEADER 1
It's a bunch of Spartans in an unmistakable condition.

ATHENIAN CHORUS LEADER 2
Aw, look at them, the miserable peckerwoods.

SPARTAN ENVOY
Could you point us to the Central Committee?

ATHENIAN CHORUS LEADER 1
You seem to be doing a good job of pointing yourselves around.

ATHENIAN CHORUS LEADER 2
Yeah, you could direct traffic with those things.

SPARTAN DELEGATE
We have some important business to take up with them.

ATHENIAN CHORUS LEADER 1
Well, you'll have to disarm before you go in.

SPARTAN ENVOY
We come in peace.

ATHENIAN CHORUS LEADER 2
Yet you seem to be smuggling spears.

ATHENIAN CHORUS LEADER 1
More like little daggers, really.

ATHENIAN CHORUS LEADER 2
At any rate, they look lethal.

SPARTAN DELEGATE
Well, they're certainly killing *us*.

(The Athenian Chorus Leaders exit.
The Magistrate enters in a similar condition.)

MAGISTRATE
Is this the Spartan delegation?

SPARTAN ENVOY
(To his men) Stand at attention!

MAGISTRATE
No need to salute, soldier.

SPARTAN ENVOY
Can't help it, sir.

MAGISTRATE
I see, so the situation on your end is just as tense as it has been
here.

SPARTAN DELEGATE
Pretty thick. There's been a general uprising across Greece.

SPARTAN ENVOY
We've all been on high alert for weeks now.

MAGISTRATE
As have we. It's this damn Lysistrata making everything so
tough for all of us. But I didn't realize your people were also up
against it.

SPARTAN DELEGATE

It's been very hard for all of us. That bitch Lampito's convinced all the women to shut down relations. There has been great suffering on all fronts.

MAGISTRATE

The damage these women have done to male morale has been just appalling. We've been very hard-pressed.

SPARTAN ENVOY

Indeed. Luckily, we've been able to maintain a firm resolve.

MAGISTRATE

As have we. We stand resolute.

SPARTAN ENVOY

It requires an iron self-discipline.

MAGISTRATE

Yes. And stiff determination.

SPARTAN DELEGATE

Absolutely.

MAGISTRATE

Have we done enough dick jokes?

SPARTAN ENVOY

I think we have, Your Excellency.

MAGISTRATE

All right, then let's get Lysistrata out here so we can wrap things up.

(Lysistrata sails on cheerfully with the rest of the women.)

LYSISTRATA

Oh, you don't all have to stand on my account, boys. Though it's certainly heartening to see you so alert. Do I have your full attention? *(Groans from the men)* Are you ready to make terms?

SPARTAN DELEGATE

You don't give us any option.

LYSISTRATA

(To the Magistrate) And you, sir, have you finally seen reason?

MAGISTRATE

Do I have a choice?

LYSISTRATA

Well, I suppose you could try homosexuality.
(To the audience) (It's very popular in Ancient Greece.)

MAGISTRATE

If I could adopt it at this late date, believe me I would. Nothing would make me happier. It just doesn't seem to do it for me.

LYSISTRATA

I see your point.

(Everyone groans.)

All right, boys, here's the deal. You've always let your peckers do the talking in the past, why stop now? For the first time in history they're talking sense. Listen to them, they're saying, "Lay down your swords and lay down with your wives."

MAGISTRATE

You still fail to grasp the complexity of the thing.

LYSISTRATA

Oh, it's not so very complicated. In fact, it's so obvious that even your dicks can think it through: Sex is good. War is bad.

Look at your women. We want you to live, we want to love you
long and hard, and night after glorious night. We want to grow
old beside you, sleeping in our own warm beds and happily
bonking away with great regularity until all our teeth fall out
and we have to gum each other. It's very simple. The choice is
yours. All you have to do to embrace us again is to embrace peace.

SPARTAN DELEGATE
We'll do anything—

SPARTAN ENVOY
Please, just put us out of our misery.

LYSISTRATA
(To the Magistrate) How about you, big boy?

MAGISTRATE
I must say it rankles to be forced to submit to this female
conspiracy.

LYSISTRATA
But don't you see? It's women who have given you everything
you've ever had that's worth having. Sex. Love. Children. And of
course your very existence. Some woman took her own life in her
hands and endured some very long hours of excruciating pain to
work your body through her own and out into creation.
Face it. *It has always been a female conspiracy!* We conspire for life!

WOMEN *(All but Lysistrata)*
WE CONSPIRE FOR LIFE!

LYSISTRATA
And now you get to keep your end of the bargain. How about it,
fellas? Will you swear to it? Just say: "YES."

MEN *(All but the Magistrate)*
YES!

LYSISTRATA
LET'S STOP THE KILLING AND START THE LOVING!

MEN *(All but the Magistrate)*
LET'S STOP THE KILLING AND START THE LOVING!

LYSISTRATA
(To the audience) Does that go for all of you, too? Just say: "YES."

(Audience presumably says: "YES.")

LET'S STOP THE KILLING AND START THE LOVING!

(The audience responds accordingly.)

(To the Magistrate) How about you, sunshine? Come on, buddy. There's a lot more fun to be had at this party than there is standing out in the cold. Want to join us?

MAGISTRATE
Oh, all right.

LYSISTRATA
You're looking better already. In fact, that's a beautiful smile when you give it a chance.

MAGISTRATE
You think so? My mother used to tell me that.

LYSISTRATA
And mothers never lie.
LET THE PEACE BEGIN!

(Cheers and music as they all dance out in pairs.)

THE END

The Persians

Introduction

The Persians is the first extant full-length play in the Western canon, and the only surviving Greek tragedy that treats a contemporary theme. Aeschylus was a soldier at Marathon (where his brother was killed) and no doubt participated in the battle of Salamis, the nearly miraculous defeat, against seemingly impossible odds, of the Persian navy. Rather than writing a straightforward triumphalist play from the Athenian victors' perspective, he sets the play in the Persian court, where the queen mother and the men who sent the army to conquer the last holdouts of the Greek opposition wait for word of their assured success. Instead, a herald arrives and reports the almost incomprehensible news of the battle of Salamis and the wholesale disaster that means for all their hopes.

The Persians is an imaginative act of extraordinary compassion and originality. Yet it is typical of all the Greek plays that have survived for us in its unsentimental and clear-eyed view of politics and war. The great Greek dramatists were citizens in a unique political experiment—a burgeoning democracy, newly minted, unsettled and constantly under threat, from both within and without. All of them were active in that experiment. As playwrights, they were far from marginal figures in their society. And all of them served their time as soldiers. When they write about freedom, they know from vital experience the price of that freedom. When they write about war, they know its terror, no matter which side one is on.

Yes, this is an antiwar play, but it is complex, sophisticated, and far from naive. All Greek plays are antiwar plays because they were written by veterans, men who knew, firsthand, the real face of battle and the pity of war. This is a play written by a man who participated in battles that changed history and preserved his fragile country with its unlikely notions of freedom in the face of overwhelming odds. Nevertheless, because he was there, he knows the horror of such a war and he never deludes himself that it was anything other than a nightmare, both for the victors and for the defeated.

Such astute sensitivity and wisdom have never graced the theatrical literature of war since. We have much to learn from the founders of theater now. Ideology has overtaken experience in our age: the truth of war is so drowned in bombast and vague polemical notions that we can forget the magnitude of its terror. We forget the real color of blood.

This version of the play is a direct response to the American invasion of Iraq in March 2003. In a rare act of political conscience on the part of an artistic director, Tony Randall canceled his spring season at the National Actors Theatre once war was declared and decided to do *The Persians*. He also wanted to mount it as quickly as possible. He hired Ethan McSweeny to direct and they managed to find a team of extraordinary designers, who were enjoined to work as fast as I've ever seen designers work. Given the scale of the project, the speed with which they came up with a magnificent production was astounding. Ethan, who was familiar with some of my adaptations, called me and basically said, "How fast can you write?" He'd been looking at all the available translations and found them terribly difficult. He wanted a new version that could blow the dust off what is, after all, an almost unfathomably old play. But the desire was always to do justice to this primary source and not torque it excessively toward easy relevance.

Since few of the rest of us were particularly familiar with the play, it was Tony Randall's passion for it that drew the whole community of artists he assembled into the circle around that ancient fire. Twelve years earlier, when he'd founded the theater, he'd written down a long list of plays he wanted to produce. He had, by 2003, produced all of them except for the play at the top of the list: *The Persians*. He later said that he'd been waiting for the right moment, and the day we invaded Iraq was that moment. His fervent faith that *The Persians* was uniquely suited to that terrible time in our history was a faith he converted us all to by the end of the production. It is an astonishing play and I count myself lucky to have had the opportunity to work on it.

Of all the texts I've worked with, this is the one I stayed closest to. This was partly a function of the haste I was in to get a coherent text together so we could begin rehearsal. There was precious little time to mull over the piece and toy with radically new readings. But my fidelity was also due to my desire, more than anything, to get out of the way of the play and let it speak clearly. I wanted the language to release the power inherent in the play without tampering with the basic structure. It's also such a little-known play (because of its difficulty) that I didn't feel I had the right to mess with it too much. An average audience member was unlikely to see several productions of the play over the course of a regular theatergoing life. Then too, I didn't want to make artificial parallels. George H. W. Bush is not Darius, George W. Bush is not Xerxes. We, for that matter, are neither the Persians nor the Greeks. The glib formulaic response does justice neither to us nor to the Greeks and belittles the complexity of what Aeschylus was responding to and our own distinct national crisis.

I did, however, take liberties with the text throughout, usually in terms of drawing out particularity in the character of the chorus. It was Ethan's idea to give each chorus member a specific area of authority, as if they were members of a cabinet. The allocations we arrived at for the chorus sections are suggested here but not essential if future productions wish to divvy up the lines differently. I streamlined several sections, always trying to find vivid images and clear, driving motivations to impel the language. I complicated Atossa's journey through the piece and added an entirely new choral section, the chorus's song concerning Xerxes' flogging of the Hellespont. (That material is not part of the Aeschylus; it's

from Herodotus.) I thought that section made clearer the growing mutinous feeling of the chorus toward their absent king.

Production Notes

Jim Noone designed a wondrously simple and powerful set, which
Kevin Adams lit ever so effectively. The wide, deep stage was covered with several inches of brilliant red sand. Three huge racks
of lighting instruments hung like gates across the back of the
stage. The center gate lifted to let Darius disappear into darkness
when he exited back to the underworld, but on Xerxes' entrance,
all the racks flew out entirely to reveal the upstage area, where
the sand met with an enormous tilted mirror, so that the horizon
line was exceptionally high. At the extreme back of the stage,
Xerxes stood, facing the chorus, reflecting himself in the high
mirror. It was one of the most stunning moments any production
of my work has ever given me, and I will always be grateful for it.

Jess Goldstein did the fine costumes, which were appropriately
simple and evocative. The chorus was dressed in what looked like
their own rehearsal clothes for the opening of the play as they did
the Prologue, and they carried opulent loose robes, which they put
on as the play began. The Herald was barefoot and bare-chested,
with an empty artillery strap across his chest. The ragged pants
had the look of modern fatigues, but weren't precisely identifiable
in terms of the country or even the era they evoked. Atossa
entered the first scene wearing a dazzling gold robe over a gold
dress. Her headdress was tall and gold, something like a northern
African headdress, with dangling ornaments at the temples.
When she appeared the second time, she wore a simple black dress
that bared her calves, and her head was uncovered. It was a shock-
ing transformation, which seemed right. At her first entrance,
running servants unrolled a succession of long, narrow carpets
before her (the feet of Persian royalty were never supposed to
touch bare earth), but the second and third entrances she made
alone, trudging across the sand barefoot.

Michael Roth did the music and found two tremendously talented percussionists who were onstage throughout and contributed mightily to the feel of the piece. When the chorus sang their song, a cellist appeared who then stayed onstage until the end. Information is provided (page 260) on how to secure the use of his music, should producers choose to do so.

It is important that the chorus be formidable middle-aged men. They are the men responsible for the whole massive enterprise of the Persian invasion, and however they may want to blame Xerxes for botching it, the weight of that responsibility is something they all recognize feelingly. They embody different kinds of power and their response to the crisis varies significantly from man to man, but they have all been complicit, and their remorse at the end of the play is absolutely genuine. They begin the play in various states of concern—it has been far too long since they heard anything. Whatever nagging unease they experience, they can still manage to take comfort in the thought of the overwhelming power of the force they mustered. So they rock between being troubled and being bombastic throughout the whole first section, working as a group to find a means of enduring their present disquiet and apprehensiveness.

Atossa's appearance should be stunning and the chorus should all go into full prostration in response. It is quite unsettling that she should even be there since she has never before come into their chambers. And the way she is speaking, her sudden ambivalence about her exceptional status as their queen, is further cause for alarm. Her narrative of the dream puts them in a terrible position. There is no doubt that virtually everything about it is prophetic in the worst possible way, but they can hardly react to it as such. Still, she is slightly mollified by their politic response and moves fluidly into asking the questions about Athens, which they can only answer truthfully. She may even laugh at the idea of any country being effective without slavery to fuel its power. But there is a sour note struck when the chorus has to admit that the Athenians are an unpredictable force, a people to be reckoned with. The Herald's appearance is a welcome interruption of a discussion that is not going well for anyone.

Each member of the chorus has a bitter truth to confront in the course of the Herald's terrible narrative. It should be assumed that some, for instance, have sons in the military. But much of this section is taken up with them surmounting their sheer disbelief before they can assimilate the news. Not in their worst nightmares could they have ever imagined it could have come to this. When the Herald leaves, perhaps flinging whatever remaining military equipment he still has in the dust, they are a group of generals without an army and they are all utterly disoriented. It is the queen, cursing their complicity and impotence before leaving, who brings their present misery into focus.

The quality in the air during the second chorus section is one of a burgeoning cabal. In their shock at the news of their defeat, various chorus members begin to place the blame for the calamity squarely on the shoulders of the young king, whom they now see in the light of the fiasco as feckless and fatally arrogant, though they all had a hand in fostering that arrogance. Faithful conservatives of the chorus resist these treasonous sentiments for a time, but by the end of the section, the entire chorus is united in their denunciation. Atossa's entrance interrupts this new confederacy of the aggrieved and snaps them back into line as her subjects.

What she proposes—that the spirit of Darius be raised from the dead—is an astounding notion, and I don't think anyone knows quite how to accomplish it. But it is an act of desperation on Atossa's part and she needs their help. The communal conjuring should seem improvised and somewhat dangerous. By the time of Darius' entrance, however, the queen and her chorus should have managed some kind of newly minted ritual, perhaps no more than kneeling in a semicircle and chanting Darius' name. Darius' entrance should be jarringly quiet and unexpected. (In the National Actors Theatre production, he walked in through the audience.) However he appears, it should be unsettling to the characters in its very lack of drama. (No puffs of smoke, in other words.) Needless to say, everyone hits the dirt in awed prostration in response.

According to the text, it would seem that the chorus never comes out of their full prostration, but I think, once Darius' focus shifts to Atossa, they should all come up a bit into kneeling or seated positions so they can see what's going on, and also so that they can be specifically chastised, both by Darius and by Atossa. Ultimately, this becomes a tender scene between a dead man and his widow, full of compassion and weighty with a real sense of loss. It sobers the chorus, drawing them back from their reactive rage and pulling them into a deeper sense of grief and remorse. Once Atossa leaves them with the image of the vastness of their desolation and the news of it spreading out through their now-vanished kingdom, they are poised to mourn the world they have lost in all its sweet particulars.

Xerxes should appear in the silence at the end of that ritual and there should be a long pause after he is revealed, during which the expected prostration in obeisance to a king pointedly does not happen. Xerxes should be wearing something that looks kingly and yet vaguely military, but the costume should be much the worse for wear. He should not, however, look as disheveled as the Herald— what he has gone through does not compare to that. Though his long, humiliated journey home has been arduous, he has still retained the privilege of his rank. Still, he is a changed man, diminished and chastened by what has happened. He is not the king they sent forth all those months ago. The chorus's response to him varies from glacial to contemptuous and for the most part he takes their blows as his due. He wavers occasionally into self-pity or bitterness, and his first attempt to gain their help in mourning the country together is rejected outright. He has not earned their help.

Aeschylus did not have Atossa enter to receive her son, but I believe this was only because the theater form in his time didn't allow for more than two principal actors. The actor playing Xerxes would presumably have also played Atossa. Because I could, I brought her back in. In fact, I found I couldn't do without her reentrance. To me, her presence was necessary if I wanted to turn mere catastrophe into something more like tragedy. After a certain point, it seemed the men could go no further. The flurry of accusations and reproach can only do so much. When Atossa enters, the climate changes. Suddenly, though Xerxes is still a king who is accountable for such a vast calamity, he is also a son encountering his mother, the weight of his shame on his shoulders. The personal element is suddenly present in high relief. Xerxes' shock at seeing his mother in the guise of a suppliant should be great. It may be, for instance, that he has never seen his mother with her head uncovered. When he kneels to her, it is unprecedented—a king would never kneel to another person, certainly not to a woman (mother or no)—but when *she* kneels in turn to *him*, it is an act of archetypal power. The play, among many other things, is a play about the birth of a queen. Atossa moves from perplexity at her seeming uselessness and impotence in the first scene to a final act of such compassion and might that the dynamic on the stage changes completely, allowing the assembled characters to begin to find their way toward a profound shared grief. By the time they are able to enact the last ritual, which she has suggested, in which all of them are on their knees in the sand voicing their communal woe, they have reached a true fellowship of repentance and heartbreak. That is Atossa's doing. And Xerxes, in turn, is at last endowed with genuine regal weight and substance. He is redeemed by enacting that ritual with a kind of genius of articulate remorse.

Should future producers wish to use Michael's powerful music, they can get in touch with him at rothmusik@aol.com

Guide to Pronunciation

(With thanks to Henry Chalfant and Kate Wilson)

Achaea	ancient	ah KAY ee ah
	modern	ah KEE uh
Adeues	ancient	uh DAY oh ace
	modern	uh DEAF uhs
Aegean	ancient/modern	ee GEE uhn
Aeschylus	ancient/modern	EE scoo loss
Agabatas	ancient/modern	æ guh BAT uhs

Alpistrus	ancient/modern	ahl PISS trahs
Amistris	ancient/modern	ah MISS trĭs
Amphistreus	ancient	am fĭs TRAY oos
	modern	am fĭss TRESS
Anchares	ancient/modern	ahn CAR ĭs
Argestes	ancient	are GAYST ace
	modern	are GUEST uhs
Ariomardus	ancient/modern	ah ree uh MAR doss
Arkteus	ancient	ark TEH oos
	modern	ark TEFS
Artabes	ancient	are TAH base
	modern	are TAH bess
Artembares	ancient	are tem BAH race
	modern	are tem BAH rees
Atossa	ancient/modern	uh TOSS uh
Attic	ancient/modern	Æ tick
Axius	ancient/modern	ÆX ee aws
Bactrian	ancient/modern	BACK tree uhn
Batanochus	ancient/modern	bah tah NOH koos
Bolba	ancient/modern	BOWL buh
Cilicians	ancient/modern	sĭ LISH uhnz
Dadakes	ancient	duh DAH case
	modern	duh DAH kees
Darius	ancient/modern	DAR ee uhs
Datamas	ancient	dah TAH mas
	modern	DAH tah mas
Diaexis	ancient/modern	dee EK sĭs
Hellespont	ancient/modern	HELL ĭs pont
Ionia	ancient/modern	eye OH nee uh
Locria	ancient/modern	LOW kree uh
Lydia	ancient/modern	LĬ dee uh
Macedonia	ancient	mæ kĭ DOE nee uh
	modern	mæ sĭ DOE nee uh
Magos	ancient/modern	MAH gos
Malian	ancient	MEE lee uhn
	modern	muh LEE uhn

Marathon	ancient/modern	MÆ ruh thon
Marduk	ancient/modern	MAR duk
Matallos	ancient/modern	MAT tah loss
Mysia	ancient/modern	MISS ee uh
Pangeon	ancient/modern	pan GAY on
Pelagon	ancient/modern	PEH lah gon
Perseus	ancient/modern	PEAR seh us
Persia	ancient/modern	PEAR sia
Pharandakes	ancient	fah rahn DAH kays
	modern	fah rahn DAH kĭss
Pharnouchus	ancient/modern	phar NOO kas
Phocis	ancient/modern	FOE kiss
Psammis	ancient/modern	SAH mees
Salamis	ancient/modern	SÆ luh miss
Samos	ancient/modern	SAH moss
Sardis	ancient/modern	SAR dis
Seisames	ancient/modern	SAY sah moss
Silenia	ancient/modern	sĭ LEH nee uh
Sousas	ancient/modern	SUE zuhs
Sousiscanes	ancient/modern	sue zees KAH nees
Spercheian	ancient/modern	spair KAY uhn
Tenagon	ancient/modern	TEN uh gohn
Tharybis	ancient	THAR roo bĭs
	modern	THAR rĭb ĭs
Thessaly	ancient/modern	THEH suh lee
Thrace	ancient	THRAY kay
	modern	THREE kee
Xanthis	ancient/modern	KSAHN this
Xerxes	ancient/modern	ZERK seez

Key: e = lẹt; uh = ạbove/sofạ; ĭ = sit; y = yẹs; th = <u>th</u>ink;
æ = cạt; ay = sạy; o = gọ.

Production History

The Persians premiered at New York City's National Actors Theatre (Tony Randall, Founder and Artistic Director) at Pace University's Michael Schimmel Center for the Arts in April 2003. The director was Ethan McSweeny, with scenic design by James Noone, costume design by Jess Goldstein, lighting design by Kevin Adams, original music and sound design by Michael Roth and projection design by Marilys Ernst; the musicians were Greg Beyer (percussion), Mairi Dorman (cello) and David Shively (percussion); the production stage manager was James Latus and the stage manager was Cyrille Blackburn. The cast was as follows:

COUNSELORS/THE CHORUS	Jon DeVries, Ed Dixon, Herb Foster, Michael Potts, Henry Stram, Henry Strozier, Charles Turner
HERALD	Brennan Brown
ATOSSA	Roberta Maxwell
DARIUS	Len Cariou
XERXES	Michael Stuhlbarg
ATTENDANTS	Christina Dunham, Mike Horowitz, Ben Lebish, Yueni Zander

Characters

COUNSELORS/THE CHORUS:

CHAIRMAN
STATE
TREASURY
JUSTICE
RELIGION
ARMY—GENERAL
NAVY—ADMIRAL

HERALD

ATOSSA, Queen of Persia

DARIUS, King of Persia, dead

XERXES, his son, current King of Persia

Setting

Capital city of Susa

Prologue (Optional)

written with Ethan McSweeny

The Chorus addresses the audience. They split these lines among them.

Aeschylus was born near Athens in 525 B.C.

That same year, Cyrus the Great defeated Egypt, adding it to the rapidly expanding Persian Empire.

Three years later, Darius the First became King of Persia. His empire was the largest the world had ever known, encompassing most of the northern Aegean and stretching from northern Africa all the way to India.

One of the last holdouts to Persia's wholesale dominion over the ancient world was Athens.

In 490 B.C., Darius led an expeditionary force into Greece.

A small Greek army met the massive Persian force twenty-five miles north of Athens on a plain called Marathon.

Aeschylus fought alongside his brother at the battle of Marathon and his brother was killed there.

The Greeks, despite being greatly outnumbered, surprisingly won.

Ten years later, Darius' son, Xerxes, returned to Greece with an army drawn from every corner of his empire. It was the largest fighting force ever assembled.

Xerxes and his host moved uncontested through northern Greece, easily conquering what was left of his remaining opposition until they reached Athens.

Aeschylus again fought the Persians when the Athenian navy faced the Persians in the bay off the island Salamis, within sight of their own city walls.

Eight years later, he wrote this play.

It contains the only eyewitness account we have of that battle, or indeed of any battle in the Persian Wars.

With this play, Aeschylus won first place in the dramatic competition at the Festival of Dionysus in 472 B.C.

The Persians is the oldest surviving play in Western literature.

CHAIRMAN
We are the trusted ones.
Left behind in this place, now emptied of young men.

STATE
We protect the hollow shell of a vacant city.

TREASURY
All of Persia is like a beach left bereft as a great wave slides
    back to sea,   5

JUSTICE
Sand sizzles and murmurs with absence
Wiped clean after the pounding water has pulled itself away.

STATE
We blink and stand in emptiness
Aged and alone
Waiting for our element to return to us again.   10

RELIGION
It is a city peopled only by anxious, silent women
Their eyes darting for omens.

CHAIRMAN
And by us, the trusted,
The ones who pointed west and told them to go,
Commanding them to leave us and seek conquest.   15

GENERAL
All day we watched as the host of our empire's power passed
Triumphal before us.
A clashing army, bristling with spears, arrows and axes.

JUSTICE
Horses sidling and jostling, eyes showing white as they strain
Against the tight harnesses.   **20**

ADMIRAL
It was like standing on the bank of a mighty river at high flood
As it plummets past, rolling debris and uprooted trees.
Roaring,

ALL *(Except Admiral)*
Roaring,

GENERAL AND ADMIRAL
Such was the power we let loose on the world.   **25**

JUSTICE
Until finally, at sunset, the last of the host trailed out of the
City and moved west, the thunder of stamping hooves fading until
All we could see was the great dust cloud rising miles beyond us.

TREASURY
And the silence moved in.

ADMIRAL
Strange after all the furor.   **30**

TREASURY
It is a silence we have lived in ever since.

RELIGION
Empty streets,
A cat skitters from shadow to shadow.

STATE
Here a curtain is pulled back
And a pale face appears at a window.   35
Wife or mother
She looks once again, she can't help it,
At the bend in the road where she last lost sight of him.
She knows she won't see him there, rounding that curve,
His shoulders tilted at that familiar angle,   40
His gait unique, his alone.
Once again, he is not there.
But she can't stop looking for him.
Just as she can't stop listening for that familiar tread on the stair.
Can't stop opening the closet once again   45
To smell his lost body on the clothes he once wore.
She has come to know him in his absence so much better
Than she could ever have known him in his presence.
Then she could afford to look away,
Not notice the particular way his hands hang from his arms,   50
The angle at which his body casts its only shadow.
She is haunted by his details now
And every person she sees who is not him
Wrenches her with his wrongness.
The world is so disappointing, she thinks.   55
So many people, but none of them him.
She knows he won't come into view.
It's impossible.

RELIGION
Still she can't help looking.

CHAIRMAN
What might he be doing, right now, this moment?   60

GENERAL
Sheathing a sword?

JUSTICE
Unsaddling a horse?

ADMIRAL
Threading his oar into the oarlock?

TREASURY
Swallowing hard on a piece of dried meat from his kit bag?

CHAIRMAN
It's unimaginable.   65

ALL (Except Chairman)
(Repeating) It's unimaginable.

CHAIRMAN
Our men. Where are they and what has happened to them?

JUSTICE
We spend our days, restless, waiting for news, any news, of
what has become of the men we sent to war.

TREASURY
We stand at the high walls and look for the dust of an approaching   70
herald, but there is nothing, only the humming waste of beyond.

JUSTICE
How can it be that such a great and furious force could vanish
without a trace?

GENERAL
Surely, if we listened hard enough, we could hear those
pounding hooves still?   75

JUSTICE
But there is only silence.

TREASURY
The rattle of some forgotten scrap blown into the gutter.

RELIGION
And so we wait.

CHAIRMAN
Thousands on thousands we sent out.

ALL *(Except Chairman)*
Thousands on thousands for whom we wait.   80

CHAIRMAN
From every corner of our empire they came, massing and
thronging the roiling force.

ADMIRAL
From mud-rich Egypt came Sousiscanes and his sly, agile ships.

CHAIRMAN
From India came the warriors in brilliant cotton garments
riding the ass-drawn chariots.   85

GENERAL
From Lydia, the luxuriant coast-dwellers, scented and sinuous,
their silent arrows true to the mark.

JUSTICE
From shining Sardis, the charioteers, each horse tossing its
impatient crest as it pulled past in a brilliant fury.

STATE
The Thracians in fox-skin headdresses.   90

TREASURY
The Arabians riding camels.

RELIGION
Ethiopians marched, black as night, in leopard and lion skins,
their long bows bristling, gazelle horn tipping their spears.

GENERAL
And golden Babylon emptied forth her thousands, thousands
on thousands.   95

ALL *(Except General)*
*(Overlapping in this order: Religion, Justice, State, Treasury,
Admiral, Chairman)* Thousands on thousands.

CHAIRMAN
There was never such an awesome parade of power as that
we congregated here and unleashed against our enemies.

RELIGION
And the king of kings, Xerxes, son of Darius, the power that
braids all the power together is our own, driving the glittering   100
herd as a shepherd drives his massive flock across the earth.

CHAIRMAN
He, our beloved.

GENERAL
Descended from Perseus.

TREASURY
Son of gold.

ALL
Equal to God.   105

RELIGION
He leads them.

JUSTICE
He stands high in his chariot,
Flashing eyes surveying his walking domain,
And it is as if an entire continent moves with him,
So many thousands, deafening is their number,   110
Dreadful is their strength.

ADMIRAL
Wonderful.

ALL
Wonderful.

CHAIRMAN
Defeat is impossible.

ALL
Defeat is unthinkable.   115

CHAIRMAN
We have always been the favorites of fate. Fortune has cupped
us in her golden palms. It has only been a matter of choosing
our desire. Which fruit to pick from the nodding tree.

TREASURY
When Xerxes first saw the Olympian mountains rising triumphant
From the rolling green of Greece,   120
Mighty and white, wreathed in the blue haze of God,
He thought: This too shall be Persia's.
What might such a king not encompass as his own?

GENERAL
When Xerxes saw the ocean in his way, he bridged it with
his multitude of boats, cables and boats, and marched his   125
army across the heaving, angry mass as if across dry land.
What can't such an army do?

CHAIRMAN
Nothing.

ALL *(Except Chairman)*
Nothing.

RELIGION
And yet I am uneasy at the thought of it. Might Nature be **130**
affronted by such an action? Is it right to do such a thing,
even if we prove it possible? Might we go too far? Might
we offend with our brazen confidence?

JUSTICE
All those years we spent jubilant, seeing the trifling, cowering
world from the height of our shining saddles, brawling our **135**
might across the earth as we forged an empire, I never
questioned.

ADMIRAL
Surely we were doing the right thing because it was the thing
we could do.

GENERAL
Surely anything we found a way to make possible was what **140**
we were destined to accomplish. It seemed so clear—our fate
was to rule.

STATE
That's what I thought at the time.
But perhaps we were merely deafened for years
By the din of our own empire-building, **145**
The shouts of battle, the clanging of swords, the cries of victory.

TREASURY
It is only lately that I begin to wonder if what we did was right.
If what we are doing is right.

RELIGION

Only now can I hear questions,
Pricking like stars at the fabric of the night.   150
I lie awake, looking up, listening,
And questions are all I hear.
No one, not even Persia, can escape fate if it is bent on our
    destruction.

ADMIRAL

A boat carried to dizzying heights on the back of a mighty wave   155
Has the farthest to fall when that wave is done with it.
Foolish is the sailor who thinks he is in control, even of his
Sliding toy of a ship.
No, he will learn soon enough that he is nothing but the guest of
The wave.   160
Soon enough, shedding what it has lifted
Or crushing it, unconcerned, the wave will move on.

GENERAL

Will we ever see those bright boys we sent out of the safety
of our gates again? Were we right to do so?

CHAIRMAN

What unthinkable peril might we have cast them into,   165
Pursuing our old men's dreams?

STATE

What has become of them?

JUSTICE

We can't know.

TREASURY

We can't know yet.

CHAIRMAN

Soon enough we will.   170

RELIGION
Until then, let us pray and prepare the ground for their
    returning.

JUSTICE
There is nothing else to do.

CHAIRMAN
And we must do something. Action, any action,
Is better than this fruitless worry and wringing of hands.   175
It becomes none of us.

(Atossa begins her entrance.)

RELIGION
But here is the queen.

CHAIRMAN, STATE AND ADMIRAL
She comes among us.

JUSTICE
Like a candle borne across a wasteland she shows a divine light.

STATE
Her eyes grace us, her glance traveling like a moving   180
warmth across us.

RELIGION
Do not look back at her, the blaze will blind you.

CHAIRMAN
O Queen of the Persians
We bow to you.

GENERAL
Xerxes' mother.   185

TREASURY
Consort of beloved Darius.

ADMIRAL
Mistress of Persia's god.

RELIGION
Mother of God as well.

ALL
We are your own.

ATOSSA
I don't know why I'm here. Perhaps you can tell me. But I had   **190**
to get away. The light kept caroming back and forth between
the golden walls. It made a sound, a high screech like metal
against metal. It sliced the air up into splinters. I couldn't
breathe. And the mirrors were staring at each other so that
when I passed between them I saw an infinity of my own selves,   **195**
all of us moving in dwindling concert, all of us, too many of
us, of me. I am haunted by my own useless importance. Every
surface reflects my aging worried face back at me. I rattle
around my gilded palace alone, echoing and reflecting myself.
There is not enough of me for so much grandeur.   **200**

CHAIRMAN
Yours is the grandeur, yours is the majesty of Persia.

ATOSSA
Too much. Too much. I escape by sleeping. I close my aching
eyes on all the shining, keening surfaces and slip into forgetfulness, into a world that doesn't stare at me. But now I have
such terrible dreams. Last night I saw Xerxes whipping two   **205**
frothing horses bloody, two horses he should never have put
in harness together. One a wild Grecian steed with a matted,
shaggy mane and restless knifelike hooves, the other a sleek
Persian mount, teeth clamped hard and fast on its bit. The
Greek horse bucks and whinnies, biting at its partner, kicking   **210**
at the chariot behind her. Xerxes struggles at the reins, cursing,

his muscles straining as he tries to yank her into line, but she is
ferocious, untamable and strong. She shakes to splinters the yoke
and bites clean through her own bit. Look at her buck, trampling
everything beneath her and tumbling Xerxes from on high!   **215**
Xerxes sprawls in the dust, choking and flailing, cowering
as he tries to shield his soft and fragile head from the flurry
of sharp hooves. But she breaks free at last, and leaps away,
trailing reins and blood as she goes. There is a figure, standing
in the dust, looking with sadness down at Xerxes where he   **220**
kneels. It is Darius. It is my own dead Darius, his face drained
with shock and woe. The dust settles around him as he stands
in silence. And then turns on his heel and walks away, perhaps
in despair, perhaps in disgust. Then Xerxes smashes his head
in the dust. He weeps and rips at his sullied robes, tears   **225**
running in clean lines down his battered and dirty face.
When I woke from this horror I found myself again in my
empty bed, gorgeous and vast, lights winking in the fabrics
from the dawning sun. And I remembered. I learned again
the silence of my gilded palace. Learned again that I am   **230**
alone. The dead hush of so much reflection, a shining box
of emptiness. It has become hateful to me. I went out into
the morning air and thought to wash the nightmare from
my vision in the spring and when I approached the altar to
give sacrifice, I looked up and saw an eagle flying fast. For a   **235**
moment I was heartened—an eagle, I thought, our mighty
bird, gracing me—but no, he was pursued, and by a quick,
dark falcon, talons spread, screaming vengeance.
I saw the falcon dive swift and deadly at the eagle. The two
of them fell in a spiral, while the falcon took the eagle's   **240**
head apart in a bloody fury.
The eagle did nothing but die horribly, never swung his
sharp beak back, never so much as clawed the air, just
dropped in a broken agony as the falcon did his awful work.
I can do nothing with these things I've seen but to tell you   **245**
of them.
There is no one else to tell. Nothing to do.

But I feel new dread for my country spreading within me,
bleeding a bitter warmth across my chest.
What do these horrors mean? Does Persia, even now, fall   **250**
from her heights, blinded and bloody?
Shall my son return?

RELIGION

Great queen. We are honored to be your confidants and we shall
never seek to alarm you. These are portents, perhaps, but where
there are warnings, there is always time for supplication and   **255**
redress. Your dead husband, beloved Darius, came to you. That
is an honor and a comfort. Make your libations, ask him to inter-
vene for his country's good. He cannot fail us. He is with us in
spirit even now, and even now, even dead, he is our protector. As
for your fears, calm them, these are mysteries and never simple   **260**
to interpret. Nothing will be served by succumbing to dread.

ATOSSA

Perhaps you're right. I will make my obeisance to the gods.
But first, there are things I want to know.
Where is this Athens?

RELIGION

A vast distance, it is where the sun dies.   **265**

ATOSSA

So far away. And yet my son is willing to cross the face of
creation to capture it?

JUSTICE

Once he has conquered it, he will rule the world.

ATOSSA

Are they so rich in numbers?

ADMIRAL

They have enough to have dealt us many blows.   **270**

ATOSSA

Do they fight, like us, with bow and arrows?

GENERAL

No. They favor spears and pikes.
They prefer to fight close up and face to face.

ATOSSA

Are they a wealthy people? Have they so much gold?

TREASURY

They work the silver seams that course like underground   **275**
rivers throughout their mountains.

ATOSSA

Who is their lord and master? The shepherd to their army?

TREASURY

They have no lord and master.

CHAIRMAN

They refuse slavery.

ATOSSA

But then how can any great enterprise be accomplished?   **280**
How can they withstand attack from without?

STATE

They have withstood Darius. And at a great price to us.

ATOSSA

You chill a mother's heart.

JUSTICE

But, look, news at last. A runner approaches.

(Enter Herald.)

HERALD

O Persia!   285
I am come to break you.
All is lost. Your mighty army has fallen.
All, all, they are all gone.

GENERAL
This can't be.

ADMIRAL
This is impossible.   290

HERALD
If only I were lying. If only I hadn't lived
To bring this black garland of woe to place at your feet.
But it's true. I am the last, the only survivor.
I have crossed the world to tell you this.

CHAIRMAN
We have lived too long.   295

TREASURY
Why have we lived long enough to hear this?

HERALD
I saw it all. The slaughter, the pity of it. I saw it.

GENERAL
We sent a force of uncountable strength.

HERALD
All gone.

JUSTICE
A bright storm of arrows, a rain of ruin we unleashed.   300

HERALD
Lost.

RELIGION
All for nothing.

HERALD
The shores of Salamis are glutted by a sea of bodies.
Their garments circling, they bob and butt each other
In the blood-red tide.   305

GENERAL
All our bright young boys. This was their end.

ADMIRAL
They spin and rot,
Unburied, in the indifferent sea?

CHAIRMAN
So far from home?

HERALD
They are silent now. Long after the awful shrieks of ships   310
ramming ships have stopped echoing. I hear it still. The
sound of the hulls splintering, the cries of the men as they
fell one by one into the unforgiving cold darkness.

STATE
This is what has become of all our hopes?

HERALD
Athens, you have destroyed us.   315

ALL
Athens, you have destroyed us.

ATOSSA
I must find a way to speak. There must be something fit to say at
such a time. But words are such paltry, tiny things. This ocean of

grief that I must transport and I stand at the shore with these leaking spoons. I must start somewhere. Tell us. Who is not dead?   **320**

HERALD

Xerxes lives.

ATOSSA

Ah, then. One star at least pricks through the ink of this night.
Now you can tell me who died.

HERALD

Artembares, captain of ten thousand horse,
Drifts face down in the wash, and batters Silenia's rocks   **325**
    with his body.
Dadakes, lord of the thousand, took a spear and fell from his
Ship in a screaming arc like a broken bird.
The bravest Bactrian, dark Tenagon,
Scrapes his sides on Ajax's stony island.   **330**
Argestes, his tall ship rammed and sunk, is tumbling in the
Waves around that dovecote island, butting stones.
Adeues, Arkteus and Pharnouchus too, all were lost from the
    same ship.
Like sparks spit from a fire, they all fell down, glittering in   **335**
their useless armor.
Matallos of the golden city, leader of the thousand horse, is
drifting too, open eyes reflecting a sky he doesn't see, his
beard moving around his face, streaked with salt and stained
with his own blood.   **340**
Magos the Arabian, Artabes, the Bactrian, leader of the thirty
thousand dark horsemen, both lie dead in an alien land.
Amistris and Amphistreus, of the flashing spear,
Brave Ariomardus, beloved of Sardis,
Tharybis, commander of fifty-times-fifty ships,   **345**
poor man, fine man, unlucky . . .
Laughing Seisames of Mysia, valiant, so young, who once . . .
The leader of the Cilicians, who, single-handed . . .

Name on name, it would take weeks to say them all.
So many, so many, these are only a handful of the lost.   350

GENERAL
It is too many even so.

TREASURY
The shame of it.

ADMIRAL
What was the number of their ships, how could they have
matched us?

HERALD
If numbers were all, the day would have been ours   355
     without question.
The Greeks counted only ten-times-thirty ships at most
And only ten were newly fitted.
Xerxes was master of a full thousand two hundred and
     seven, the fastest vessels ever built.   360
We were not outnumbered. No. How could we be?
Our fleet stretched wide across the horizon.
It was some vengeful god who leaned full weight against the scales
And skewed the balance of our fortune. Some god saved that city
For them.   365

JUSTICE
What? You can't mean that Athens still stands.

HERALD
Stands intact. And will stand forever, I think, as long as her
people live to guard her.

ATOSSA
Tell us this thing from the start. Was it Xerxes, glorying
in his numbers, who attacked first? How did it begin?   370

HERALD

Some malicious spirit hovered over the whole disaster from
the very beginning.
A Greek appeared, furtively stolen away from his ranks. He
approached Xerxes and then tipped the whispered venom of
deception into his ear: "When night falls," he said, "the   375
Greeks will use that cover to scamper like rats, each away,
threading swiftly out into the open sea and to cowardly escape."
Your son, unused to Greek mendacity, still confident of
Fortune's blessing, immediately rose to his command and
charged the fleet, as soon as the eye of day had closed, to   380
rank themselves in three rows at every entrance to the sea.
"If any single Greek snakes through our defenses to run
safely home, all your heads will roll," he said.
And so, sleepless, they did their work. Oarsmen plied their oars
all night long, and by the time dawn's horses began to pull the   385
light across the sky, all were arrayed in their several stations. But
it was just then, when we could finally see, that we realized our
great mistake. Not a single Greek had made a move for flight.
And as we squinted, disbelieving, in the streaky dawn, we
heard an awesome and terrible sound. A jubilant call of good   390
omen going up from the Greek ships and echoing against
all the island rocks. It chilled our spines. Because it was also
a war cry. And they were coming at us, slapping the waves
with their thousands of oars as a trumpet flared, exultant
and piercing. And then we saw them clearly, first one wing   395
and then the other, bearing down hard.
And a call went up from their ships: "Liberation!" was the
cry. "Liberation! Greeks! Free your country! Your people!
Your sanctuaries! Graves of your ancestors! Now! Now! Now!
Liberation!" And before we could save ourselves the first   400
boats rammed us.
Bronze prow clanged against bronze prow and then the
sickening sound of the splintering, the cries of panic. The
Greeks, like hunting dogs in a frenzy, circling and lunging,
circling and lunging, biting as our big ships showed their   405

bellies. We were choked in the narrows, backing against
each other until we rammed our own ships, wood screeching
against wood as we tried to free ourselves. The water was a
frothing mess of wreck and bodies.
So many, so many. Like schools of fish in the reaching nets,   410
stunned and gazing, drifting with broken oars and ships
undone, the waves rummaging through the debris.
Spread out for miles was the roiling disaster of our fleet. And
when night fell you could still hear the cries, men wounded
and flailing, calling for rescue when there was no one to save   415
them. Until, after what seemed a lifetime, the last ones stopped
calling, stopped thrashing and calling, stopped calling at last and
slipped under to silence. I hear them still. The cries of them,
men I couldn't save. Men I never knew. Men I'll never know.
All those men. Never in the history of the world have so   420
many died on a single day. That long day.

ADMIRAL
O terrible.

ALL
Terrible.

HERALD
I can't tell it well enough to make you see it. That's only a
fraction. It's all swimming in my head. Worse things happened.   425

TREASURY
There can be nothing worse.

HERALD
There is the fate of the Immortals, those finest Persians,
The excellent, pride of a nation.
Those brilliant men all met their deaths in infamy,
     disgrace and ugliness.   430

GENERAL

This is more than can be borne. What happened?

HERALD

There is an island. A stony stunted thing, harbor is impossible, where Pan rejoices and the sands are pocked with his dancing hoofprints. This is where Xerxes sent his choicest troops, thinking they could kill the shipwrecked Greeks or salvage and rescue   **435** their comrades in need. But he did not see the dark star that rose above him, because when the Greeks were triumphant that day they leapt onto the shore and tightened a noose around that thwarted place and trapped us there between them. Some of us were stoned to death, others died by arrows, snapped into our   **440** midst from the close choking ranks of our captors. In the end of it, they were just hacking at us like beaters slashing through a wood, blade on bone and flesh as they made their way from one edge of the circle to meet themselves in the middle. By then Xerxes, who saw it all, too much, from his high and privileged seat at the   **445** top of a sea wall, weeping dispatched what was left of his host. And in skittering, orderless flight, all scattered in the twilight. To nothingness all fled.

ATOSSA

(To the gods) Weren't the dead at Marathon enough for you? Haven't you exacted your price? How many Persian dead   **450** will it take to sate you? *(To the Herald)* Did any escape?

HERALD

It was panic and disorder at the end, but there were some. There were some. But it is they who deserve your pity most. A long journey home and no place of mercy. Choking on dust, men searched for water and died clutching sand. If they   **455** survived the crossing of Phocis, Locria and the Malian Gulf to find the springs of the Spercheian plain, there was Achaea and Thessaly to come. That was where most of us died. Not just thirst. Hunger gnawed our bellies, sometimes to death. Through Magnesia and Macedonia we staggered, across   **460**

the River Axius, the sucking, reed-choked marsh of Bolba,
the mountain Pangeon . . . the world is large.
And how different our retreat seemed than our advance was
so long ago in that new world, jubilant with strength.
In Thrace, winter was conjured out of season by some vengeful   465
god and we wore the night out chanting placations to divinities
we didn't know, hugging our famished ribs and weeping for mercy
from a world we didn't understand. We begged the earth, we
begged the sky, we sang for something like kindness from a
bewildering world. When dawn came, we started across the new   470
ice toward the opposite shore. Some of us were lucky. We'd
begun the journey across before the sun was high. But there
were others behind us who weren't so fortunate. We heard the
cracking of it like thunder and saw one man after another fall
beneath the bobbing white plates. That's when we began running   475
away from them in a panic, sliding and slipping as the fissures
ran beneath us. Their cries as they went under rained down
on our backs. Happiest are those who die quickly. Only a
handful of us made it through all of that, and we cannot look
at each other. We will never look at anything squarely again.   480
We have seen too much. We have outlived too much.
We are what is left of your Persian army.

(Herald exits. Silence.)

ATOSSA
Some god there is who hates us. Some divinity that leapt
among us with both feet and has trampled us down like grass.
The nightmares were prophetic it seems. But no night vision   485
could have prepared me for what has come to pass.
Suffering beyond compass.
And you, my murmuring futilities, what have you to offer now?
Prayer? By all means. Abasement? I am brought low.
Let me go prepare myself for my new life as a suppliant.   490
Should my son return in my absence, keep him from self-
annihilation. A country can only take so much. Bring him home.

(Atossa exits.)

JUSTICE
(To the gods) Why has this happened?

CHAIRMAN
(To the gods) What have we done to offend you?

GENERAL
(To the gods) What transgression could warrant such punishment? **495**

RELIGION
It is the difference between the father and the son.
When Persia belonged to Darius, the gods were content with us.
They blessed us.
But since Xerxes stepped into his father's robes, still warm with
His father's mightiness, they have turned their backs on us. **500**

GENERAL
(To the gods) Was it that boy?

TREASURY
(To the gods) Was it that boy we made king?

STATE
(To the gods) Is it Xerxes who has offended you?

ADMIRAL
But he is our king.

JUSTICE
He is king only by birth. **505**

RELIGION
And he has betrayed us.

TREASURY
That moon-faced boy.
Lit only by the borrowed light of his father's sun.

STATE
He has destroyed a world
Beautiful, ordered and serene.   510

JUSTICE
Destroyed his father's world
With one short life.

TREASURY
One proud life.

STATE
One brief life.

JUSTICE
Of insolence.   515

CHAIRMAN
But we adored him.

ADMIRAL
Abased ourselves before him.

GENERAL
Clothed him in power.

JUSTICE
Yes, and he mistook the gold of the armor we gave him for
the shining skin of a god.   520

RELIGION
As if he was divine, he flogged that countless force across the
breast of the earth, and drank the rivers dry as he went.

JUSTICE

Even from the height of heaven, the gods could look down
and see his scorched path of dust across the map of the world.

GENERAL

How could we have thought that such a desecration of the   525
earth would find the favor of the gods?

RELIGION

But that is not all we suffer for. We are paying for his flagrant
sacrilege.

JUSTICE

So different from his father's justice and tolerance.

RELIGION

The gods remember what he did to that mighty icon, sacred   530
to Babylon. Marduk of the golden hands. He swaggered into
the temple, blind to God, and broke the icon to pieces, then
melted its divinity down into nothing but money.

JUSTICE

When priests tried to shield their holy statue with their naked
arms, he dragged them out to the open street and silenced their   535
cries of warning by slitting their throats like goats in a marketplace.

RELIGION

(Sings) You have undone us
God-mocking boy,
Xerxes, O Xerxes
You have destroyed us   540

RELIGION AND JUSTICE

(Sing) You have forgotten
Only Nature
Only God
Is immortal.

GENERAL

No, it was the Hellespont. That was his great offense.   **545**

In contemptuous folly he sought to enslave even Nature.

RELIGION

Even Nature, he thought, should bow before his mortal boy's body.

GENERAL

And when the Hellespont shrugged off the first bridge he
    built across her back,

He commanded that an iron yoke of fetters be laid across the water   **550**

And that the sea be flogged for its rebellion.

JUSTICE

Three hundred strokes he gave the mighty water.

Beat it until the beaters' arms gave out.

GENERAL

And then he cursed it.

Bitter, muddy water, he said   **555**

You will not defy your master again.

TREASURY

I flog you, vile river

You will submit to me

I will cross you whether you will or not.

STATE

Bow down before your master   **560**

Know that you are my slave.

GENERAL

(Sings) You have undone us

God-mocking boy,

GENERAL, RELIGION AND JUSTICE

(Sing) Xerxes, O Xerxes

You have destroyed us   **565**

You have forgotten
Only Nature
Only God
Is immortal.

STATE
And the waters coursed beneath his golden slippers   570

TREASURY
Rolled beneath his mortal feet as she will roll
In a thousand thousand years

RELIGION
When the name of Xerxes is forgotten

TREASURY
When all our works are dust.

STATE
She is uncaring and mighty   575
And she will never bow to man.

CHAIRMAN
And Xerxes, when you lie unmourned
The dust of the earth you have dishonored
Will sift your bones to sand.

ADMIRAL
And the water you flogged will flow on, on   580
Into eternity.

ALL
(Sing) You have undone us
God-mocking boy,
Xerxes, O Xerxes
You have destroyed us   585

You will be forgotten
Only Nature
Only God
Is immortal.

Only Nature   590
Only God
Is divine.

*(Atossa enters, dressed as a suppliant, in black, bareheaded and
barefoot.)*

ATOSSA
I am lost in this mortal wasteland.
I can see no farther through this black confounding sorrow.
All I can think to do is beg my dead king to return to us.   595
Let him speak unearthly wisdom to these rudderless times.
Darius, I entreat you.
Ascend the steep and harrowing path from dark ease.
Clamber up from forgetfulness into this harsh new day.
We stand in confusion, gasping forlorn in the upper air.   600
Light the lights!
Blaze him a beacon to the shell of his city,
This woe-struck memory of his former home.
Can you see it, my king?
Follow the pinprick of light that dances at the end of your   605
    hard journey.
Can you hear me, my king?
Follow the anguished voice of this lost wife who calls to you.
Deep in the secret chambers of the earth's heart, listen.
Darius!   610

CHAIRMAN
Darius! Beloved leader so mourned.
Your children, bereft and confused, are calling to you.

STATE

Help us, speak to us, lead us again.

JUSTICE

All the truths we lived by died today.
The only certainty left to us is the memory   615
Of your justice, your kindness and your flawless rule.

TREASURY

Days of promise and joy
A world of order and clarity
Lit by the divine warmth of your guiding grace.

GENERAL

Come back to us.   620

ADMIRAL

Let us tell you of our woe.

RELIGION

Let us weep for the suffering,
Weep for the dead,
Weep for the ruin of the beautiful world you made for us.

CHAIRMAN

O King, all is lost.   625

ADMIRAL

All your tall ships are gone.

ALL

(Repeated under the following speech) Darius, Darius . . .

ATOSSA

Darius! It is your own queen who cries your name.
The queen who shared your noble bed and watched the long

Nights in your arms. 630
We are blinded by misery.
Grace your broken kingdom once more.
Only you can give us succor now.
Come home! Come home.

(Darius enters. Everyone goes into full prostration.)

DARIUS
Persian sun, how brilliant you are. 635
And the color of your sand, how bright.
I had forgotten.
Why have I been summoned from the wandering darkness
    and silence?

CHAIRMAN
O King. 640

GENERAL
You have come back to us.

DARIUS
My friends, my generals, comrades in arms.
Rise and tell me why you called for me.

ADMIRAL
Great Darius.

TREASURY
You have come. 645

DARIUS
I cannot stay. It is only by some aberrance I am permitted
this air again. It shall not last. Even now the darkness pulls
me like a sucking tide back to emptiness.
Speak! Rise and tell me why I stand in the upper air again.

JUSTICE

We cannot rise. **650**

RELIGION

Your greatness overwhelms us.

DARIUS

Wife. Your grieving voice was what pulled me up the steep and
narrow ascent. It was the sound of you that brought me this
unfathomable distance. Can you tell me what these men cannot?

ATOSSA

It is not hard to say. It is only impossible to comprehend. **655**
Persia is lost.

DARIUS

O my people. How could this have happened?
Some dreadful plague? A famine?
What unearthly terror could have destroyed us?

ATOSSA

Athens. She has destroyed your mighty host. **660**

DARIUS

Not all. It can't be all of it. They were a world of men.

ATOSSA

All.

DARIUS

Which of my sons led them to destruction?

ATOSSA

Xerxes. He rashly emptied a continent of men into the maw
of death. They lie unburied on Attic soil or drift in salt **665**
nothingness, eaten by the voiceless fish of alien seas.

DARIUS

How could he have even brought the army to stand in
such peril?

ATOSSA

He flung a bridge of boats across the Hellespont and
marched them over it.   670

DARIUS

To do such a thing he must have been goaded by some black
madness of ambition. To risk so much, so many, defies all
human sense.

ATOSSA

Yes. I think no god could have wrought a greater ruin.

DARIUS

O my goodly host! My men.   675
Cut down before they'd even begun. All that youth and hope.
The underworld will be flooded by a sea of boys, wailing
Confusion and fear in their new shadow home.
But death will muffle their cries soon enough
Dim their bright eyes   680
Dip their cooling bodies in blank forgetfulness
Until they skitter in silence, glazed with eternity,
Shifting with the countless others through the dreadful calm of
That gray nothingness.
The obscenity of it. The disgrace.   685
To have brought such a murdering fool into the world.
A monstrous, brazen boy who could cast away so many lives
So many lives,
And for nothing.
Where is he?   690

ATOSSA

Homeward bound.

DARIUS
He lives?

ATOSSA
So I am told.

DARIUS
I pity him.
Better to have died than to live with this.   **695**

ATOSSA
He is not solely to blame. He was goaded to leave his gilded life.
Rousted from his pillows by unscrupulous counselors, fevered
by their own ambition. They taunted him to impetuosity.
They shamed him, saying that he was only half the man
you were, and disgraced your memory with his inaction. Or   **700**
they puffed him full of delusion, telling him he was a god,
son of a god, that he should rule the earth. Accomplish what
even you could never have done.

DARIUS
And so he has. He has emptied an empire. Poured the youth
of an entire world like so much water into desert sand.   **705**

ATOSSA
My dead beloved. Tell us.
What must we do?

DARIUS
Mourn the dead of this great country.
Those poor bodies, our sons,
Those terrible human reefs that bank themselves against the   **710**
Stony shores of Attica and glitter now with the dead lights of
All their open eyes.
They shall lie in the restless waves as testament
To what horrors an overweening pridefulness can reap.

This is the harvest of such insolence and grasping.   715
Never again squander the grace of good fortune
In lusting for yet more.
A brutish discontent and greed will render you first monstrous
And finally bereft.
Seek humbleness and repentance.   720
Atone to the gods we have offended with this unholy arrogance.
Yours, my queen, is the hardest task.
When he returns, the shock of his shame shall be appalling.
He will long for the forgetfulness of death.
Your voice alone will be recognizable.   725
Your voice alone will be bearable.
Only you, only his mother, will be able to speak to him in the
Terrible solitude of that disgrace and confusion.
Lead him to the unmarked place in his bewildered heart,
The crossroads of his own self-knowledge.   730
Let him stand there and look down the long road
Of the journey ahead of him.
My dear old wife. I am sorry for you.
I must go.

ATOSSA
I have missed you so long. And now I must lose you again.   735

DARIUS
Yes, I am lost again.
Life! The air filled with birdsong, the color of the sky . . .
Grasp the joy of things while you can, my friends.
The end will come soon enough.
Death is long and without music.   740

(Darius exits.)

ATOSSA
God pity us.

ALL
Pity us.

ATOSSA
Even now, murmurs of calamity, havoc and shame
Mass and lift, like startled birds.
They jibe and circle   745
In a terrible moving cloud of jagged sorrow.
They darken the sun, cawing lament
Spreading the truth of this nightmare
Across the breadth of Persia
Even out to the ends of the earth.   750
We cower under their flickering shadows
And shudder beneath their sharp cries of doom.

(She exits.)

JUSTICE
We have lost the sun.

STATE
Unimaginably vast is the world that has been vanquished.

TREASURY
The pine-black chill mountains of deepest Europe.   755

GENERAL
The dry hill towns of the northern Aegean, spiked with towers.

RELIGION
The isles of the gentle headlands,
Washed like pebbles to shimmer in the western sun
As they nestle in the crook of the sea's arm.

CHAIRMAN
The shining olive groves of Samos.   760

JUSTICE
The cattle-dotted hills of Thrace.

TREASURY
Ionia, splendid in wealth, perfumed by ease.

ADMIRAL
Salt-tossed islands, far flung,
Specks of promise that shimmered at vast distance,
Then rose from the waves to greet the ocean-weary sailor.   765

STATE
On, on to all our southern empire,
Where mighty rivers wink out to their deaths in the desert sand.

ALL
*(In a round, Chairman, General, Religion, State, Treasury,
Admiral, Justice)* Lost, lost
All our cherished kingdom
Gone.   770

(Xerxes enters. Silence. Stillness.)

XERXES
You do not bow before me, my fathers.

CHAIRMAN
All Asia staggers and kneels, mangled beneath you, King.
We do not.

XERXES
You are right not to do so.
I am accursed.   775
Hated by gods and men alike.
No place on earth can hide the shame of me.

Even the deepest caverns of death's secret chambers
Are not black enough to hide me.
But how I yearn for their coolness and silence even so. **780**
How is it I was spared to stand before you, my fathers?
Why should I alone be deprived of the mercy of death?

RELIGION
You have given Death enough.
Glutted his dark kingdom with all the sons of Persia.
Thousands on thousands **785**
Row on shining row of them
You threshed like golden wheat to lie beneath us in silence.
Your bloody hands have beaten your great country to her knees.
Look upon her.
See the devastation you have wrought. **790**

XERXES
O Persia. My country.
What have I done to you?
Help me to mourn her, my fathers.
Cleave the air with keening
For the thousands lost. **795**
Send up to the furious heavens a howl of grief
For the greatness that has passed from the earth.
Never to return.

GENERAL
Never to return.

ADMIRAL
Thousands on thousands. **800**

XERXES
Thousands on thousands.
The numbers of the dead are awesome.
The mind reels at the magnificence of our destruction.

JUSTICE
Where are your comrades, King?
Those who were closest to you?   805
Where is Pharandakes?

ADMIRAL
Where is Sousas?

STATE
Where is Pelagon?

CHAIRMAN
Agabatas?

TREASURY
Datamas?   810

GENERAL
Psammis and gentle Sousiscanes?

JUSTICE
What has become of those who walked beside you?

XERXES
All my companions are gone.
The friends of my youth.
My comrades-in-arms.   815
All lost.
I abandoned them there where they fell from the ships
To carpet the rolling blanket of the sea as far as the eye
    could compass.
They hammer the rocks in bloody silence.   820
All the men I loved.
Or they gasped their last breaths choking on the dust they
Kicked up in their final struggle
On that cursed island of thorns.

The last thing they saw was Athens.   825
They looked up and saw her ancient ramparts glimmering
above them in the dusk before they plummeted into her
watery lap or beneath her warriors, their open eyes
reflecting the bristling bronze helmets of the men who
chopped them to pieces as the bloody sun fell down the sky.   830

JUSTICE
You could not have left them all behind.

CHAIRMAN
It is impossible.

RELIGION
Even your favorite? Even he, your right arm, the man you trusted
above all? Even Batanochus' son, fine and kindly Alpistrus?
You could not have left that noble son to rot on the alien dirt.   835

XERXES
Do not ask me! I can bear no more.
This horror tears and bites within my chest like a maddened dog.

GENERAL
But there are so many others missing,
So many others beloved,
So many who once graced your train.   840
Xanthis, Diaexis and Anchares . . .
It cannot be that you stand before us utterly alone, utterly
Stripped of your goodly host.

XERXES
I come naked and empty-handed. Stripped of all my men.
They were the finest sons of Persia.   845
And they have met their end.
All.
All.

TREASURY
What life is left is not long enough to mourn them.

RELIGION
Age upon age until the end of time.   850

ADMIRAL
Never can this dreadful knot of sorrow be untied.

STATE
Never can this weight of grief be lifted.

CHAIRMAN
Woe never ending for Persia's lost hope.

*(Atossa enters. Silence. Xerxes kneels to her.
Atossa goes to him, kneels and touches him.)*

ATOSSA
My shattered son.
Shatterer of my shattered country.   855
My heart is broken with pity.
Pity for all of us.
Dead and living.
We are Persia's orphaned children.
Let us take her dust in our hands   860
And ask forgiveness of her holy ground.

(He spreads his hands in the dirt.)

XERXES
Mother forgive me.
I have wronged you.
O Persia.
Pity me, your destroyer.   865
O pity for the suffering I have unleashed.

Pity for all your dead sons.
I weep for what is lost.
Help me!
Help me honor them with grief.   **870**
O my people!

ALL
O my people!

XERXES
O my Persia!

ALL
O my Persia!

XERXES
O my people!   **875**

ALL
O my people!

XERXES
O my Persia!

ALL
O my Persia!

XERXES
Lost! Lost! Lost!

ALL
Lost! Lost! Lost!   **880**

XERXES
In bitterness we sing to you!

ALL
In bitterness we sing to you!

XERXES
We fill your empty city with our cries!

ALL
We fill your empty city with our cries!

XERXES
All our hopes scattered!   885

ALL
All our hopes scattered!

XERXES
All our grace destroyed!

ALL
All our grace destroyed!

XERXES
Misery falls on us!

ALL
Misery falls on us!   890

XERXES
We are blinded by woe!

ALL
We are blinded by woe!

XERXES
O Persia, O Persia, my mother,
Magnificent and vast.

How I have betrayed you.   **895**
Terrible the darkness into which I have plunged you.
Lead me home.

ALL
We lead you home.

XERXES
Lead me home.

ALL
We lead you home.   **900**

ATOSSA
Home.

XERXES
Take my hand and lead me home.

(All exit.)

THE END

Oedipus

Introduction

Part 1

I was commissioned in early 2004 to write a new version of *Oedipus* for the Guthrie Theater in Minneapolis, to be directed by my old friend and collaborator, Lisa Peterson.

It was Lisa who had the idea for the production and Lisa who brought her suggestion to Joe Dowling, who not only took her up on it, but scheduled a slot for it in the next season, script unseen. I'm tremendously grateful to Lisa for her inspiration and to Joe for his faith in me and for the chance to work on the play.

To be honest, I had never been particularly drawn to *Oedipus*, though it is probably the only Greek play of which a majority of any audience would at least know the basic plot. My reluctance may have had to do with precisely that phenomenon—the prospect of coping with two thousand plus years of scholarship and reverence was quite intimidating. But Lisa's interest in the play as a means of confronting the issue of American identity at this moment in history intrigued me. She felt that the play would provide a lens through which to look at our deep aversion to coming to terms with our own past and the consequences of our actions. That notion inspired me to look at the play differently.

I began to read translations and do research and, in April 2004, I wrote Lisa a letter, focusing on the aspects of the play I was beginning to be most interested in exploring.

I enclose an edited version of the letter below:

Dear Lisa,

Just thought I'd put some notes together, the kinds of things I've been thinking about as I mull over the play and get to know it better. They are in no particular order.

• I've been trying to understand why I find this play somewhat repellent, and perhaps why I haven't approached it before. I suppose that there is something disturbing to me about what I sense is a sort of ancient Greek version of original sin. The idea that this particular child at least is *born* a sinner, born doomed. He is fated not only to suffer—as are all men—but to do terrible things even as he thinks he is doing right. What should we learn from this? That the gods are to be feared? That when we search for the transgressor, the source of our sorrow, we must search first the house of our own soul?

Or is it that we learn from Oedipus the true price of self-knowledge—that to be human is to be both entirely innocent and entirely guilty, the holy/accursed thing that so few of us ever have the courage to confront in the mirror? Is the point that by the end of the play, Oedipus finally must acknowledge himself, for the first time, as being truly and simply human—the solution to the riddle—no longer exempt, no longer exceptional, except in the sense of being the most radical example of the constraint of being human? I am still quite flummoxed by this and expect to be thrashing it out for some time.

• I'd like to focus on telling the story so that it's more of an effective mystery. Time after time in the Sophocles, Oedipus is presented with so much information that it seems impossible he doesn't put the mystery together. The denial is so great as to defy credulity.

The first moment that would demand rethinking would be Tiresias' contribution to the story, such that he's not quite so explicit, so spang on the head about what will happen to Oedipus. What seems most important about what he tells Oedipus about the future is (a) that Oedipus is in fact the blind man and that his blindness will be manifest in time, and (b) that he is the monster he seeks. Similarly, I'd like to look at Jocasta's contribution to the revelation and think in terms of honing down the information she gives, perhaps to the single revelation of the killing taking place at a crossroads. Otherwise there's just too much of what she says that Oedipus simply can't hear and believably still fail to put it together. I'll be looking throughout for such opportunities, but these are the obvious ones at the moment.

· Considering the business of contemporary relevance— how does this play speak to our times? Well, how did it speak to its own times?

Oedipus was born of the dreadful combination of a plague year and a war year. The plague is attributed to Ares, the god the gods would exile if they could, who presided over "death breeding death," both war and pestilence. The play was, we think, written in 430 B.C., the plague year that was the second year of the Peloponnesian War, the war that would prove in time to be the undoing of the Athenian people and their civilization. The way the plague is described—this consuming, rampant image of death moving through the city— makes one think at the same time of what the war was doing to Athens. This must have had resonance for the audience, as it will have resonance for us, in the second year of what looks to be an unending war, as will the idea of a political leader who is, knowingly or not, the cause of his people's suffering.

· Numbers thread through the text. The three roads, the riddle of the Sphinx. But it is a rather crude math—no numbers over four, the number needed for a child's locomotion—and that rudimentary, brutal math matches the blunt riddle of his life. The basic math of a normal life keeps eluding him. There should be *two* women—mother and wife—rather than one. The puzzle of his existence keeps confounding him, because it is so obviously wrong, I suppose. One plus one keeps equaling one in his case. It happens again and again. He is the investigator of a crime, the prosecutor and the judge, but then he also turns out to be the criminal he has been pursuing and has already condemned. Similarly, he turns out to be both the physician and the disease he is attempting to eradicate. There is something about numbers counted out of sequence that may be of use. Oedipus is presented as a mathematician working out the fact that he is himself the solution to his own horrible problem.

· I am increasingly fascinated by the phenomenon of the crossroads—the place where all the various paths of a life, all the possibilities, converge in one fate. I think it may have something to do with the perception of the female sexual organs, that site of mystery and origin, the place where the line between the legs meets the V of the pubis. There is a Pan-African notion of the trickster, a figure who is always linked to the crossroads. He is the figure who is unavoidable, the figure to be placated and feared. There's something archetypal about this that I want to explore.

· The text is filled, of course, with notions of sight. Oedipus, who thinks he is enlightened, clear-eyed, is relying always on the most overwhelming of the senses, the sense with the greatest capacity to fool, whereas the real prophet and seer, Tiresias, is blind and thus undistracted by that most facile and untrustworthy sense.

What Oedipus deprives himself of—his sight—is what has betrayed him. He didn't *see* himself.

His great mistake (and he makes it twice) is a failure, not just to recognize himself, but to recognize himself *in others*—not to see his father as his father, his mother as his mother. He treats strangers as kin and treats kin as strangers. This is a failure of sight. But it's also a failure of instinct. One prizes intellect over instinct at one's own peril, it seems.

Idea for the blinding: We see Oedipus far upstage, with his back to us, holding the brooches up. He extends his arms up, then, as he's stabbing them down—full blackout. Lights up as he extends his arms up again. Once again, as he brings the pins down—full blackout—all of this accompanied by the chorus somehow.

Here are the three best translations I have of one cogent section of the choral ode in the Sophocles that takes place presumably at the same time that the blinding is occurring offstage.

1. Bernard Knox:

> O son of Laius,
> I wish I had never seen you.
> I weep, like a man wailing for the dead.
>> This is the truth:
> You returned me to life once.
> And now you have closed my eyes in darkness.

2. Robert Fagles:

> I tell you the truth, you gave me life
> my breath leapt up in you
> and now you bring down night upon my eyes.

3. Stephen Berg and Diskin Clay:

> I wish I had never seen you
> I grieve for you
> wail upon wail fills me and pours out
> because of you my breath came flowing back
> but now
> the darkness of your life
> floods my eyes.

In each of these translations, the content seems to be that the chorus are addressing their desire for blindness, which is not so terribly different from Oedipus', because sight is unbearable.

What I think we can articulate, if we have the blinding onstage and it is accompanied by full blackouts and by something along the lines of this text, is the deep identification the chorus and audience by that point have with Oedipus, such that we are blinded with him and by him.

· The notion of exile interests me because the play hinges on Oedipus' two exiles, both voluntary, which frame the tragic action of the play.

1. He exiles himself from his parents in Corinth so as not to hurt them.
2. He exiles himself from Thebes because he is the source of his city's misery.

Both are exiles self-imposed by a man attempting to render himself harmless and justly homeless.

We are all products, like Oedipus, of an unlikely act of mercy. The incident of the shepherd who cannot bear to kill a helpless infant and who makes that pivotal choice—to give him, cursed though he is, to a life of unknowing exile—is resonant for all of us, since to be human is to be in exile.

We are all exiles from our mothers, sent out into the world in innocence of our dreadful fates.

Homesickness is the human disease. We wander the world, homesick for a home lost before memory but which we can't help missing—a sense that we have been cast away from our true nature, our true selves. We seek the truth of our origins, no matter what it is, and will die in the search for it. This is the home we are sick for, but terrible the story of the man who lives to recover that lost home. It is not for us to find.

· I'm interested that Jocasta's stated belief—that life is all
based on chance and randomness and nothing can be pre-
dicted—is a kind of precursor to existentialism and mod-
ernism. There is no meaning to the way things happen
and thus, weirdly, nothing to be feared except the rather
dispiriting sense that nothing matters or makes any
sense—the old existential dread problem. There is some
parallel here with the current phenomenon of our dwindling faith in an intelligible moral universe and a consequent self-conscious cynicism (as opposed to irony) that
pervades the culture. The American ethos at the moment
seems to me to be a combination of desperation and rapa-
ciousness tricked up to look like recklessness and expedi-
ency; whatever it is, it provides no sense and no solace.
I suppose the appeal for us, as for Jocasta, has to do with
the seduction of forgetfulness. If we can manage to
remain inside the present moment, we never have to
answer for our actions in the past, never need to succumb
to the pull of the subconscious, which is, in part, the pull
of history and hence accountability.

In Jocasta's case, and in the plague-ridden Athens of
the first production of the play, the nihilistic philosophy
must have been a common response to the crisis of the
times. There must have been a growing conviction that
in the face of the chaos they were enduring—so many
were dying and every death was inexplicable, the just
and the unjust equally vulnerable—worship was futile
and the cosmos utterly arbitrary. Perhaps we share some
of that despair and it manifests itself similarly.

Jocasta's baldly heretical statement of her acquired
philosophy leads, in a way I haven't quite figured out, to
Oedipus' triumphal claim that "Luck is the goddess who
gave birth to me."

· I find this section fascinating, and not in any straightforward way, because Oedipus becomes lighter, more excited
and positively exuberant at the point just before the shep-

herd arrives and after Jocasta has gone to kill herself. A huge part of this must be his anticipation that he is about to learn the truth. This is the sort of man he is, and it is what makes the tragedy that much more vivid, that he would be at his most exalted just before the worst news is to come.

What I am particularly interested in at the end is that transformation of Oedipus into what Creon calls a "cursed, naked, holy thing," that Greek idea of the *agos*—something both sacred and cursed. That's the concept most remote for a modern audience, I think, and it's the concept most crucial for us to come to terms with.

- I was struck by the statement in Aristotle's *Poetics* that the kind of learning peculiar to tragedy is the recognition of blood ties.

Hence the prevalence of recognition scenes in Greek tragedy's dramaturgy. But the hat trick is, I think, that there has to be a corresponding *frisson* of recognition on the part of the audience. We must, for instance, understand our kinship with Oedipus at the end of his cruel story, when he has become literally unspeakable (there was no Greek word for incest) and rendered inhuman, no longer a man—a thing. His crime has tainted him so indelibly that he is beyond the reach of any kind of spiritual cleansing or worldly purification and can never hope to live among men until his death. He must be in permanent, comfortless exile for the rest of his life. And it is at this point that we must recognize him, despite this, to be our own. He is of us, the monster we are in the darkest chamber of our being.

More anon, my friend.

I just wanted to get the conversation rolling and let you know what's going on for me at this point.

Love,
Ellen

Part 2

I write this in January 2005, in the last week of rehearsal for a production at the Guthrie Theater in Minneapolis.

Despite my initial reluctance, I've come to appreciate this play as I have no other, and believe I have some understanding of its enduring status over the centuries. I'd always been put off, I think, by the terrible rigor of the cosmology of the play, an alien cosmology for most modern people. The bleakness of the worldview put forth by the horror of this play can be crushing and confounding. But Lisa Peterson's continuing fascination with the play and her deep belief that *Oedipus* is uniquely relevant to our time kept me open to the power of it and finally overwhelmed any doubts I had.

My way into the play was directly related to my having seen, in the 1980s, several performances in different cities of Lee Breuer and Bob Telson's *The Gospel at Colonus*, a magnificent interpretation of Sophocles' *Oedipus at Colonus*, which struck me then, as it still does, as the best modern adaptation of a classical Greek text ever done. Part of my admiration is due to the work's unapologetically religious bent. I finally understood in a palpable way what had always seemed a rather intellectual notion—that these plays were originally performed as part of religious festivals. And the god honored in the great Athenian festivals was quite specific—Dionysus—who is present in tragedy but also presides over ecstasy. The religious aspect of these plays can be felt in the ruminative way they circle around mystery. What human beings cannot understand because of the limitations of their consciousness and their mortality drives them to grapple with the divine. All tragedies have a spiritual quotient, because all tragedies are encounters with what human beings can't, for all their gifts of rationality, understand. *The Gospel at Colonus* is clearly centered on the mystery of death. *Oedipus*, it began to seem to me, can be understood as a meditation on the mystery of birth.

What is human life at its essence? We are all walking miracles, no less than Oedipus is, all of us saved by a strange mercy for an obscure purpose. We are alive against all odds, each of us having made the perilous journey from the womb. The naked vulnerability of the human child, dependent on mercy for life, is at the heart of human consciousness and informs everything we do thereafter. It is a memory we embody rather than remember, that primary truth of our existence, and I find it particularly resonant in this play. We are strangers in the world at birth, and we are dependent for our survival upon the kindness of the strangers we meet upon our arrival. The image of the newborn Oedipus, whose life hangs in the balance on the slopes of Mount Citheron, became central for me. I intend that image of the naked child in the fetal position as a sort of physical and metaphysical question mark poised at the beginning and end of the piece.

Similarly, I want the riddle of the Sphinx, her question: "What is this thing?" to echo throughout the play, because it is so crucial, not only to Oedipus' identity, but to the nature of the riddle the play takes on. Her riddle acts like all the riddles of the play in that it is circular. Oedipus' answer: "It is man," cannot be said to "solve" the riddle, but only to force the restatement of her confounding question: "What is this thing?" and I mean that question to resonate throughout, which is why we return to it in the climactic choral ode. Oedipus is presented with circular riddles continually, even when he doesn't know he's being presented with them. It is the way the gods speak in this play. When he goes to the shrine of Apollo and asks: "Whose son am I?" he thinks he doesn't receive an answer to that question when the god responds that he will kill his father and marry his mother, but he is in fact receiving an answer to what the god interprets as a riddle Oedipus has asked. Whose son is he? He is the son who will do these unthinkable things to his parents. It is only at the end of the play that Oedipus can realize the divine circular logic he has been trapped in from the start.

The chorus is engaged in the Sophocles play in a journey that parallels Oedipus' journey but brings in larger spiritual issues throughout. The members of the chorus are representatives of a people in severe crisis—the shadow of the plague is present at all times—and their only hope in assuaging their suffering seems to be the extraordinary king they love so unreservedly. Lisa said in the course of rehearsal that the play could be understood as a love story between the chorus and Oedipus. The course of events disturbs them and forces them to confront issues of faith and to question the very nature of the cosmos. Caught in the increasing darkness and confusion of their time, they must choose, again and again, to ally themselves with their mortal savior. But the play doesn't make it easy for them. The sense of being on the wrong side of God, transgressing as a people against the divine by giving their allegiance to a great man, is extremely difficult and constantly disturbing. They are forced, in the third ode, to contemplate a world without God and they find such a world unbearably pointless and brutal. But such is their desperation that they still cling to Oedipus, even in the face of a harrowingly empty vision. I take liberties with the Sophoclean odes, but I'm not departing completely from what is present in the original text. That sense of the chorus struggling throughout with the larger spiritual questions provoked by the dramatic action is very much in place in the Sophocles. I'm just taking those questions on as a person of my time, steeped in the welter of what the modern world has given me to think *with*—everything from Freud to existentialism, chaos theory, Brecht and Beckett. With all of this, the essential question: "What is this thing?" is as alive as ever. And we are no more at home in the world, no more comfortable with the inescapable fact of human suffering and the silence of the gods, than our ancient forebears were.

My major cautionary note about staging this play concerns the common practice of simplifying the scale of the play to create an easy contemporary political resonance. It is important to me that Oedipus be an extraordinary man, a paragon of leadership. Any attempts to *explain* his tragedy as being the direct result of flaws in his character drastically skew the logic of the play and reduce a complex, deeply disturbing work to a smug, tidy puzzle that can be snapped together and forgotten. Sophocles, it seems to me, takes great pains to establish not only Oedipus' unique brilliance and appeal as a leader but the inscrutable nature of his fall to ruin. Even by Greek standards, this play is opaque concerning what spiritual lesson, if there must be such a thing, one should glean from it. Formulas of sin and consequent divine punishment are not valid here. For example, Sophocles downplays aspects of the myth (which would have been familiar to the Greeks) concerning Laius' morally dubious actions during his rule (aside from directing the murder of his own son) specifically, I think, in order to discourage an interpretation of the tragedy as a consequence of the sins of the father being visited on the son, a kind of tragedy Greeks were quite familiar with. Sophocles allows us no simplistic formula of divine retribution. This is what has made this play so maddening and compelling for all of us since. The gods are offstage and inaccessible, no matter how fervently we call them to account. The divine is palpable only in oracles, which speak not of justice but only of what is inevitable.

The presence of God in this play, more than in any other Greek play I've worked with, is chilling in its disinterest and indifference. The gods merely state what will happen but never why. The chorus is caught in a world so horrifyingly hostile and apparently devoid of divine justice that they are continually forced back upon the only thing they are left to believe in—their king. The chorus speaks continually about silence. It is a world of silence and they are haunted by it. It is the silence of the dead, and not just the human dead who surround them; the whole of nature is dead and dying—they are even bereft of birdsong in this plague-ridden world. But the chorus comes to recognize the silence as even more cosmic in scale than that of their natural world; they are experiencing the silence of the divine itself. It is perhaps not accidental then that silence is what, more than anything else, provokes Oedipus. Silence always encircles mystery, and mystery is anathema to him, probably because he embodies it.

Much has been made of the legal language and procedures that pervade the play. The Athenians were an enthusiastically litigious people and would have recognized themselves in Oedipus, who is continually cast in the role of the quick-witted prosecuting attorney, questioning, more often than not, a reluctant witness. It is the silence of what is known but actively unspoken that infuriates him again and again. It is his stubborn inability to accept such silence that he has to thank for the very unfolding of his life story, since he would not accept, as any other man would, the silence of God itself when he asked his question: "Whose son am I?" at the shrine of Apollo. I've heightened and elaborated this episode because I think it elucidates Oedipus' extraordinary nature. The idea of a man who refuses to be content with silence, even when it is the silence *of God*, is so impressive and utterly characteristic that it sets up everything to come. He is revealed in that moment as the sort of man who will pursue the truth, break down reluctant witness after witness, no matter what the personal cost, no matter who is telling him to stop, because the silence of the unspoken is that abhorrent to him.

The oracle he receives at the shrine, that answer in the form of a riddle, bears no fingerprints. It is distinctly inhuman. There is no making moral sense of it, no negotiating for another life story, and no escaping it. It simply *is*. It also seems outside linear time, as if it has already happened, or rather that it may as well have already happened, since it is inevitable. There is a stark clarity to the bald fact of Oedipus' tragedy that strikes me as very Greek and quite alien to our far more human-centered logic.

We are often reminded that the Greeks anthropomorphized the divine, the implication being that they were more childish and less sophisticated than we are in their faith. I think this play puts the lie to that rather self-aggrandizing notion. The unsentimental, clear-eyed Greek vision of the divine is something the modern world cannot accept, not because it is too human, but rather the opposite. I write this in the immediate aftermath of the Indian Ocean tsunami, a catastrophe modern religion seems helpless to make sense of. What kind of god would inflict such suffering? And if there is divine intention evident in such an event, how are we to think of such a god? The Greeks never shied away from a recognition of the inscrutable nature of the divine, the apparent indifference of nature, and the tenuous place human beings have in the structure of things. The divine is continually invoked, but the gods are anything but reliable, and never subject to human notions of justice. The chief characteristic of the gods is their very inhumanity, indicated not only by their immortality but by their inaccessibility to human logic, their incomprehensibility. One of the major points of the tragedy of Oedipus seems to be that even the most magnificent of us, the greatest of men, cannot claim to be exempt from the dark workings of the divine. No human conduct can ensure us the benign glance of the immortals, and our only guarantee is suffering and death.

Since civilization lost hold of that stark understanding of our relationship with the divine, we seem to be increasingly like gamblers who go to Vegas convinced that we've finally discovered the system. The Greeks never flattered themselves that if such a system even existed, it could be worked out by human reason. But I think they would have found the hubristic gambler's plight wonderfully tragic, wonderfully, and horribly, human. And they would have watched with compassionate awe as the roulette wheel relentlessly finally rattled to its confounding conclusion and the death of all such delusions.

All that being said, I don't believe, as has often been proposed, that the Sophocles play sets out to prove the point articulated in his final choral ode: that there is nothing like human happiness to be found in the world, and that it would be better never to have lived at all, the suffering of the human condition being what it is. The play presents a city in the grips of a profound and inexplicable natural crisis, and a leader who spares nothing to meet that crisis. Oedipus is compelled by greatness of intellect, but also by greatness of heart. He acts for others with the sense that he is uniquely suited to lead and he musters his gifts for the sake of his city rather than out of any desire to find favor with the gods. He is compassionate rather than self-interested. And he is the victim of a terrible fate nonetheless. The reason for his tragedy is nothing we can comprehend; all we can be sure of is his greatness. And his greatness is a result of his humanity rather than any reliance on the divine. He is a uniquely secular hero in Greek drama. It is his secular nature that makes him vitally important to us, his tragedy something we cannot help but identify with. Whatever the chorus can make of his fate, what is undeniable is that he saves them. Saves them twice, in fact, first by answering the riddle of the Sphinx and finally by exiling himself from the city. He unflinchingly pursues the truth and, once he attains that knowledge, does what he must do in accordance with a human sense of justice and the need of his people.

It is the stunning power of his character even more than the awesome nature of his tragedy that makes him impossible to categorize, impossible to forget. His tragedy is certainly far more spectacular than the common round of human suffering, but we share a bond of mortality with him and love him, not just because he is greater than we are but because we are, at essence, like him, and, like him, sure to die, no matter what we achieve. The Greek audience knew that the workings of the gods were inscrutable; they didn't need a play to prove that bleak fact. The amazing accomplishment they were faced with in *Oedipus* was the presentation of a character who, despite the familiar limitations of our mortality and for the sake of his people, battles the silence of the world and makes it speak.

Part 3: Production Notes

This play, more than any Greek play I've ever dealt with, works as a music-theater piece—the scenes provoking odes, which in turn provoke scenes. There are five major choral odes and I think they need to be approached as pieces of music whether they are completely scored or not.

We were fortunate indeed to snag the talents of my dear friend Gina Leishman to act as a composer for the Guthrie production. We could afford only two musicians and Gina's instinct was to go with a percussionist, who could provide a world of sound and determine rhythm, combined with a reed player, who could provide not only melody and pitch but also a sonic color closer to the human voice. In a serendipitous coincidence, it turned out that the Minneapolis-based new music ensemble Zeitgeist was interested and available to work with us, and its core musicians, Heather Barringer and Pat O'Keefe, just happened to be a percussionist and a reed player, respectively.

It was important to us that the chorus be a group of people who look as if they might be members of the audience, representatives of the local community, mostly middle-aged, but ethnically and physically diverse. I would suggest that there not be fewer than six chorus members; one can't really achieve a critical mass otherwise. Gina was adamant that the chorus's first ode, their first utterance: "Save Us," be scored and sung in order to make clear immediately the theatrical universe we are in. We are in the realm of ritual, and when that is unapologetically embraced from the beginning, it saves one a great deal of trouble; one need not attempt to realistically justify behavior that is frankly formalized, such as speaking or singing spontaneously in unison. That said, only select passages of the odes were sung, though most were underscored. The stanza of the second ode specifically intended as an ode to "the holy siblings" was the only part of that ode that was set to music. The bulk of the third ode was set, but even that one, which was the most heavily scored, contained passages spoken by a single voice rather than sung. The fourth ode, which begins: "Gods, are you listening?" was not sung at all but was spoken by a series of individual voices. The fifth ode: "Let the storm break," was, in our production, largely an improvised piece relying on the gospel-influenced singing abilities of one of the chorus members. It became a dance that not only the chorus but Oedipus himself participated in, which was wonderfully jubilant and unique in the play. "What is this thing?" was not sung at all but was spoken, mostly in unison, as was the ode that ends the play, though I do recommend letting a single voice speak at least the last phrase of it alone.

In terms of divvying up the chorus sections, I recommend using a variety of techniques, from single voices through canons to unison, depending on the people who make up the chorus. An example of a canon would be the phrase: "We must drive him / out" spoken in sequence by six people. The second person would begin to overlap the first after the word "him," the third likewise, and so on, until the phrase has been spoken six times, the first: "We must drive him" and the last "out" being the only words spoken by a single voice in the clear. Like any musical skill, it takes practice to get a canon right, but the technique can be quite effective with this kind of material if used judiciously.

An example of dividing a choral section, given six chorus members, might be:

(1) A killer stalks the desperate city.

(2) A monster, unpunished, lives in our midst.

(1–6 Canon)We must drive him / out.

(3+4) We will do our work. (5+6) It has been shown to us.

(2) But, oh gods, we are not equal to all.

(1+3) We are only mortal,

(1) and the darkness of our time has overcome us.

(3+4) Look down upon us.

(5) See the harrowing woe of all we suffer now.

(1+2+3) Death breeding death. (4+5+6) Confusion and horror.

(2+4+5) Pity us. (1+3+6) We can only do so much.

(1–6) Help us.

It is important to explore the possibilities of this kind of choral speaking since so much of the play hinges on it and the effect can be extremely powerful if it is done properly, with sensitivity not only to the text but also to the sensibilities and vocal qualities of the performers.

Should future producers wish to use Gina's remarkable music, they can get in touch with her at gleishman@earthlink.net

Production History

Oedipus premiered at Minneapolis's Guthrie Theater (Joe Dowling, Artistic Director) on January 21, 2005. The director was Lisa Peterson, with set design by Riccardo Hernandez, costume design by David Zinn, lighting design by Christopher Akerlind and sound design by Scott W. Edwards; the composer was Gina Leishman, the musicians were Zeitgeist: Heather Barringer (percussion) and Pat O'Keefe (reeds); the dramaturg was Carla Steen and the stage manager was Chris A. Code. The cast was as follows:

OEDIPUS	Peter Macon
TIRESIAS	Sandra Shipley
CREON	Stephen Yoakam
JOCASTA	Isabell Monk O'Connor
CORINTHIAN MESSENGER	Tom Bloom
THE SHEPHERD	Richard S. Iglewski
A BOY	Dylan Frederick, Ryan McCartan
THE CHORUS	Barbara Bryne, Benny S. Cannon, Wayne A. Evenson, Emil Herrera, Richard Ooms, Regina Marie Williams

Characters

OEDIPUS, King of Thebes

TIRESIAS, a revered blind prophet

CREON, a respected statesman, the Queen's brother

JOCASTA, Queen of Thebes

CORINTHIAN MESSENGER, a middle-aged man, once a
   shepherd

THE SHEPHERD, a middle-aged man

A BOY

THE CHORUS, made up of at least six people, mostly middle-
   aged and elderly; they split the lines among them

A naked child is lying in the fetal position, his back to the audience.
Dim light.

A VOICE
Here is the riddle, mortals:
What is this thing?
It moves on four legs in the morning
Two at noon
And three at evening   5

The answer is as close as breath.
Tell me or die. One by one.
Tell me and die. One by one.
I eat ignorance.
One, two, four, three, two, three, one, four . . .   10

(A cry. The Sphinx's? Oedipus'? A singular, piercing cry of woe
becomes a muted communal lament as the Chorus enters from
different sides and obscures the naked child. Dawn.)

CHORUS
Save us. We suffer.
Save us. We are dying.
Save us. We walk in confusion.
Save us. We are blinded by fear.
Save us. Save us.   15

(Oedipus appears. Silence.)

OEDIPUS

Citizens! You know me.

My people, my children. I was not sleeping. I cannot sleep.

I close my eyes and the multitudes of the suffering close

around me in the darkness. You are always with me. I feel

your mingled breath on my cheeks, your uncaught tears on   20

my chest and face. And the smell of the pyres finds me

where I lie. I open my eyes and stare into the blackness and

think, Now, now, now, someone is suffering.

So I have come out alone to meet you in the dark.

Rise up, my friends.   25

Speak to me. Tell me of your woe.

CHORUS

O King. We are frightened.

The ship of Thebes is ghosting in alien waters.

She is silent, her sails tattered.

No one is left on the tilted empty deck.   30

We are dying in the red waves.

We have done all we can:

Sacrificed and prayed.

Atoned for what sins we know.

Even now, hordes of the lost kneel at temples across the city.   35

Blinded by the smoke of our own pyres.

We cling to the altars, like sailors to splinters from a wreck.

Hands empty, we reach toward nothingness.

We are suppliants to the silence that lies beyond us.

We beg without knowledge of what is killing us.   40

Beg until our voices close in raw silence.

But still.

But still.

But still.

The plague stalks us, ravaging the city,   45

And death is everywhere.

The bodies of men, women and children lie like lumber

hastily stacked for burning.

Every day, more die, faster than we have time to mourn them.
And still the pestilence swings wide and blind. Nothing escapes   50
the compass of it. The hills are silent. Birds fall from the sky
and lie like so much flyblown fruit. All the animals are downed
and rotting, their legs rigid, their eyes open and lightless.
In our fields, the crops curl, heads stooped to the gray earth.
Every wind rattles the black stalks. Mothers, in agony, bear   55
corpses. After their labors, they hear only silence, and look
upon the curled stones they have delivered in pain.

OEDIPUS
This is what I feared. This is what I knew.

CHORUS
O King. You are the greatest of men.
You are the one who saved us.   60
It was you who answered: "It is man," to the Sphinx and
freed us from her. We remember how it was before you came
to us. Still hear her terrible scream of prey as she fell upon
us one by one. It was you, the Stranger, who released us from
the darkness of that terrible time and led us into the light.   65
It was your courage, it was your brilliant mind, that shifted
the stone from the black cave we were trapped in. We know
you now. We know your strength and power.
Speak to the darkness once more.
Free us again.   70

OEDIPUS
My children. I see all.
Each of you stands in the single light of your own catastrophe.
I am the night sky. Every burning star exists in me.
A mass of searing pain, countless shining, spinning torments.
My night mind has wandered over all the paths to find a cure.   75
And I have already acted.
I sent Creon, my brother-in-law and most trusted statesman.
I sent him in my stead to Delphi

To ask the god Apollo what I must do to save my city.
Every day that has gone by has been torture.   80
I pace this palace like a limping lion.
Watching the light edge across the floor of my cage.
I shift and turn, waiting, impatient, for action.
And always the smoke curls through the bars to find me,
The smoke of the burning bodies of my own people as they die   85
One by one, day after day.
It is agony.
It is agony.

CHORUS
Here, here, we are released from doubt.
He is coming, King.   90
At last.
And he smiles, look he smiles.

(Creon enters.)

CREON
Good news! All will be well!

OEDIPUS
What do you mean? How can that be?

CREON
Shall we go inside? You cannot wish to discuss this in the open.   95

OEDIPUS
Why not? Anything you have to say affects everyone here.
I am not for secrets.

CREON
In the presence of all these people?

OEDIPUS
In the presence of all.

CREON
I had thought to speak to you alone.   100

OEDIPUS
No, say it to all of us.
I share their suffering. They will share my truth, whatever it is.

CREON
All right. If that is how you want it done.
Apollo has spoken.
He says: 105

> There is a corruption.
> Seek it and drive it out.

OEDIPUS
But we know this. Corruption. We feel it.
Does the god give us no more help than this?

CREON
It is a man.   110

OEDIPUS
It is a man?

CREON
It is blood.
It was a murder. A murder long buried in the body of the
state. At last, after festering for years, the poison has broken
to the surface and it wracks the body. It kills us now. 115

OEDIPUS
What murder? When? Who was the killer?

CREON
It happened before you came here.
Our late King Laius was murdered.

OEDIPUS
I never knew Laius, never saw him, only knew him dead.

CREON
It is his killer who must be found.   120
He is the corruption.

OEDIPUS
But that was years ago. Nothing was done at the time? How
are those ancient footprints to be traced?

CREON
He is here. In Thebes.
Apollo said it: 125

> What is neglected lies obscure yet never loses power.
> But whatever is sought can be found.

He is here. Born of this soil, he stands on it still.

OEDIPUS
The man lives? He is among us?
Tell me of this crime. Where did it happen?   130

CREON
It was the time of the Sphinx. A time of riddling, death and
confusion. Laius went out from the city to seek Apollo's voice,
just as you have had me do. He never returned. Nor did his
train of followers.

OEDIPUS
There were no survivors? No one who saw this?   135

CREON
Only one. A slave. And he was so terrified by what he saw
that his only wish was to slip away into obscurity and silence.

OEDIPUS

But he must have been questioned. What did he say?

CREON

His terror destroyed his mind. He could remember nothing.

OEDIPUS

Nothing?   **140**

CREON

There was only one thing he said he could be sure of.

OEDIPUS

Anything, even the smallest detail, would be better than
nothing.
What was the thing he could remember?

CREON

That there were many. Many killers. They fell upon the king's   **145**
procession, he said, like a hailstorm upon a stand of wheat.

OEDIPUS

But killers, a killer, would never attack a royal train alone.
No, there must have been real power, here, in Thebes, compelling the crime. No one works singly. The murder of a king
is never uncomplicated by larger designs.   **150**

CREON

There was talk of this at the time. But we were sunk in
confusion. It was chaos.

OEDIPUS

I don't understand you. Your king had been murdered. No
investigation could be more important. How could you let
the trail go cold for all these years?   **155**

CREON

The Sphinx was on us then. We could see no further than
her blinding, killing riddle. Until you came and delivered us.
And then we were happy to forget.

OEDIPUS

Then it is for me to bring this thing to light.
A killer lives.   160
Wherever he is, he is a menace.
He is a shadow lurking in wait.
I will bring him to light.
Not just for my city but for myself as well.
A man who could kill a king and go unpunished   165
Could kill another.
Laius' blood sings to my own.
I will start at the beginning, all alone.
It is time, long past time, to seek the truth.
This city shall not die of ignorance.   170
Arise, my people, and pray.
Live in hope.
I am here.
The hunt is on.
Whatever is sought can be found.   175

(He exits into the palace. Creon exits.)

CHORUS

A killer stalks the desperate city.
A monster, unpunished, lives in our midst.
We must drive him out.

We will do our work. It has been shown to us.
But, oh gods, we are not equal to all.   180
We are only mortal,
And the darkness of our time has overcome us.

Look down upon us.
See the harrowing woe of all we suffer now.
Death breeding death. Confusion and horror.   **185**
Pity us. We can only do so much.
Help us.

O Shining Ones, we call to you:
We sing to the holy siblings,
Athena, Artemis and Apollo,   **190**
Ringed with light
Ringed with immortality
Holy ones
We beg you.
Save our city.   **195**
She is clenched in the black jaws of our savage time.
Those who still live beseech you.

There is a god we cannot honor, though he is in your number.
He is the god the gods would exile from their midst.
Ares, god of war, Ares, the ruthless, it is Ares who has   **200**
    visited this plague upon us.
We hear his voice in the roar of the funeral pyres.
He screams there.
He is dreadful.
Sower of havoc.   **205**

Great is man, able of mind, heroic and subtle.
He comprehends the waking world and orders it.
He can be good, he can be great.
But two things even man cannot outstare.
Pestilence and war.   **210**
In these Ares resides.
The god of war breeds chaos and butchery.
Unleashes anarchy in minds and bodies.
He stokes the fires of madness, fans the flames of brutality.
He plunders peace, lays waste to joy.   **215**

The voice of human reason cannot be heard above his
   howls for blood.
The mind of man is helpless against him.
It is Ares, the god, Ares, the ravager, who plagues us.
O Shining Ones, he is too much for us.   220
Unseat him, pluck him from his throne and hurl him
Sprawling through the depths of air
Until his scream dies forever.

Man is staggering under his iron weight of woe.
Drive him out   225
Drive him out
Drive him out.
He is accursed though he is holy.
He is holy but accursed.
He is accursed though he is holy.   230
Drive him out.

(Oedipus enters.)

OEDIPUS
I hear your prayers and they move me.
And now I've come to ask you to join me in lifting this
Sickness from our beloved city.
I came as a stranger to this country.   235
I knew nothing of your king's death when I entered this
   valley for the first time, alone, to meet the Sphinx.
But this I cannot do alone. I will need your help.
Each of you is the vessel of the history of your city.
One of you knows the truth.   240
Where is the murderer?
Tell me.

(Silence.)

Let him who knows speak.
Who is the murderer?

(Silence.)

I will not harm the one who speaks. Even he who did this.   **245**
All he will receive in return for this knowledge is banishment,
unharmed. He will go with a king's thanks. Though he has
blood on his hands, he will merely leave us.
That is all I ask. Who is the man?

(Silence.)

Whoever did this thing, whoever lives silent, his crime now   **250**
poisoning this city, let him know this: He will find no shelter
here, nothing will be given to him, no one will pray for him.
He has no recourse here, he is accursed.
I drive him out, comfortless, into eternal exile.
He is the disease. He is the corruption.   **255**
I speak for Apollo. I speak for my city. I speak this for myself.
As far as I cast my eye, even on the clearest day, my power is
absolute. I will find him out. He can no longer shelter in
shameful obscurity.
The light of my eyes is searching and, like an eagle, I will   **260**
plummet down upon him unsuspecting.
My justice is wide.
Whoever he is, I curse him.
Let his days be cruel, burning in nullity and under the lash
of hatred. Let his life be long and terrible, leached of any   **265**
human happiness. Let him find kindness nowhere.
And if I unwittingly sheltered this man, if I have ever offered
him comfort, however unknowingly, let this curse fall on me.
Let me suffer what I demand in justice. The curse is
complete and knows no rank or border. The curse is eternal   **270**
and binding, no matter where it falls. Let it pursue the guilty
unto the gates of hell itself.
A king! A king was murdered!
How could a single citizen sleep while this killer slunk free?
I walk that king's very halls, sleep in his bed, share his queen,   **275**

planted the seed of my children in the same furrow where he could have planted his. I live in his shadow, sleep within the echo of the footsteps of his unquiet ghost. I will fight for him. Fight for him as if he were my own father. I will see all. I will know all. 280 Nothing will stop me.

CHORUS
O King. May I speak? Your curse has emboldened me.

OEDIPUS
Speak. What do you know?

CHORUS
I know that I was not the murderer. I know that I do not know who was. But Apollo does. He must. Why should we 285 not ask the god to reveal him?

OEDIPUS
The gods have given me my orders. They need not give me anything else.

CHORUS
Might I speak again?

OEDIPUS
Again and again. I am open to all counsel. 290

CHORUS
If we cannot speak to Apollo himself, might we speak to one who hears him? I'm thinking of Tiresias, whose eyes were blasted blind by the fire of the divine. He withstood that blaze and now he hears the god speaking. Might he be questioned?

OEDIPUS
I have thought of this already and have called for him. Called 295 for him twice. I am not used to being ignored when I command.

CHORUS

Look, King, he comes at last.

See, see, he is ageless, majestic and awesome.

Woman and man, both, nothing human is alien to him.

Yet though he is mortal, the divine rings in his ears.   **300**

The voice of God hammers in the blackness of his skull and

sounds him like a bell.

With his sightless eyes he stares directly into eternity.

(Tiresias has entered. Silence.)

OEDIPUS

O Tiresias. You are master of mysteries.

You alone can untie the dreadful knots of our terrible time.   **305**

Your ears are licked by the flames of blazing divinity.

Your eyes, dead to the passing world, are open to the immortal.

You see the truth.

You know the agony of your city,

You can feel it singing in your own bones.   **310**

We have heard Apollo and he has told us:

Bring the murderers of Laius forward into the light
And cast them out.

O Tiresias,

Spare nothing in your city's aid.   **315**

We are in your hands.

Do what only you can do.

Rescue your city.

(Silence.)

TIRESIAS

It is a curse. To know too much.

Why did I forget this?   **320**

I should never have come.

OEDIPUS

I don't understand you. I called for you.
I have asked you, humbly, for your aid.
What do you mean you should never have come?

TIRESIAS

Let me return to silence.   325
Let me go home.
I will live on, you will live on.
Leave the truth unspoken.
It would be best.

OEDIPUS

This is a strange cruelty.   330
This is your answer to a desperate city?
To clench your teeth against the voice of God within you?

(Silence.)

This is an obscenity.
This silence is an offense against the city that gave you
     birth, the very earth on which you stand.   335

(Silence.)

What more can you want from us?
Do you want us to kneel to you?
This we do.

(Everyone kneels.)

We kneel to you, mortal prophet, we bow in supplication.
All Thebes crouches at your feet now.   340
We are shattered by our troubles,
We kneel in the dust of this dying city,
Dust washed by the hot torrents of our own tears.

Our hands are open to you.
We beg you.   345
Do not turn away from us now.
A terrible mystery clutches us in its grip.
Holds us fast in torment.
In the name of the gods
Tell us what you know.   350
Speak.

(Silence.)

TIRESIAS
You kneel to me in ignorance.
But I will not deliver you into knowledge.
No. Never. I will not speak.

(Oedipus leaps up.)

OEDIPUS
You know and will not speak?   355
What hateful arrogance fuels you to refuse such frank supplication?
You'd enrage a man of stone!
You are heartless and insolent.
You have betrayed us, the dead and the living.
Speak, damned monster, speak!   360

TIRESIAS
I withstood the blaze of God, I can withstand this tantrum.
All I say to you, Oedipus, is look to your own heart.
I am not your scourge.
Put your own house in order before you try to dismantle another's.

OEDIPUS
You are speaking to your king. When you insult me, you   365
insult your country. Beware.

TIRESIAS

I am not your subject, sir, nor any man's. I belong to God.
I do not speak because there is nothing for me to say.
What will happen will happen. Truth does not need prophets.

OEDIPUS

All the more reason to speak then. If it doesn't matter what   **370**
you say, what prevents you doing your king's bidding?

(Silence.)

Practice your trade, prophet. Your king commands you.

TIRESIAS

Rage, Oedipus, rage. It is useless. Wind across a wasteland.
I shall not speak.

OEDIPUS

Yes, you will have all my fury, and let the force of it wake   **375**
your leaden conscience. Let it whip the dust from your buried
infamy, lay it open in the air and read it in the noonday sun.
This is what your shameful silence has led me to believe: It is
guilt that seals your faithless mouth. A king's murder is on
your eyeless head. A king's murder. Whether you raised your   **380**
hand or not, you had a part in it, this I now know.

TIRESIAS

What you know, what you know. Fool. Bloodstained fool.
Ignorant as an animal of your own crime.

OEDIPUS

What? You dare slander me? You're smart enough to know
what you're doing. That's outright treason. I could have you   **385**
killed for that. Where is your fear?

TIRESIAS

Why should I fear you? The truth is all my safety. And I live
in the shelter of it.

OEDIPUS
Who are you speaking for? Is it Creon? Whose devices are
you working?   390

TIRESIAS
Blame yourself if you must blame someone for this. I warned
you not to force these words to light, but you wouldn't listen.

OEDIPUS
Spit it out then, creature.
Indict yourself and be done with it.

TIRESIAS
All right then. Listen.   395
This is the truth you bully me to utter, against my will:
You do not know the shame you live in. You are steeped in
pollution. You swim in it, wallow in your own filth and know
nothing. Nothing.
You are the corruption that has brought a curse down upon   400
your people. Thousands have already died for your ignorance.
Yes, the royal hunt is on, but you, sir, are your own prey. You
are the man you're hunting.

OEDIPUS
Say that again.

TIRESIAS
The murderer you seek is here. He is you.   405

(Silence.)

OEDIPUS
Designs and deception. My eyes are adjusting to the murk
of this high treason. You know nothing of God. You rattle in
blackness inside your unlit skull and lie and lie. Your only
allegiance is to Creon. He is behind this, I see it now, only he

could have goaded you to spew this grotesque slander. I have 410
been a fool to trust him. He has always envied me my power.
How could he not? And you were always his flunky, weren't
you? You stood beside him from the first, mouthing what he
told you to say. When have you ever been a true prophet? When
Thebes teetered in crisis in the dark days of the Sphinx, did 415
you come to the aid of your suffering city with all your
mummery? No. You two formed a cabal to topple your country
entirely with the murder of a king. I was the unexpected savior
who wrecked that plan with my arrival. It was left to me, a
stranger, to defend your city. I, whom you call ignorant. I alone 420
matched my mind against the mystery. And I did it without any
of your hollow sorcery and cant about God. I didn't need to disem-
bowel birds and finger their blue guts to do what was right.

CHORUS
O King, you go too far! This is dangerous insolence!

OEDIPUS
This wanderer, from parts unknown, walked into chaos 425
empty-handed and defeated it with nothing but a human
mind. Now, in your country's second moment of peril, the
two of you seek to carry through on your original plan by
fanning the flames of fear, you seed your great sorrowing
city with this suspicion of a beloved king. But you have under- 430
estimated your city and you have underestimated me. This is
where the trail of infamy ends. Of course I have found you
out. It was just a matter of time. What did you expect me to do?

TIRESIAS
Just this. What you have done. You cannot help yourself,
you are what you are. You have always been a stranger, it's 435
true. But not as you think. A stranger to yourself.
You do not know yourself, Oedipus. Even who you are.
Never having sought this knowledge, I know. You do not.
Whose son are you? Ask yourself that.

OEDIPUS

Whose son am I? What do you mean? 440

TIRESIAS

Today you will find out.

Today is your birth, your mother and your father.

And today you will finally meet the real stranger.

Today he will kill you.

OEDIPUS

Leave with your life, and never cross my path again. I won't 445
waste my time with you. I will deal with Creon, your taskmaster.
You are not worthy of even the back of my hand.

TIRESIAS

I'll leave you with a riddle, King, and be gone. You're fond
of riddles, and you're good at them. No one better. It is your
killing gift. As you will see. Let this suffice: 450
What is that thing which, once born, eats its own father then
climbs back into the womb from which it came and sleeps
there in bloody ignorance?

OEDIPUS

No more of your riddles, monster. Leave my sight.

TIRESIAS

I leave your sight forever, King. No, you shall never see me 455
again. Though there will come a time when you will weep for
the sight of me. Even me. But I will not come. Even you will
not be able to bid me to your sight again. Nor anyone else, King.
Never again.

(He leaves.)

CHORUS

O King. This was not done well. The voice of God has left us in 460
anger. Rage crackles in the raw air, spreading terror through the

miserable streets. Now is the time for temperance and reverence.
Now, more than ever, we need the tender glance of the divine.
Without it we are lost in mortal turmoil and confusion.

OEDIPUS
That blind schemer has nothing to do with God and never did.   **465**
He has just fooled you with his sanctimonious charades for
years. We are well rid of him. It is good he has gone.
Now I can think.
Rejoice, my people, your savior has returned to himself. Never
again will he seek in others what he need only find in himself.   **470**
All you need of the divine is here. The mind of a leader, search-
ing, searching, moving swift as thought, unencumbered by super-
stition and fear. My whole life has drawn me to this moment.
I am keen as a knife edge now, free in my knowledge.
I will act.   **475**

(He leaves.)

CHORUS
Listen to the running footsteps.
A killer runs.
In his head the blood is drumming.
    "Seek him out."

Running, running, he gets nowhere.   **480**
Desperate, jagged is his flight.
Still the voice of the god pursues him,
    "Seek him out."

Panting up the slopes, he scrambles.
Printing blood on every rock.   **485**
In the aching air he hears it
    "Seek him out."

No one, no one, can outrun the voice of God.

Look up, murderer, look up.
The Fates are circling.   490
They have found you.
Soon their shadows will rush cool across your shoulders.
And in an instant, they will fall.
Flickering silence, they will fall.
Wind in black feathers, they will fall.   495
    They will cut the thread.
    This is what God said.
    They will cut the thread.
    Welcome to the dead.

No one, no one, can outrun the voice of God.   500

Under the white shafts of the holy sun
We all dodge and run across a broken land
Under the gaze of God's unblinking eye.
And all that is mortal shall die.

There is no hiding from the Fates circling above us.   505
Every man shall feel the plummeting shadow of his death
    spread across his back.
For all that is mortal shall die.

I cannot place my faith in prophets,
For even the best of them walk beneath that flickering light. 510
Just as I do, just as I.
No one can outrace that hovering shadow.
For all that is mortal shall die.

I have a king
And though he too is mortal, he is great.   515
When he faced that singing terror
When his brilliance drove her from our land
Then we saw our dreams embodied
Then we saw the best of man.

I can't abandon   520
Won't desert him
Not this king I've come to love.
He's the only hope that's left me
As the Fates hang up above.

There they are hanging   525
Clicking their scissors
One two three
They bide their time
Making slow circles
In wait for me   530
Clicking their scissors
They flap and climb
Clicking their scissors
Watching me running
Riding the currents of timeless time.   535

(Creon enters.)

CREON
Citizens, I come here in disbelief and shock.
Can it be true? Can Oedipus have accused me of such—
I can't even say it—is it possible?
As I made my way here through my own beloved city
streets, streets I have walked with honor all my life, rumors   540
murmured in my wake. Everywhere I turned, people
cupped their hands to speak of me to others, or stared at me
in stony silence as if I was a stranger.
This is a kind of nightmare.
No slander could ever cut as deeply as this.   545
Nothing worse could ever be said of me.
And from *him*, my brother, the man I've served loyally all
these years.
Can this be?

CHORUS

Lord Creon. Our king is distraught. He did strike out, and   550
like a child, hit the one who stands closest to him.

CREON

He actually said this? That I compelled Tiresias to lie?

CHORUS

He did.
We heard him. But we cannot speak for his intentions.

CREON

So the rumors are true. This was his accusation. I couldn't   555
believe it.

CHORUS

Lord Creon, his words were spoken in fury, not in consideration.

CREON

The shame. How can I outlive this?

CHORUS

But we needn't speak for him. He is here.

(Oedipus has entered. They stare at each other.)

OEDIPUS

You. Sir. That you can stand before me. Brazen and unbowed.   560
Oh, look at him. What a performance. What a mockery.
All sanctimony and innocence. You are good, I'll give you that.
You have taken me in for years. But no more.
It is your king, not your fool, who is looking at you now.

CREON

You have judged me without hearing me, sir.   565
This is no justice. I have a right—

OEDIPUS

What right can a man like you claim in such an hour?

CREON

I have a right to know what I'm accused of.

OEDIPUS

First tell me of your dead king. Be useful to me in this if
nothing else.   570

CREON

My dead king? You mean Laius? I don't understand.

OEDIPUS

Then I will make you understand, Brother.
How long ago was his murder?

CREON

You don't need me to tell you that, it's common knowledge.
Not long before your crowning. The crime is old. A year   575
older than your oldest child.

OEDIPUS

A dark time. A time of crisis.
Yours was the hand at the helm. But you had help, even then,
from your minister of smoke. Didn't he stand by your side?

CREON

Minister of—? Who do you mean, sir?   580

OEDIPUS

The blind one. King of Cats.

CREON

Tiresias?

OEDIPUS
Yes.

CREON
He was by me, yes, my trusted aide through evil times.

OEDIPUS
And evil times need their professionals. What a sorry state **585**
you were in. First the Sphinx preyed upon you, feeding one
by one upon the people. Then the murder of a king. Almost
more than a country can bear.
I am curious. It puzzles me. Why was there no inquiry into that
crime? Why was no one tracked, no one brought to justice? **590**

CREON
But I have told you this already. We could get no answers. All
were dead. Or so we thought. Only one survived and he was
so blasted by terror that nothing could be wrung from him.
He staggered into the city, wild with horror, weeks later, just
in time to see you crowned. He went speechless from the **595**
shock of all he'd seen.

OEDIPUS
So many speechless, so many silent. Odd when there is so
much to tell. Odd too, your wise man's silence. He who says
he hears the gods. He had nothing to say? Why was that?

CREON
I don't know. **600**

OEDIPUS
But you know much.

CREON
What do I know?

OEDIPUS
You know for whom Tiresias has always spoken. It is not
the gods he listens to. He does not work for them. It's politics,
not God, that murmurs in his ear. And he works for the man   605
who pays him. He works for you.

CREON
Me?

OEDIPUS
You were the one he spoke for today. He named me as the
murderer. The killer of a king.

CREON
If that is what he said, he said it for his own reasons. I had   610
no hand in it. What would it profit me? *(Oedipus laughs)* I'm
serious. I have never sought it, never wanted kingship with
all its troubles and weight of care—

OEDIPUS
All its power—

CREON
I have power enough. Power on my own terms. I have only   615
ever wanted what I have.
I have rank, through position and blood. The queen is my
sister, you, then, my brother. I have sway, entrance to any
majestic hall I choose to enter. I am fawned upon, but never
held ultimately responsible. Favors, tokens, prayers and   620
benedictions reach me on their way to you. I bask in your
reflected light. I do not need to shine perpetually and, like
the moon, I can be as changeable as I choose. No one relies
on my warmth or my steady light.
I am liked because I am not feared.   625
I am liked because I never have to stand the final test of my
mettle.

I prefer it so. It is an easy, comfortable life and I sleep long
and soundly.
Treason? It is not in my nature.   630
I know who I am. I am content. I am the moon.
Do not mistake me for something I am not.

OEDIPUS

The moon is subtle, untrustworthy and devious. It dips
behind clouds to plunge the world into darkness when it
sees its moment. If you are the moon, I know your tricks.   635

CREON

I have not lied to you, King. Think through this rash injustice.
If you must pursue this, at least do one thing first. Ask at
the shrine of Apollo if the message I brought you was the
one the god imparted. Then, if you insist on accusing me of
conspiring with a soothsayer, I will account for myself in a   640
due process of law. And if I am still found guilty, this
I promise you right now: If you let me choose my own mode
of death, it will be far more terrible than any court could
devise. This crime you tag me with is that hateful to me.

OEDIPUS

Oh, but you are cunning. You want me to falter in the pace   645
of this inquiry. Run to temples, drag through a trial. No. I'm
sure you have covered all your tracks. There is no time for this.
The city is in crisis. Such wicked doings must be stamped
out as quickly as possible, or else the spark will blaze into a
consuming wild fire. Is that all you have to say?   650

CREON

No, King. There is more. If I have only this moment to speak
in this mad pelting race to ruin, I will say this: Since I stand
accused, I accuse you in turn. In my own voice. Face to face.
You have done me two injuries. The first is a petty, dreary
crime: the crime of slander. You have done me harm in the   655

eyes of men and that matters to me, it stings, and all the
more deeply since it is provoked by a wild falsehood. But
your second crime is unforgivable in one so freighted with
honor as a king: you have mistaken a good man for a bad one.
This shows want of character, want of judgment, want of   **660**
common sense. I am your friend. I am your kin. I am your
ally, none more steadfast, none more true. And this is how
you treat me? Better to slash off your right foot and fling it
in the mud. It is madness.
I have stood by you for years. Time has proved me.   **665**
You should have known me better.

CHORUS
Listen to him, King. An honorable man is speaking.
Rise above your anger and hear the truth.
Nothing is gained by rashness.

OEDIPUS
If it is rash to act quickly in the moment of inspiration,   **670**
and in the swiftness of thought to take the challenge, then
I have rashness to thank for my every accomplishment.
My success has been the child of the lightning pace of my
perception.
Quick with the Sphinx.   **675**
Quick with traitors.
Quick to grasp and quick to act.
Your city was saved by the speed of my thought.
I do not wait for knots to tighten.
I cut the knots before they're tied.   **680**
And to this your city owes its life.

CREON
Quick then, reckless King. What will you do to me? Banish me?

OEDIPUS
And let you wait out another string of years in darkness until
your moment comes again? I know better this time. No.

Death. 685
Quick justice. Quick death.

CREON

Think, King. Do not race to error. Act your part.
If you must judge me, be judicious.
Give evidence. State your case.
What have I done? 690

OEDIPUS
You are a traitor.

CREON
So you say. You are a man.

OEDIPUS
I am a king.

CREON
You are a man. You could be wrong.

OEDIPUS
I am not. 695

CREON
And if you are?

OEDIPUS
I am a king. And a king must rule.

CREON
Not for long if he rules unwisely.

OEDIPUS
Do you hear this, my city?

CREON

It is my city, too. That you haven't taken from me yet.   700

CHORUS

Sirs, sirs, stay your wrath before you break us in two. This is
not right. Ah, but here is order and calm. Let the queen
come between you and return you to yourselves.

(Jocasta enters.)

JOCASTA

What is this mad clamor? Have you forgotten yourselves?
Have you forgotten your city? Is this a time to be shouting   705
in the streets in some petty dispute? When your people are
in anguish? Shame on you. Think! Think of who you are.
Oedipus, come inside. Brother, leave us.

CREON

Sister. Your husband here just condemned me to death.

JOCASTA

What?   710

OEDIPUS

I did. This man has plotted against my life.

CREON

Never! You know me, Jocasta, you know your brother's
nature. Is this thing possible? You saw the dread in my eyes
when you were made a widow, those dark days when
I thought the crown would come to me. I never wanted it.   715
You know that, Sister. This is the truth. I stand here, before
my gods and my people, and I swear it.
Let me be damned, may the gods destroy me, if this is not
the truth.

JOCASTA

O Oedipus, believe him. He lays himself open to the infinite   720
power of the beyond. His words are sanctified by this nakedness.
For your own sake, for the sake of your people, believe him.

CHORUS

Believe it, King. Give way to reason.
Temper your rage.

OEDIPUS

I have caught this wickedness with my own hand. I feel it   725
writhe in its captivity. Why should I loosen my grasp?

CHORUS

Loosen, release. Open your hand. Have mercy.

OEDIPUS

Do you know what you're asking?

CHORUS

Yes, King.
Creon has sworn his innocence before the blazing eye of God.   730
Hear him. Honor that vow. He is your kinsman. Don't cast
him off.
He is unworthy of such disgrace. Yours would be the betrayal.
On your head, the crime.

OEDIPUS

Let me be clear then. In asking for this, you ask for my death.   735

CHORUS

Never, by the sun itself, never do we wish for that.
O King, remember your city. Thebes is dying, life by life.
And now this fury between you sickens us further,
Drags us under the bloody waves. Release us.
Let him go.   740

OEDIPUS

If that is what you want, so be it. I release him, though it
may mean my destruction. I do it for you, out of pity for you,
not, never, for him. He has my undying hatred, let him track
it like soot with every footstep for the rest of his days.

CREON

If this is what you know of mercy, may you never be in need   745
of it. Yours is a terrible nature, Brother. I would not have it
for the world. Your great head is a locked box where you
nurture grievance and shadow, startled by the echoes of your
own frantic whispers coming back to you. Your reckless fury
crackles like lightning through all your dark rooms. No,   750
I don't envy you, and never did, for all your power.

OEDIPUS

Get out of my sight.

CREON

With pleasure. The world knows me, though you do not.

(Creon leaves.)

CHORUS

Lady, why do you wait? Take him inside and comfort him.

JOCASTA

Not yet. I will know first what happened here.   755

CHORUS

This poisoned time breeds suspicion and malice in the
troubled air. They breathed it and fell upon each other.

JOCASTA

Both? They were both to blame?

CHORUS
There was injustice on both sides, anger on both sides.

JOCASTA
What did they say?   760

CHORUS
Enough, lady, we are sick of words.
We reel and stagger in misery.
Calm your raging king.

OEDIPUS
I hope you're satisfied.
Blunt my righteous anger and see where it gets you.   765
Glory in your ignorance. Enjoy your make-believe peace.

CHORUS
King, do not mistake us, we are your loyal subjects,
We cling to you, our only pilot in this storm of blood—

JOCASTA
I must know. What happened here?

CHORUS
Let it rest, Queen. Nothing can be served by—   770

JOCASTA
I will not let it rest. My brother has been banished.
I have a right to know what could have warranted such disgrace.

OEDIPUS
Yes, he is your brother. And I am your king.
He is guilty of high treason. I have been accused, here, in
front of all, of murder.   775

JOCASTA
My brother said this?

OEDIPUS

Oh he's too smart for that. He sent his soothsayer in to do
the dirty work.

JOCASTA

Tiresias?

OEDIPUS

Yes. He said I killed Laius.   780

JOCASTA

The prophet said this?

OEDIPUS

In front of all.

JOCASTA

But this means nothing.
Prophets and prophecies . . . they spawn nothing but mayhem
and misery. I have learned this too well. The scars of that   785
lesson still burn across my own beating heart. It is prophecy
I have to thank for my greatest sorrow, my deepest regret.
I will tell you a story I have buried in memory. All the years
of our happy life together, I couldn't bear to think of it. But
I'll tell you now and let you judge for yourself the truth of   790
prophecies.
When I was first married to Laius, I had a child, a boy. He
was born with open eyes and we stared at each other in
amazement. He lay on me and I kissed his smooth feet, feet
that had never touched earth. Three days I had him, that was   795
all. On the third day, a vile prophecy was delivered to us. Not
from God, you understand, just some old charlatan, jingling
charms, but it was enough to wreak havoc. This child, this
wide-eyed, wordless stranger I held in my arms, would be his
father's murderer, the prophet said. The utter horror of it.   800
Laius believed him. Panicked, he wrenched the baby from

my breast and gave him over to the winter night to do its
work. The last time I saw my child, he was curled naked in
his father's arms, staring up at him in confusion, one tiny
hand splayed above his father's thundering heart, as if to   805
calm it. It was brute fear that killed that child. To trust that
prophet was a terrible sin. No man can speak for the gods,
no man can speak for the future. Nothing could be clearer—
just look at what happened. For all his lethal caution, some
group of men he never knew butchered Laius at a crossroads.   810
Fortune-tellers lie. And those who believe them are fools.
My child was taken from me, his life was flung away on the
bare rocks of Citheron as the winter night howled his tiny
bones to ice. I have so little of him, just three days, nothing
to remember. Only the glitter of his open eyes. When the   815
nights are darkest, when the cold moves in, I feel the glint
of them on me and I shudder for what he suffered, what
I couldn't save him from.
My unlucky stranger. My King, why do you shiver?

OEDIPUS
A crossroads, you said.   820

JOCASTA
That's where the murder happened, so they told me. A place
where three roads meet.

OEDIPUS
Oh God, oh God, the light. This is all too clear. I have cursed
myself.

JOCASTA
What is this terror? Tell me. How has this story upset you?   825

OEDIPUS
Where is the man?

JOCASTA
What man?

OEDIPUS
The one who survived. Who saw it. Who couldn't speak?

JOCASTA
The slave? He's off in the mountains, a shepherd, I think.
He asked to be released from the household when he returned   830
in the first great days of your reign. It seemed a small thing
to grant, after all he'd been through.

OEDIPUS
Could he be found?

JOCASTA
Probably. He's not far from the city. No one has spoken to
him in years, but we know where he is.   835

OEDIPUS
I must see him. I must see him.

JOCASTA
And so you will, if you want to. But talk to me. Tell me
what makes you shake. I've never seen you like this.

OEDIPUS
The terror courses through me again, that familiar fear. I've
lived under its shadow so long I grew used to it, could almost   840
forget it. But I feel it once again, darkness hovering.

JOCASTA
Tell me, my love, tell me from the beginning.

OEDIPUS
I will. Who better than you to tell at last?

My father is Polybus, king of Corinth. His queen, my mother,
is Merope. They raised me as a prince of the land and my   845
days were easy and bright until something happened. Perhaps
it was a trivial incident, perhaps I shouldn't have treated it
as I did, but I am what I am, and I did what I did.

JOCASTA
What happened?

OEDIPUS
I was at a banquet. It had reached that pitch in the evening   850
when noise and chaos were overtaking the party. Someone
I didn't know, a drunk, yelled something, a wild insult,
I almost didn't hear it above the din. But I did. He jeered
that I wasn't the son of my own parents. Another man would
have let it go, the brute was red-faced, spittle flecked his lips, 855
he was blind drunk, but it shook me. The next day, I went
to my parents and told them of it. They were shocked and outraged and told me to put it out of my mind. But I couldn't.
The insinuation curled inside my brain and fed there like a
worm on moss. I left after dark, telling no one, traveling   860
light, and walked all night, walked all day until I reached
Apollo's shrine. I asked the god: "Whose son am I?" Silence.
The god wouldn't speak to me. Priests tried to send me
away. "If the god won't tell you, it is not for you to know."
But I wouldn't leave, just crouched there, my back against   865
the damp walls, and waited, I don't know how long it was,
for an answer. I was alone with the mouth of God, listening,
the dripping in deep caverns, the long silence. I could wait.
Then there was a rumble, the hiss of steam, I stood for it
and at last it came, the divine rock spoke, a keening, eerie cry.   870
Worse, worse, than anything I could have imagined. There
in the darkness I heard it: "You will kill your father. You
will breed with your mother to spawn a host of monsters."
I ran, ran for the light, ran in panic, across a wilderness I did
not see. All I knew was that Corinth was behind me and I was   875

fleeing it, running north, never to see it again. Never to see
my dear parents again, running from the country I knew
into the world I did not. I would be an exile for the rest of
my life. That was all I knew.
Feet bleeding with every step, I lived by the North Star.   880
Across mountains and through forests I trudged, never looking
back. Until one day at noon, I came to a crossroads, a dismal,
forked place, overarched with twisted pines, near a river that
trickled through sucking mud and reeds. Three roads met
and mine was the north one. And as I reached the crossroads   885
a carriage came barreling down toward me, the driver
whipping his horses and cursing at me to give way. I would
not. And then I saw the man sitting behind him, an older
man, wielding a long pike. This he thrust at my head, his
eyes flashing with malice as he struck at me. I can see him   890
still. The blunt stake darting toward my eyes. I saw blood.
I wrested that pike from the old man's grip, swung it at his
head and toppled him from his seat. He fell hard into the
dust and lay still, staring up, unblinking. Then the driver,
I beat him to death with his own whip. Then everyone, every   895
single one of them. I was lit with rage, unstoppable, like a
wild fire leaping up the dry brush of a mountainside. Until
I was left in silence once more, standing on blood.
O my Queen, I have cursed myself, done this thing. I murdered
a king, I know it. Then, like a thief, rolled in my victim's   900
bed, laid with his wife, stole his kingdom. It must be so.
And all to outrun a prophesy that has hung over my head all
these good years. That, at least, I have evaded, nothing could
be worse, but still, I am a murderer. I am the thing I cursed.

Let him have nothing, no word, no comfort, no prayers.   905
Cast him out from this suffering city and cleanse it with
his absence.

I am the corruption.

Back, back, to exile, Oedipus, you have no home again.

CHORUS

O but, King, let us hear the shepherd.   910
You remember, sir, there is some hope.

OEDIPUS

You're right, I can live in that.
Until he comes I can live on that hope.

JOCASTA

Hope?

OEDIPUS

The only thing he remembered, the only fact he uttered   915
was that there was more than one killer, more than one.

JOCASTA

He said that. That's true. Said it more than once, it was all he
said. It is on record. The only eyewitness. You see it will come
out all right. Calm your fears, my love. And as for prophecies,
you know my mind on them. My dead king's killers prove it,   920
my baby, dead for all these years, proves it. These things
cannot be told. These things cannot be known. Believe me.

OEDIPUS

I believe you. But call the shepherd. I will not rest easy until
I look him in the eye, hear it from his own mouth.

JOCASTA

Yes, yes, we'll send at once. But let's come inside, away from   925
the heat of the day, the sounds of the tormented city, the
smell of the pyres. You must rest.

(They exit into the palace.)

CHORUS
Gods, are you listening? Gods are you there?
Is there nothing higher than us?
Is there no law greater than what we cobble together with   930
   our own human hands?
Is there no shining order, no light of divine reason?
Are we alone in this shimmering silence?
Is there nothing eternal?
Is there nothing here that will not die?   935
Where are we to seek the truth if not in you?
If nothing, nothing is sacred
Why tell the story? Why sing? Why dance?
Without God, we are just beetles
Scrambling, mindless, over rubble.   940
And the world of men
Nothing but tyrants and fools
Shaking their sticks or rattling their chains
From pointless birth to pointless death.
Nothing matters if all we thought was true   945
Has only been a lie.
The ground is strewn with blood and bodies and there is
   nothing but heat in the vault of the sky.

(Jocasta enters.)

JOCASTA
God. I am unused to calling for you.
But an old grief has risen from the waves of memory   950
Where I buried it so long ago.
And guilt surfaces with it.
The crime I didn't prevent.
Innocence murdered.
They bound your legs together and flung you into black   955
   oblivion and forgetfulness.
But you have risen again and found me here.
My baby. Your eyes shine in wordless terror once again.

O the loss. O the loss.
The world is in blank confusion once more.   960
My husband is a stricken stranger
Haunted by ghosts.
His great mind shreds itself in this new horror.
The familiar scent of disaster is in the air.
And here I am again.   965
Stopping nothing.
Helping no one.
Once again my love is useless
As fate rumbles toward me, bearing down.
I stand at this crossroads and wait.   970

(The Corinthian Messenger arrives.)

MESSENGER
Good news. All will be well.

(Silence.)

Where is King Oedipus? I have news of great moment.

JOCASTA
You speak to his wife and mother of his children.

MESSENGER
Blessings on you, Queen, and on your house.
Blessings always.   975

JOCASTA
That is kind. We are in need of them.
Where do you come from?

MESSENGER
Corinth.

JOCASTA
And what is the news?

MESSENGER
Your husband is exalted. And though there is some sting to   **980**
his triumph, it is slight—it is in the nature of things.

JOCASTA
What do you mean?

MESSENGER
King Polybus is dead. The throne belongs to Oedipus.

(Jocasta laughs.)

My lady?

JOCASTA
(To the gods) Such a swift return for such a meager prayer?   **985**
I thank you.

MESSENGER
(Confused) I am out of my depth.

JOCASTA
Prophecies, prophecies, all of them hollow as babies' rattles.

(Oedipus enters.)

My King, I am confirmed in my confident scorn, listen to
what this man has to say.   **990**

MESSENGER
I bring you news, King, of bitter joy. King Polybus is dead.
Yours is his vacant throne.

OEDIPUS
Lady, you laugh?

JOCASTA
Is it not as I told you? Look on your old terror and smile.

OEDIPUS
Yes. Yes. But wait. *(To the Messenger)* How did he die?   **995**

JOCASTA
What does it matter? Not by your hand.

OEDIPUS
I can't explain it. The terror lives. How, sir?

MESSENGER
(Confused) He . . . he was old. That's all.

OEDIPUS
And I never touched him. Never laid a hand on that dear
head. All these years. Never even saw his face. I fled him to   **1000**
save him and ran straight into my life. It is all . . .

JOCASTA
Senseless! Embrace the mad indifference of the world and
rejoice. You are released from fear.

OEDIPUS
But that keening voice in the cavern of God, it still howls
in my blood.   **1005**

JOCASTA
It is just noise, love. There's no meaning in it—no more to be
feared than the whistling of the wind across an empty bucket.

OEDIPUS
But my mother? But the queen?

MESSENGER

She lives. And longs to see your face.

OEDIPUS

Ah, but that she cannot. Never. Hers is the last knot in that   **1010**
bloody noose around my neck. The rope I've trailed behind
me all these years.

JOCASTA

My King! Don't you see? You can do your mother no harm!
There is no truth to be found in these mutterings and useless
oracles. It is all just nonsense and superstition. The world is   **1015**
ruled by chance. Nothing more. We cannot know the future,
and even the past is lost to memory, that old fabricator who
unravels every stitch, invents as much as she recounts. All you
can trust is the present moment, the pulse that counts the seconds out. Everything else is like a dream you wake from and   **1020**
cannot quite recall. We shed these shadows in the light of the
day, they lift like mist in the morning's heat and are forgotten.
This. Just this—now—is all we can lay claim to. This is the
only solid ground. Plant your feet on this and be happy.
Plant your feet on this and be free.   **1025**

OEDIPUS

Yes, my Queen. But my mother, my mother lives. And while
she does, I cannot risk it. The fear lives with her.

MESSENGER

What fear, if I may ask, sir, in that lady?

OEDIPUS

An oracle I was given—the voice of God itself—that
I would do my parents unspeakable harm.   **1030**

MESSENGER

Your parents, you say?

OEDIPUS
Yes, Polybus and Merope. Dearly as I loved them, I fled from
them to protect them from that crime.

MESSENGER
And that's why you never came back to us? I never knew.

OEDIPUS
Yes, I ran, abandoned them to let them live safe from their   1035
only son.

MESSENGER
But sir, if you'll permit me, you are not that. Never were.

OEDIPUS
What?

MESSENGER
Whoever's son you are, they are not your parents. No more
than I am.   1040

OEDIPUS
No more than——? What do you mean?

MESSENGER
You do not know? And to think that I, of all people, should be
the one to tell you. No, your love could not hurt Merope. You
could never have harmed Polybus. You were not born of them.

OEDIPUS
Be clear, man. What do you mean? How can you know   1045
something I do not?

MESSENGER
Because I was the one who gave you to them.

OEDIPUS

You? What are you saying?

MESSENGER

Yes. Me. It was on the thorny slopes of Citheron. I was a shepherd.
You were a tiny baby, bald head lolling on a neck, staring eyes. **1050**
You'd been left there. Such a cruel thing. This naked mite.
I wrapped you in a lamb's pelt. You weighed nothing at all.
I went to the palace at dawn. There she was, walking the halls,
as she always did, like a sleepwalker. Years had gone by, years
of disappointment. The gods wouldn't give her a child and the **1055**
queen had grown old with it. She would walk back and forth
all night, pounding her fists on her stubborn empty belly,
tears streaking her lean pale face. Poor dear. I entered the
palace with this little bundle—you—and found her there.
I didn't say anything—just held you out to her. Like this. She **1060**
looked at you and, oh, the smile. I've never seen anything like
it. You peeped out of that wool. Like a face in a cloud. She
took you in her arms and then, I'll never forget it, she licked
her finger and gently stroked the dirt from your forehead. It
was all so silent, like a dream. And then she was walking, **1065**
swaying down the hall with you, humming some wordless
song, lost in your eyes. The eyes in the cloud.
It's the best thing I ever got to do in my life. You.
Giving you to her like that.

OEDIPUS

(Amazed, quiet) I was never their son. I was never their son. **1070**

MESSENGER

It changed everything for me, I can tell you. No more shepherd-
ing for me. That was all over. I was indoors now. Walking down
those shiny halls. Wearing good-smelling clothes. Ordering
people around. I liked that. And when I'd see you running
past me, flailing some toy sword, frowning with some **1075**
imaginary story, I'd put a hand out and skim the top of your
head—you never noticed—and smile to think of what I'd done.

OEDIPUS
But who am I then? What kind of mistake am I born from?
Who left me there? Who would do that?

MESSENGER
Oh, I don't know. But I know the man who might.   1080

OEDIPUS
Who?

MESSENGER
The man who found you.

OEDIPUS
I thought you said you found me.

MESSENGER
No, I wasn't the one who saved you. I just delivered you, deposited
you into that good life. The one who saved you was another   1085
shepherd. I came upon him just before dawn. It was a cold
morning, the sheep were snorting steam, their hooves making
sharp marks in the ice. He was standing there, still as a post,
bent over something. I thought, something is wrong, poor man,
maybe one of his lambs has died. Maybe a dog. But when I got   1090
to him, I saw he was holding this naked creature—you—staring
down at it, dazed. He kept saying: "I don't know what to do.
I don't know what to do."

OEDIPUS
Who is this man? Where is this man?

MESSENGER
He was one of Laius' slaves. I knew him from the mountains.   1095
He drove the largest of the flocks.

OEDIPUS
Does anyone know who this is?

CHORUS

Yes, King. There's only one man it could be.

OEDIPUS

Does he live?

CHORUS

Yes, King. In fact, I think he is the very slave you've already **1100**
sent for. The eyewitness to the murder. Isn't that so, Queen?
You would know.

(Jocasta does not speak.)

OEDIPUS

Jocasta? You must know.

(Jocasta does not speak.)

Why don't you answer me? Is that the man?

JOCASTA

I don't know. I don't know. **1105**

OEDIPUS

You know. You must.

JOCASTA

No. No.

OEDIPUS

I have to find him. Ask him.

JOCASTA

Don't. Please. Don't.

OEDIPUS

But I have to. You must see that. He's the only one who **1110**
can tell me who I am.

JOCASTA

Why ask? Why know? Live without knowing. I beg you.
Live, Oedipus.

MESSENGER

Oedipus. Swollen foot. That's right. That's how you got your
name.   1115

OEDIPUS

What do you mean?

MESSENGER

Whoever it was who left you, they'd done this thing—horrible,
really—they'd pierced your little ankles, run a leather thong
through them, bound them together. Gave you one leg instead
of two, so you couldn't crawl. I saw the bloody cord hanging   1120
down when I went over to the shepherd. It was me who cut
it, released your legs, before I wrapped you in the fleece.
Poor thing. It hurt so much you didn't even cry.

OEDIPUS

My old wound. My limp. Now I know.
Who would do that? What kind of parents—?   1125

(A cry escapes from Jocasta.)

What is it, Queen?

JOCASTA

You must not know. Promise me, it's all I ask. Promise me
you will not look further. Let it rest here.

OEDIPUS

How can I promise you that? Why would you ask me to?
You know me. Is it that you fear what I'll find out?   1130

JOCASTA
Yes.

OEDIPUS
I see. You think I'll discover I'm some backstairs bastard. Is
that it? You think I'll find out that I'm some poor mother's
sordid little secret? Well, of course I am. I must be. Why else
would they do that to me? But why let that bother you? I am   **1135**
still who I am. Your king. Your husband. It doesn't bother
me. I feel better than I have in years. I'm free at last. This
is so good. For the first time in my life I am utterly myself.
Born of nothing. Beholden to nothing. I am my own man.
Now I must find out. I'm hungry for that knowledge. It's   **1140**
all so improbable. I'm alive, against all odds. I must find out
what kind of miracle I am.

JOCASTA
Never. Leave it in darkness.

OEDIPUS
That is not who I am. You know that. I will know the truth,
whatever it is.   **1145**

JOCASTA
I beg this from love, for your own good.

OEDIPUS
My own good? Let me be the judge of that. No more darkness!
Give me light! How could you think I would ever choose
ignorance?

JOCASTA
Ignorance was your only hope.   **1150**
My unlucky stranger. Good-bye again.

(Jocasta exits. Silence.)

CHORUS

It's a strange silence she leaves us in. Like that stillness, that
hush before the storm rushes in.

OEDIPUS

Let it come! Let the sky break to pieces and wash the face
of the world! Pound this hard ground into pocked mud;   **1155**
level us; batter all the windows; rattle all the gates!
I am going in at last. Turning the handle on my last door,
stepping across the threshold to meet my fate in the dim
room. There he is, the stranger, standing in the dark corner
next to the closet door, I will see his face at last.   **1160**
I have no fear of him. She is afraid of what I'll see there
—an ignominious birth. Child of a slave, child of some
drunken nobody. I don't care. I know who gave birth to me.
I've always known: Chance and Fortune, luck and the roll
of the dice—these are my real parents. Always were. Who   **1165**
could ask for better? They have given me everything. No one
has been luckier than me.
I will know who I am. I will know who I am.
I am not ashamed.
Let the knowledge fall on me like a summer rain.   **1170**

CHORUS

Yes! Yes! Let the storm break!
Let the secret of your birth
Thunder out of the silence.
Let it echo across your mighty mountain home.
Let great Citheron ring with it.   **1175**
Let the wide earth sound with it.

We always knew this.
Knew that you were the child of mystery.
Your parents could be nothing mortal, nothing common.
No, you are too strange and wonderful for such a birth.   **1180**
The gods have had their hands on you from the first.

Your eyes glitter like the surface of the sacred mountain
    stream.
Your mind darts like golden arrows loosed from the god's own
    bow.   **1185**

Was it the nimble god Pan who begot you with some
    dancing nymph in the wild?
Was it Hermes, swift spirit of the lightning ridges, who
    mated with some bride of the high peaks?
Or did Dionysus leave his wine kisses on some daughter of   **1190**
    the mountains?
Or are you the child of light, begotten from the scattered
    brightness of Apollo's passing grace?

All of these are worthy of the story of your birth.

Your greatness will sound at last, loosed from its divine   **1195**
    captivity in the stones of great Mount Citheron.

(The Shepherd enters, hesitant, reluctant.)

OEDIPUS
The stranger approaches. Is this the man? Yes.
This is the man. At last.
So slight a person, yet he carries everything I need to know.
All my secrets are shining like jewels in the darkness of that **1200**
ancient skull.
Look. They light his eyes.
Come to me. Stand before me. I will ask you at last.
Did you serve King Laius? Were you his slave?

SHEPHERD
Yes. But I wasn't bought from an auction block.   **1205**
I was born and bred in this palace.

OEDIPUS
What was your work?

SHEPHERD
I drove the flocks.

OEDIPUS
Where?

SHEPHERD
I grazed them on Mount Citheron.   1210

OEDIPUS
(Gesturing to the Messenger) Do you know this man?

SHEPHERD
Which man?

OEDIPUS
This one. Right here. Did you ever see him there?

SHEPHERD
On Citheron? I, this man? I couldn't say. My eyes are bad.

OEDIPUS
Look harder then. Take your time. Do you know his face?   1215

(The Messenger goes up to the Shepherd. They stare at each other.)

MESSENGER
It has been a long time, old friend. We were young men together, mingling our flocks, we drove them up into the high
pastures when the spring began. We talked, perched on some
high rock, watching over them below us. Through the hot
summer, the buzzing in the air, the sound of all those   1220
creatures, cropping the grass, all those long days, we kept
each other company. And when the winter came we parted,
driving the herds down different faces of the mountain.
Until the spring came round again. You remember.

SHEPHERD
Yes, I guess . . . It's all so long ago.   **1225**

MESSENGER
You remember. We were great friends.
And then there was that cold morning. I found you with
the child?

SHEPHERD
Child?

MESSENGER
That poor baby. You'd found him, you said. You didn't know   **1230**
what to do with him. You were crying. I said: "Give him to me.
I'll take care of him." And you did. You remember.

SHEPHERD
Terrible secret. Why do you speak of it now?

MESSENGER
Look, here he is. Standing in front of you. That baby survived.
Grew up to become a king. Isn't that something?   **1235**

SHEPHERD
Shut up, you idiot!

OEDIPUS
Don't you yell at him, old man. What's wrong with you?

SHEPHERD
He's talking nonsense. It's all just noise.

OEDIPUS
I am your king. You will say what I brought you here to tell me.

SHEPHERD
But I have nothing to tell you. Really. I'm nobody. I never   **1240**
saw anything.

OEDIPUS
You saw it all. You were there at every crossroads of my life.
You will talk. You have no choice. Pin his arms.

(Two members of the Chorus take hold of the Shepherd.)

Twist them.

SHEPHERD
God help me. Why? Why are you doing this to me?   **1245**

OEDIPUS
Did you give him that child?

SHEPHERD
Yes. I wish I'd died that day.

OEDIPUS
We'll happily kill you now, if you like.

SHEPHERD
Yes. Kill me now.

OEDIPUS
Not before you tell me what I summoned you to say.   **1250**

SHEPHERD
Oh, please. Just let me die.

OEDIPUS
Where did you find the child? Did someone give it to you?
Did you do that to it yourself?

SHEPHERD
No. I didn't do that. It was someone else.

OEDIPUS

Who? Whose child? **1255**

SHEPHERD

I beg you. No more.

OEDIPUS

You have no choice in the matter. Speak. Where did you
get the child?

SHEPHERD

It was from the house. This house.

OEDIPUS

Was it some slave's baby? Was it someone who worked here **1260**
who gave it to you?

SHEPHERD

I can't say. I can't say it.

OEDIPUS

You can. And you will.

SHEPHERD

It was of this house. Born here.

OEDIPUS

Yes. But whose? **1265**

SHEPHERD

His.

OEDIPUS

Whose?

SHEPHERD

The king's.

OEDIPUS
The king's?

SHEPHERD
Laius. He was the king's own son. 1270

(The Shepherd is released by his horrified torturers.)

I couldn't do it. They said he was cursed. Fated to murder his
own father. Said that I must kill him, leave him on the rocks.
They'd mutilated him, pierced his ankles, then strung them
through and bound them, to keep him from crawling. Someone
said: "It'll be faster that way." They kept saying: "We're 1275
trusting you to do what's right. Take him up there and leave
him. Don't come back until you've done it." I took him into
the night. It was so cold. I held him to my chest, tried to
keep him warm there. He didn't even cry. It was as if he knew
what was happening to him. I couldn't see. Stumbling as 1280
I climbed up in the dark until I got to the top. I knew what
I was supposed to do. Just put him down and go back. Put
him down, leave him, leave him. But I couldn't do it. I pitied
him too much. His eyes looking up. Trusting me. I couldn't put
him down. And then the shepherd came. I gave him to him. 1285
Knew he'd take him to the other side of the mountain,
another country, let him live. Let him live. Anything would be
better, I thought. So, empty-handed, I went back down the
mountain, back to the palace. And I thought, I'll never see
him again. But he will live. 1290

OEDIPUS
But you did see me again.

SHEPHERD
Yes, at the crossroads. When you were killing me. But I was
saved by a strange mercy. I lived. To return to my city, and
look upon my new king.

OEDIPUS

Light. Light. Light. I can see too much.   **1295**
All of it. All of it. This open book of infamy.
My sordid stain of a life. Open to the light.
Enough. No more. Where is the darkness?
Let it swallow me. *(Oedipus hurtles into the palace)*

*(The image from the beginning of the play appears: the child
curled, his back to the audience. The same out-of-sequence
counting begins, and continues under the length of the following.
The Sphinx: One, two, four, three, two, three, one, four . . .)*

CHORUS

What is this thing?   **1300**
What is this thing?
Child of nothingness.
Child of chance.

(We hear long ripping sounds, sheets being ripped.)

Creature, animal, naked to the air.
It shivers in the darkness of the world.   **1305**
It knows too little.
It knows too much.

(Dimly, we begin to make out that Jocasta is ripping sheets.)

It doesn't know why it was saved.
But it knows it will die.
It doesn't know why it lives.   **1310**
But it knows it will die.
It tells stories to itself in the darkness.
Making things up.
Muttering in the darkness.
The story of happiness.   **1315**
The story of fame.

The story of heroes.
Tells its beads.
Makes gestures in the air.
Makes promises.   **1320**
It thinks. It thinks.
It thinks it has done something.
It thinks it can be safe.
It thinks. It thinks.
It thinks it can be happy.   **1325**
It thinks that something of it will last.

(Jocasta hangs herself, using the strips of the sheets as a rope.)

Listen to it muttering.
Telling stories in the dark.
What is this thing?
What is this thing?   **1330**
This cursed and holy thing.
This holy accursed thing.

(A cry. Oedipus finds Jocasta.)

Everything that can be suffered, it suffers.
Oedipus. Oedipus.
How we have loved you.   **1335**
And when we loved you, we loved ourselves.
How we have praised you.
And when we praised you, we praised ourselves.
No man has meant more to us.
No man so envied.   **1340**
No man so honored.
And now.
And now.
And now.

(His back to the audience, Oedipus holds the brooches up.)

We wish we'd never seen you.   **1345**

(He plunges the brooches down into his eyes. Full blackout.)

God forgive us all.

(Lights up. Once again he holds the brooches up.)

You gave us the light.
Now you plunge the world into darkness.

(He plunges the brooches down into his eyes. Full blackout.)

A VOICE
The queen is dead.
The queen is dead.   **1350**
The queen is dead.
And the king . . . the king . . . the king . . .

*(Lights up. The palace doors open. Oedipus is revealed, standing
in the threshold, blinded. Silence.)*

CHORUS
Your eyes. Your eyes. What made you do that?

OEDIPUS
Nothing. No one. My own hands.
They chose this. The blind need blindness.   **1355**
It was right.
Someone is speaking. He's making sound.
Listen to him. Speaking in the night.
As if there was anything to say.

(The Shepherd approaches him.)

I am being seen. I can feel it on my face.   **1360**

(The Shepherd touches him.)

You. The one who always saw me. The only one who ever did.
The one who saved me. For this.

*(Oedipus spits at him. The Shepherd doesn't react. Oedipus falls
into his embrace.)*

I beg you. You are the one who must do this.
Deliver me now.
Deliver me to obscurity at last.   **1365**
Lead me to the mountains again. Take me there once more.
But this time, this time, leave me there.
You promised. Leave the cursed creature there.

(Creon enters.)

CREON
This is obscene. No one should look on this.

OEDIPUS
My brother moon. Forgive this broken monster.   **1370**
Let me go.

CREON
It is not for you to say. Not for me to say.
You belong to the gods now.
We will ask them what to do with you.

OEDIPUS
They have already spoken: Drive him out.   **1375**

CREON
Do not seek to command. That time is gone, Oedipus.
You are no longer a king.
What you are now, no one can say.

OEDIPUS

I am the walking corruption.
I beg you. Save the city.   **1380**
Banish me and live.

CREON

Your fate is something I cannot determine.
I will not touch it. We will wait. Go inside.

OEDIPUS

No, no, not inside! Please. Exile is all I can bear.

CHORUS

Lord. Take pity. Let him go.   **1385**

CREON

All right. Yes. Sightless, leave our sight, Oedipus.
Never return.

(The Shepherd begins to lead Oedipus away.)

CHORUS

We have seen this. We have seen this.
We are cursed now with knowledge.
We can never return to innocence.   **1390**
Go, King. Go.
We will live in your absence, we will go on.
And for the rest of time, all we will be doing is trying to forget
    you.

THE END

ELLEN MCLAUGHLIN's plays have received numerous productions throughout the U.S. and internationally. *A Narrow Bed*, *Infinity's House* and *Days and Nights Within* all premiered at Actors Theatre of Louisville, the latter winning ATL's Great American Play Contest. *A Narrow Bed* was subsequently produced by New York Theatre Workshop and received the Susan Smith Blackburn Prize. *Iphigenia and Other Daughters* was written for The Actors' Gang in Los Angeles and received its world premiere there. Later, it was produced in New York City by Classic Stage Company. *Tongue of a Bird* premiered at Intiman Theatre in Seattle and was subsequently produced by the Almeida Theatre in London, Center Theatre Group/Mark Taper Forum in L.A., The Public Theater in New York City and Oregon Shakespeare Festival, among others. *Helen* was produced by The Public Theater. *The Persians*, commissioned by the National Actors Theatre in New York City, received its world premiere there. *Oedipus*, commissioned by the Guthrie Theater in Minneapolis, received its premiere there in January 2005.

McLaughlin is an NEA grant recipient and winner of a writer's award from the Lila Wallace–Reader's Digest Fund. In 2000, she won the Berilla Kerr Award for Playwriting.

She has been teaching playwriting at Barnard College since 1995. Other teaching positions have included Princeton University and the Yale School of Drama.

McLaughlin is also an actor. She is most known for having originated the part of the Angel in Tony Kushner's *Angels in America*, appearing in every U.S. production from its earliest workshops through its Broadway run.

She is married to Rinde Eckert and lives in Nyack, New York.